Esther Fairfax

£1

GW00746071

Ego at the Threshold

EGO AT THE THRESHOLD

Edward E. Sampson

DELACORTE PRESS / NEW YORK

Designed by Deborah Speed

Library of Congress Cataloging in Publication Data

Sampson, Edward E.
Ego at the threshold.

Bibliography: p.
1. Ego (Psychology)   2.   Philosophy.
I.   Title.
BF175.S23   154.2'2   74-11095
ISBN 0-440-03385-3

To
M
and
M and **M**

Contents

Ego at the Threshold

Introduction

The restless, curious mind of man has never ceased exploring the outer reaches of his existence, seeking ways to transcend the routines of everyday life. Today, the need for this quest seems to have reached crisis proportions. All of us feel the need of salvation from the tragedies that the promise of our civilization has also brought. Little solace is to be had from searching the archives of history to learn how enduring such feelings have been. For many in the Western world, the search has turned toward the ways of the East, in the hope that the philosophy, religion, and life style of Asia may offer escape from the pains of Western civilization.

Stereotypes are difficult to abandon. Western man's view of the "mysterious" Asian mind tends to make two related errors: Like the people themselves, to the Westerner, all Asian philosophies look alike. Moreover, to the unschooled Westerner, the Asian outlook seems to differ markedly from his own view. Some even suggest that there is an Asian mind on the one hand and a radically contrasting European or Western mind on the other.

While such stereotypes fail to grant a fair hearing to either the Eastern or the Western perspective, they are especially in error in homogenizing the Eastern mind. Many philosophies and cultural styles characterize the Western world. Similarly, there is no single Eastern outlook. Instead, philosophies, religions, and life styles abound, including among others, the classical Indian views contained in the Vedas, Upanishads, and the *Bhagavad Gita*; the various perspectives of Buddhism; two dominant, yet contrasting Chinese philosophies of Confucianism and Taoism; and the different forms of Zen.

On closer examination, even the supposedly radical contrast in outlook between East and West fades somewhat as we recognize many parallels in the European and Asian worldviews: the samsara of the East can be compared to the Western concept of everyday life as a round, a rat race; the Buddhist belief in the power of knowledge and understanding finds many representations in similar Western views; the maya of the East emphasizes what we in the West see as a difference between the many appearances of reality and the underlying reality itself; the pursuit of an eternal, universal truth that characterizes several Eastern perspectives has its parallel in the philosophical visions of Plato and Kant; the loving practices and morality of Buddha and the philosophy and life of Jesus likewise contain significant similarities.

Of course, it is possible to slough off the differences *within* the perspectives of the East and West in order to highlight the differences *between* them. Even then, however, we do not uncover two totally different systems of belief; rather, what is revealed are similar cultural themes which, as Lewis Mumford has suggested in his analysis of the distinction between the Old and the New World cultures of the West, have coalesced uniquely in the West into a single, mutually reinforcing context that serves to "overwhelm human consciousness."[1] What I am suggesting is that the apparent differences between the Asian and Western perspectives primarily reflect differences in the objective conditions of life in these areas. In the West, science, urbanization, and technological advance have coalesced to produce what might be called a near-total mechanization of all human life. It is the confluence of these objective social forces that has created what we take to be the Western mentality; their absence in concert has provided the contrasting context of Eastern life.

Starting about the fourteenth century, reaching a clarity in the seventeenth century and approaching its zenith in our contemporary world, Western consciousness is characterized by its

rationalism, utilitarianism, [and] scientific positivism. Objectivity and causality were the dominating principles of the new ideology: only those aspects of human experience that were external and repeatable, open to the inspection of other men, verifiable either by experiment or strictly controlled induction and deduction were treated as real . . . subjectivity and teleology had no place in this new framework.[2]

This consciousness evolved from and was sustained by machine technology and the scientific-manipulative powers it gave Western man. The demands of the machine became the demands for man: "organization, standardization, regularity, control [were] applied to every manifestation of life."[3] While rural man lived in harmony and understanding within nature, urban man sought to control nature, and soon, to control other men as well. The methods of science offered verifiable, external means for seeking and establishing truths about reality; thus did man turn from the subjective and inner world toward this more readily understandable external world. Man thereby acquired a sense of an objective reality that helped salve the wounds of strife and insecurity that the idiosyncratic and too-personal subjectivist frameworks had provided.

As science, urbanization, and mechanization more recently have begun to sweep eastward, we witness a transformation of the Asian consciousness; the tenets of Eastern belief as well as the Eastern life style become increasingly like their Western counterparts. The reverse trend, however, is also to be noted, especially among the young counterculturists of the West, who have turned toward the East seeking a human answer to the problems of their mechanized world. So East meets West as objective social forces converge upon the East; while West meets East as those forces in their extreme drive man near the brink of his own destruction. And yet it is unlikely that the Westerner will find directly translatable answers to his quest through the wholesale adoption of the ways of the East. That millions of persons in Asia, for example, have spent their daily lives engaging in practices that today tempt the imagination of Western youth and others seeking a better way does not mean that those same practices can either fit into or be sustained by the mechanized context of Western consciousness and life.

The application of Western science and technology to the physical world, while profoundly transforming man's consciousness, never had a more profound impact than when it was applied to man himself, as in psychology and sociology. The demand that man be studied in the same manner and with the same techniques used to study physical objects drove out or forced underground the subjectivist and humanist themes of Western thought, which still survived in the less scientific East. The renaissance in Western circles of an interest in Eastern perspectives is paradoxical yet understandable. Western science itself has evolved techniques with which to study man's more subjective and private psychological experiences: physiological recording techniques that measure brain activity, record dreams, and other states of consciousness, for example. It has thus become increasingly possible to translate into the terms of Western science some aspects of Eastern thought and experience. And such translation, of course, legitimizes what was subjective and illegitimate by bringing it within the purview of proper science. The paradox, however, is that the very scientific and mechanized system that made such experiences illegitimate for inquiry is now being used in their study.

It is by no means clear that the experiences and life styles characteristic of the nontechnological East can ever become a major life theme in the West, even though Western science can study them scientifically. Thus, paradoxically, one may scientifically study experiences that will forever remain alien to the system studying them. Or, perhaps as with the scientific study of humor, the process of subjecting "Eastern experiences" to scientific study may destroy their richness and thereby render them meaningless.

That the Westerner should turn East, or for that matter, seek to bring to light those Western systems of belief that contain parallel themes (e.g., the turn to the practices of Jesus), suggests a strong human tendency toward balance in life. The Westernization of consciousness, its mechanization and routinization, has extended beyond the boundaries of humanity, draining persons of those very qualities that distinguish them as human. Many have been cast back upon a search for that part of themselves lost in the smoky, concrete canyons of the city and in the routine of a dehumanized life style presumably created to make life more comfortable and equitable for all mankind. The search is not for the Eastern way as such, but rather for a way of reclaiming one's eroded freedom, one's lost creativity, a spirit that has been threatened by the very system that once lifted it elegantly from the crises of man's earlier existence. We intuitively sense our need to restore the balance that has been lost in our world of mechanization and efficient rationality.

The essay that follows reflects this growing search in the West for a perspective on human life that has been profoundly eroded elsewhere but has been nurtured within the East. We search for the bases of human freedom and transcendence in a world that is now, and for all practical purposes will remain, intensely governed by Western consciousness-shaping forces. Our search is for that point of balance between the Westernized pursuit of mechanization, stability, and order and the Easternized pursuit of subjective enlightenment and personal freedom. We search for the true shape of human nature within the social order, one that reflects both the Western and the Eastern aspects of human existence.

1

The Nature of Persons:
An Image for Man

What, then, is the fundamental nature of man? Who are we and what are we really like? "The merriest species of the creation"? "The slime of the dung-pit"? "God's ape"? "Nature's sole mistake" "but breath and shadow and nothing more"? "the measure of all things"? "a bubble"? "the only animal that blushes, or needs to"? "political"? "rational"? "tool-using"? "treacherous"? "noble"? "ridiculous"?[1]

The answers culled from daily experience vary extensively, revealing both the peculiarities of the individual's life history and the proverbial wisdom of society. In search of a more fundamental truth about man's real nature, we turn to the theories and findings of the social sciences, hoping to discover answers.

Amid a confusing array of data and concepts is a semblance of order concerning man's *true* nature. As with all things, however, our true nature is not necessarily true, but merely a point of view about the fundamental nature of human reality. Although two dominant views emerge, the *behaviorist* and what I term the *constructivist*, one basic image for man is revealed, as we shall come to see.[2] The behaviorist view[3] argues forcefully that, fundamentally, we are like machines, shaped and conditioned by the world around us to be the servants of its demands. The constructivists, in apparent contrast, see us as free agents who define and shape the reality about us; we construct the reality to which we then respond. What passes for contrasting perspectives on our fundamental nature, however, illuminates only one side of the picture; our search for man's true nature must carry us to the dark side, the face of which, while hidden to our everyday view, nevertheless remains a present and active part of each and every one of us. But here I get ahead of our story.

The behaviorists maintain that we are what we are and learn to be what we become not because of some mystical mentalistic power of free choice, or even because of genetic endowment, but because of the conditions of our social learning experience. Society and its agents of socialization use rewards and punishments to reinforce certain behavior patterns, shaping each of us usually in ways of which we are only vaguely aware.[4] We are fundamentally plastic and malleable things to be shaped to grow this way or that: figurines of clay, carved to fit a social mold.

The world of stimuli out there, the bells and buzzers, the coins, the grades, the praise and ridicule, write upon the blank tablet that is our mind at birth, determining the responses we make and the life we come to lead. Like machines, we are complex circuits of connected associations between stimuli and responses that have been properly reinforced: rewarded or punished. The socializing agents—parents, teachers, advertisers, social scientists, the government, the media, and so on—reinforce the response they want us to learn. On repeated occasions, such reinforcement finally solidifies the circuitry that connects that response with this stimulus; on future occasions, when that stimulus is presented, our response emerges neatly, predictably, and mechanically. We are shaped by those who shape, and into shapes *they* desire.

The father of behaviorism, J. B. Watson,[5] maintained that the behaviorist principles of Pavlovian conditioning could be used to make a young child into anything one wished. Surely, if Pavlov could condition a dog to salivate to a bell rather than to food directly, then persons could be made to acquire through the same processes of conditioning those skills needed to become doctors, lawyers, or whatever. The principles of learning were the same for man and beast.

Based on his rigorous and inventive work with animals, B. F. Skinner concluded that we can be trained through positive reinforcement techniques to do what the experimenter, trainer, or teacher wants us to do. Just as the rat learns to press a lever in the Skinner box to get a pellet of food, or the pigeon to peck his beak at a particular spot on a radarscope to receive his bit of foodstuff, so will Johnny learn if he is given bits of candy, the promise of an *A*, a pat on the head, or whatever reinforcer is being employed to help stamp in the new habits.

It was but a tiny step from the animal laboratory to the real world of people and their problems. Behavioral-shaping techniques could be and were employed in the development of teaching machines designed to teach Johnny to read, learn history, do his math, or whatever. From the classroom, the Skinner box next moved into the therapy hour. Homosexual males were shown photos of naked males and electric shocks used to stamp out their erotic responses; when they were shown photos of naked females, on the other hand, they were rewarded. Troublesome children were candied their way to health, M & M's becoming some behavior therapists' trademark. Hospitals based on token economies were established; for proper behavior the patients received tokens to exchange for goodies in the hospital canteen. Bed wetters, always a nuisance to themselves and others, completed an electric circuit when they wet, thereby ringing a bell or producing a mild electric shock that awakened them and taught them to stop wetting.

From the behaviorist's perspective, our personalities *must* be tampered with in these ways; after all, our personality is not our own, not a personal possession to do with as we please. To imagine that our personality is our own is a luxury both illusory and dangerous.[6] J. V. McConnell,[7] a famous student of the behavior and life of the flatworm, noted that our so-called unique individuality was actually forced upon us by our genetic heritage and social conditioning; only fools and foggy idealists could imagine that we built up our personalities out of choice and the exercise of free will. We are who we are not by choice but by factors well beyond our personal desire or control; thus, if what we are is deemed not healthful or useful to the good society, behavioral techniques must be used to change our personalities. We are a social and a biological product and have no right to the ownership of this product; we have no right to refuse to have this personality-product reconditioned if it is not a proper one. Wooldridge's[8] aptly titled book, *Mechanical Man*, seconds this behavioristic thesis, noting further that since we are nothing more than complex machines, surely someday soon we will be able to manufacture persons who in all ways will be indistinguishable from those created by nature. A product created by nature and one manufactured by man are, after all, both products.

The behaviorist image sees persons as *shaped by* an objectively given reality; the constructivist says that we are the major *shaper of* that social reality.[9] The constructivist position goes by many names, and as with the behaviorist view, has several important variations; but whatever its form and whoever its proponents, it argues that we are not a passive receiver of stimuli, not a blank tablet to be molded and shaped; we are always actively engaged in creating and shaping the world to which we then respond. If we appear to be machinelike, then surely it is we who have constructed ourselves in this manner.

Larry was a student in a sensitivity group I organized some years ago during the heyday of the Haight-Ashbury district of San Francisco. Larry was much older than the others in the group (in his late fifties) and more into wine than dope. The ethos of this group was openness and honesty, but Larry refused to play along. He would impatiently ask us, "Well, when are we going to have our encounter?"; but when we impatiently asked him when he would participate, all he ever said was, "What's an encounter anyway? How do you do it?" In time, we learned from some of Larry's questions what he thought an encounter was: "Isn't an encounter when you skewer someone and pass them around for everyone else in the group to look at and analyze up close?" "Isn't an encounter when you chop through the brick and cement fortress that we each have around us, in order to try to get a look inside at the real person hiding in there?" "Isn't an encounter when you peel away the onionlike layers of the person, ripping each layer off, one by one, until you get down to the core, down to nothing?"

Look at the terms that mean sensitivity group and encounter to Larry: skewer, chop through, peel away to nothingness. These words help us get inside Larry's head to see how he defines a sensitivity session; and equally important, once we are inside his head looking out at us—those who would skewer, chop through, and peel away—we gain a keen sense of why Larry was so hesitant about joining in. Who but a fool would want to play a game defined in that manner?

The constructivist viewpoint tells us that the way a person defines a situation is basic to understanding how that person will behave. Larry's defensive behavior was consistent with his definition of the group situation as dangerous. There is no such thing as an objective world of stimuli containing the same meaning for all persons; rather, the subjective, psychological meanings and definitions of the situation must be taken into consideration. A stimulus is not a stimulus is not a stimulus. If we are ever to understand human behavior, we must first understand how each of us subjectively defines and thereby uniquely experiences reality.

It is as though we each are wearing glasses of different sizes, shapes, and colors that actively filter the world we experience. We live in different realities. To understand behavior, we must understand the glasses people wear, through which they look out on the world.

On first glance, there is a certain excitement and humanistic quality in this constructivist image; it seems to give our inner world a chance to play a meaningful role in our daily life. It seems to permit my moods and my feelings to influence my behavior. The stimuli to which I respond are under my control; I am the creator of the world in which I live.

Our personality, which the behaviorist tells us is not ours at all, the constructivist appears to treat with respect and dignity. After all, our personality is something we ourselves create, carving it out of the matrix of our experiences; our personality is unique, never to be surrendered or cast aside in the name of social therapy. We are the authors of our fate, the shapers of our destiny. When it is written, we are the ones who have written; we are the ones who have chosen to respond to the writing or to ignore it. Hurray for us! See, we have dignity; we are free! Or are we?

Dignity, individuality, freedom, and creativity are the magic words of the constructivist perspective; control, reinforcement, predictability are the behaviorist's watchwords. They seem worlds apart, aliens to one another. Yet, place the constructivist in his laboratory and see the transformation occur. They call themselves constructivists and speak of man's freedom and authorship of his own fate; yet they act like the behaviorists they must be in order to manipulate and create the kinds of persons they too wish to see happen. They criticize the behavior therapist who conditions health into his patients,[10] and the teaching-machine practitioner who mechanizes the learning process, while applauding the open classroom that likewise shapes its students into having to like doing their own thing because, after all, that is what is rewarded. In the organization of business and industry, the behaviorist view emphasizes the need to manipulate conditions of work and incentive to improve performance; the constructivists, while emphasizing the need to create an atmosphere conducive to the worker's sense of personal identity and growth, nevertheless manipulate conditions and symbols in order to transform him into the desired image: both hope to get more work done.

In terms of the practical matters of our everyday lives, and in spite of all rhetorical distinctions, the behaviorists and the constructivists have the same image of our fundamental nature. The two views may differ in their detailed analyses of the mechanisms of human development and change;[11] nevertheless, in the daily conduct of our lives we function more or less as sophisticated machines. Lest we be deluded by the apparent attractiveness of the constructivist position into thinking that it provides a real alternative to the sense of dehumanized sterility which the behaviorist perspective of human nature conveys, it is important to become clear about the illusory and limited freedom and individuality which the constructivists' view offers: it is not the alternative, transcendent view of human nature that we are seeking in our quest for freedom.

Skinner is correct but incomplete in his proclamation that human freedom and dignity are illusions;[12] in our everyday affairs, "freedom of choice" is the master illusion to which most of us are utterly blind. The constructivist model reinforces our desire to be deluded, to live in a fanciful world of never-never, while concealing the real character and true width of our freedom. The behaviorists' truth is hard to hear and accept; yet the deceptively humane constructivist version imprisons us within an illusion. In either case, our individual freedom is gone even as we hope it is within our grasp.

The constructivists paint us as the shapers of our reality, as the authors of our own life stories; yet when we look at the end-product of our years of "self-made" socialization, we find that we have all ended up more alike than different, more routinized and mechanical than unique, spontaneous or creative. Regardless of whether we have shaped our world or it has shaped us, practically speaking, within any given cultural and linguistic community, persons are *destined* to shape and construct their worlds in relatively non-unique ways; the building blocks for construction are much the same. While the limits of human freedom offered by the constructivist position are wider and more substantial *in theory* than those of the behaviorists, these limits do not extend us far enough. There is more to us than either perspective reveals; it is this something more that motivates our search.

When we ask how we can accomplish this shaping of reality that the constructivist position suggests, we must turn to the notion of the symbol or the symbolic form, and in particular, to language, for our answers.[13] The world out there is not experienced directly, but rather exists for each of us as a product of symbolic processing. That processing, in turn, relies on language.

Naming and The Word take on substantial mythical and religious significance in all societies. Even today, for many persons,

His name is not mentioned except under special circumstances and with feelings of respect, lest the name bring His Presence to us. Naming and the entire symbolic process capture the flux of reality and place it in a fixed position within our consciousness. Symbolization gives us a reality in which to live, to notice, to recall, to fantasize, to project into the future. To name something is not simply to attach a neutral tag, label, or symbol to a ready-made, already existing empirical object; rather, the process of naming or symbolizing *re-presents* the object to us. The symbolic process actively *constitutes* the objects of our empirical world, restricts our focus, calls our attention to one aspect of the totality over another, shapes our experience.[14] Research has demonstrated[15] that the way persons experience the figure O——O is influenced by the name it is called— *eyeglass* or *dumbbell*. Is the figure ⋈ the *sun* or a *ship's wheel*? The name shapes the way we experience the object.

Between us and reality lies the filtering and shaping system of language. Language exists in an ongoing historical and social context; it is neither unique to the individual nor an individual accomplishment. Language serves a channeling function, selecting certain aspects of reality and certain relationships for our attention while rejecting and ignoring other possible distinctions. Language gives social relationships to us; it provides us the categories for experiencing and knowing ourselves. As such, our constructions of reality are from their outset constrained and channeled into a particularistic perspective which the symbolic forms have already formulated for us. Our experiencing is a social, a cultural, a historical experiencing. Even our innermost thoughts, revealed to no one, partake fully of this social-linguistic process.

Research in psycho- and sociolinguistics[16] has repeatedly demonstrated the importance of language in providing the categories within which our world is experienced. In its strongest form, what has been called the Sapir-Whorf hypothesis of linguistic relativity[17] argues that our entire worldview, or *Weltaunschauung*, is determined linguistically. Speakers of different language systems thus live in different social realities; their language systems cut up and reformulate reality into uniquely different bundles. Speaking a given language involves more than saying a different word or constructing a different sentence from the speaker of another language; the language we speak creates the world in which we live.

In learning a new language, we have to struggle for some time to equate the new with the known, and we never grasp the full reality of the other's perspective until we learn the new tongue so well that we come to think in its terms. The world we now experience is different from the world our mother tongue revealed. The greater the difference between the language systems involved—as, for example, between Indo-European and American Indian forms—the more strikingly different is the new reality experienced.

Yet even speakers of the *same* language deal with a reality that has already been predetermined for them; they are constrained thereby to confront a similar social reality. Regardless of how we learn, for all practical purposes, symbolic forms give us a historically differentiated world.

If there is a clearly demonstratable historical and communal unconscious filled with archetypical images, as Jung[18] maintained and as myths, dreams, and symbols suggest, it must surely lie within the language systems into which we are socialized. They contain within them our ancestors' ways of constructing and relating to reality; in the present we also live with the past, because of our linguistic heritage.

Symbolic forms not only create and objectify the particular conception of social reality shared by all speakers of the same general linguistic community; in addition, language itself forms an immediate, usually unconscious basis for legitimating specific aspects of social and physical reality.[19] The act of naming which differentiates one part of reality from another, thereby objectifying it for us, at the same time legitimates that part by declaring it real, valid, and proven to exist. Kinship terms, for example, define one part of a total collectivity as belonging together, and as separate from other parts. The word *cousin* defines a particular relationship between two persons; it objectifies this relationship as something real and informs each of us that Joe and Jane are uniquely related as cousins. A specific set of expectations concerning the manner by which these two persons may or ought to relate to one another is thereby brought into play.

The process of naming or giving a symbolic form to some event, aspect of reality, or relationship thereby establishes that aspect as having an objectivity and an existence apart from the very human activities and historical process from which its existence originally derived. We respond to named things as though they were intrinsically or independently real rather than as symbolic representations of something more fundamental: as representations of an aspect of the never-ceasing, ongoing activity of human minds.[20]

Labeling theory as it has been applied to social deviancy is a case in point.[21] Varieties of acts take place every day; some are labeled delinquent by parents, police, teachers, judges, and others; and those who engage in these acts are labeled delinquent or deviant. Having been so labeled, these people become objectified; they have a reality status apart from other persons; labeling likewise legitimates a particular kind of treatment for them. As Becker[22] has suggested, labeling begins the individual on his career as a deviant. We begin to relate to him as a delinquent, as though delinquency were an intrinsic quality. Similarly in the area of mental illness,[23] a schizophrenic is no longer a person, but rather is a case to be legitimately dealt with in such and such a manner.

And, perhaps most importantly of all, the person so labeled can readily come to believe, "If I've got the name, I might just as well play the game." In other words, if I'm thought of as bad, delinquent, crazy, immoral, or whatever, then I might just as well begin to perform that role and reap whatever benefits it may hold. The mother who, distrusting her teen-age daughter, continually refers to her as a whore, even though her daughter in fact has done little to warrant that label, may thereby help create a daughter who comes to feel, "If that's what you think I am, in spite of all evidence to the contrary, then, what the hell, I might just as well be one!"

Those who hold power in a society, and thereby have ready access to the public labeling machinery, often utilize it to objectify some element as bad, evil, dangerous, or criminal, and thus legitimate the manner by which that element must be treated. Calling young people "student agitators" permits us to handle them differently than we could were they defined as "sons and daughters." Calling the Vietnamese "gooks" facilitated a different kind of treatment for them than they would have received had they been called "Vietnamese peasants." Calling a person a "patient" permits a different form of relationship than would exist were he called a person or a friend.

Becoming socialized within a society involves learning the symbolic forms and the labeling processes of that society; we are thus constrained to confront a world that is not individualistic even if the learning was guided by constructivist rather than behaviorist theories. Both the behaviorist and constructivist paradigms manage social control and social change by modifying the external situation in which we find ourselves. In both cases, the controller of those situations, including the symbolic forms and labeling processes involved, can manage thereby to exercise substantial control over us.

The typical manner of describing the behaviorist view makes it sound more blatantly manipulative than the constructivist; after all, the behaviorist consciously attempts to rig reinforcement schedules in order to produce particular kinds of persons. But the constructivist, who creates or controls persons by manipulating their symbolic universes, is indeed as manipulative, if not more so. For while giving each of us the sense that our choices have been made freely and we are the creators of the world to which we respond, the constructivist in fact manipulates the symbolic forms which constrain us to see things in particular ways while we remain unaware that we are so constrained.

Which is the more manipulative? The behaviorist who says, I am going to change your behavior, or the constructivist who says, you are free to see as you want to? Of course, neither the behaviorist nor the constructivist so boldly proclaims his intentions; rather they conduct their manipulations outside the awareness of those whom they seek to influence. While the behaviorist changes the schedules of reinforcement of whose existence we may even be unaware,[24] the constructivist changes the symbolic forms and thereby objectifies and legitimates the new reality that we adopt and to which we respond, again without much awareness.[25]

In essence, those who can control symbolic forms within a society can influence the behavior of the citizens of that society as much as can those who control the power to reward or punish; and the former can do so without causing as much of an outcry as those who would more boldly apply behavior-modification techniques.

If "our side" wins a battle, it is called a *victory*; if "their side" wins, it is called a *massacre*.[26] Within those words is contained two entirely different senses of moral rightness concerning the battle itself. A victory is righteous and good; a massacre is a devilish act of fiends.

We could develop a new dictionary of synonyms, pairing linguistic concepts that, while ostensibly referring to the same behaviors, reflect distinctly different experiences and responses. The housewife in Northern Ireland who refuses to abandon her besieged home—is she *courageous* or is she *stubborn?* Or is she *foolish?*

On all levels, governmental and personal, symbolic processes provide control, or at minimum, attempts to control persons and situations. The process depends on (1) agreeing to the labels used to describe others, thereby (2) agreeing implicitly to the treatment of those others, and (3) agreeing to see ourselves in the manner by which we have been described or symbolized by others, including agencies that control symbolic processes.

When I come to use *their* label for myself, I have come full circle and have fallen completely within their system of control. Nor can I readily disengage myself; for if I am what they say I am, then their treatment of me is proper. I find myself arguing fruitlessly to justify my action within their system of labels—a losing battle, as anyone who has tried it can testify. If I am labeled sick or deviant and I try to justify my behavior by calling upon unique circumstances that motivated me, I remain, in the end, sick or deviant. I have accepted their view of me and am only trying to add more to the justification scheme. I am still sick. The only way out of this dilemma, of course, is not to play their game, but rather to play one's own game and attempt to induce the inducers to accept one's symbolic universe.

Do we refer to what happened in Watts in 1967 as a *riot* or a *civil insurrection?* The term *civil insurrection* connotes an entirely different set of causes and cures from the term *riot*. In the majority's terms, it was a *riot*, probably instigated by hotheads and outside agitators. Interestingly enough, the most militant and organized blacks called the events in Watts a *civil insurrection*, thereby refusing to play the game by white rules.[27]

"A little revolution is a good thing." That statement attributed to Thomas Jefferson is experienced much differently than when it is attributed to V. I. Lenin.[28] The act becomes a different act when it is placed into a different symbolic universe.[29] And the treatment it is accorded varies depending on the symbolic universe into which it is placed. Robbery is not robbery; murder is not murder; violence is not violence. Each is accorded a different perspective and reaction as a function of the category of experience into which it is received. And those categories are symbolic and social, part of a society's learned and shared language system.

Language and symbolization play a vital role in our entire process of experiencing and understanding reality. The connections we make between symbol and reality instantaneously and unconsciously mediate our experience in such a way that we do not even see the mediating symbolic universe that carries our experience to us and shapes our reaction to it.

Once learned, our symbolically mediated reactions are as immediate and rapid-fire as a reflexive knee-jerk. And yet we imagine ourselves to be free and self-determining, especially at those very moments when our reflexive blindness is at its peak. We fail to see the manner by which the symbolic forms have shaped our view of reality and molded our reactions to the things named; rather, we imagine ourselves to be living within an objective world, given to us as it really is.

The constructivists inform us that we construct the reality to which we respond; but they fail to inform us that the building blocks for that construction are cultural and historical products. Thus, while we imagine ourselves to be the authors of our own life stories, which indeed we are, we fail to see that our story is composed of sociohistorical characters doing the same kinds of things and living the same way as other's stories.

It is our story, but it is not uniquely ours; not an original. Our limits are broader than strictly mechanical linkages would suggest; but the limits are real and function more mechanically and reflexively than our lofty ideals and values would find comforting.

We live in a forest and rarely see the fence that surrounds it. For us the forest in which we dwell is the entire universe; within it we carry on the affairs of our daily lives, unaware of what lies beyond the fence, unaware even that the fence is there. Within that forest, we walk on paths laid down for us. It is we who walk; that is our accomplishment, and no mean achievement at that. Our lives as lived convey one dominant image of our fundamental nature: intelligent, thoughtful, reflective, complex, we may be; but machines we clearly are.

2

The Person as a Machine

In saying that we are essentially mechanical or machinelike, what do I mean? According to the dictionary, mechanical refers to action without spontaneity, spirit, or individuality; mechanical action is habitual, routine, automatic. When I say that we are like machines, I am talking about the routine, habitual, predictable, nonspontaneous quality of human life, about order and predictability, about acting routinely and out of habit.

The preceding is so obvious that it hardly needs a comment. It is also so abhorrent to the average man that he automatically bristles with anger or becomes defensive when he hears it. Yet, our machinelike nature is not only a fundamental proposition of social scientific theory and investigation, it is also a fact of our daily lives. If it were not so, we could not engage in our everyday encounters with others; all would be chaos and confusion; we would not know ourselves—let alone anyone else— so unpredictable, even random and chaotic, would everything be.

Nevertheless, our everyday world is an ordered world: things fit into a place; we and other persons fit into a place; events make sense. Even moments of confusion are readily understood. We do not wander about looking puzzled, always wondering about or questioning the world. The world makes sense; it is coherent and understandable; we take it for granted. We know it to be located out there, existing as a reality apart from us; we know it to have a past and an emerging future. We know its routines and recipes for living and perform them without question, without doubt, without wonder.[1]

When the student takes a beginning class in social psychology he learns that one aim of the field is to predict and to control human behavior, and that one substantial body of work that seeks to achieve this aim is called *role theory*.[2] According to the first statement, social scientists need people who are machinelike in order to be able to carry on studies of human behavior. The entire field is built around this supposition.

When our lesson plan turns to role theory, we cannot suppress a yawn as we learn how much time and effort has been put into developing a language that describes our everyday world. We yawn because we know role theory intuitively; it is a part of our everyday lives applied in each and every encounter. Even the most deviant and revolutionary student in the classroom, taking notes or muttering under his beard, is playing out his role, known and predictable, in this setting.

Role theory reveals that society consists of various positions, or roles, defined in terms of the sets of expectations held by the role-holder and his audience for proper behavior in that position. Father, mother, son, daughter, teacher, doctor, undertaker, dentist, fireman, policeman, patron at a restaurant, audience in a movie theater, fan at a football game, football player, referee—all are social roles. And each of them contains a description of the behavior expected from the role player and from those with whom he is linked in a relationship. The professor stands up front and lectures while the students sit back and take notes; the fan sits in the stands and cheers or boos while the players run about on the field. All is in order and chaos is kept at a minimum.

Of course, role-deviant behavior does occur; but, in general, we enact our roles in a known and predictable manner. We know this intuitively and so are not amazed when we encounter this material in a course in social psychology. In fact, the only time amazement occurs is itself a testimonial to the behind-the-scenes power of the role model in everyday life. We experience amazement, anger, puzzlement only when the role game has been violated,[3] only when the role occupant does not play his part as expected. Yet, even our amazement is predictable; hardly amazing to the social scientist who, once again, has robbed us of our uniqueness just at the moment we thought we had him backed up against the wall.

The social-psychological laboratory has been one useful locale for demonstrating both routine adherence to role behavior and predictable response to role-deviant actions. In the lab, one can generate deviant acts at will rather than awaiting their occurrence in the outside world. The lab researcher simply hires his stooge to play a deviant role and then notes the reactions of uninformed subjects.

In one such effort undertaken by Stanley Schachter,[4] groups of students came together to discuss the case history of a juvenile delinquent and to decide on treatment for him. The experimenter, aware that he was dealing with "sophisticated" social science students, knew in advance just what treatment policy they would recommend. Thus, when he presented them with a rating scale to use in guiding their judgments, he knew that the majority would opt for a generally "loving and compassionate" treatment. This in itself is a prediction concerning the role behavior of students who nevertheless feel independent and free.

Knowing in advance the attitude of these students permitted the experimenter to include in his group persons paid to take different treatment positions. He hired one person to enact the role of deviant: to adopt a punitive approach to the treatment of the delinquent. Another was instructed to adopt the same punitive position but to change it toward the group's dominant position of love and compassion during the discussion. A third was instructed to adopt the dominant group position.

The discussion began, and lo and behold, the "deviant" was the center of discussion; person after person tried to convert him, to shape him up, to get him to see the world properly—

that is, as the majority saw it. The second stooge, who, as ordered, changed his position halfway through the discussion, was received with a hero's welcome. And the third stooge, who went along with the majority, aroused no comment at all. After all, he was like everyone else—he was simply fulfilling his part in a predictable manner.

In another laboratory investigation,[5] the deviating stooge had been instructed to enact the role of a bigot in a group of otherwise rather enlightened, liberal-minded students. The views of this deviating character were met with hushed silence, anxious withdrawal, and active avoidance. Rather than attempting either to convert the deviant or to discover the reasons behind her deviance, the students actively avoided the deviant, as though she carried the plague. This reaction, too, was to a certain extent predictable. The presence of one who deviates will be met with amazement, puzzlement, anger, or some effort to place him so as to restore the known and predictable order of everyday life, i.e., so as to eliminate anything that is problematical and causes thinking and effort to handle.

Perhaps the most frightening demonstration of the machine-like nature of persons who are simply performing their roles and doing their jobs was a recent experiment in which persons were to use what was described to them as electric shock to teach another person how to learn better.[6] In this situation, the experimenter cast the subject in the role of teacher and asked him or her to use an increasingly high "voltage" (up to 450 volts) to punish a student for every error in learning a list of words. The "student" was the stooge in this case, instructed to make errors at certain points during the experiment and finally to complain bitterly about the painful nature of the shocks. At one point, the student complained of having heart trouble and asked that the shocks be stopped. Finally, at another point— about 300 volts—the student stopped responding altogether. The subject-teacher was instructed to keep applying shocks. When he heard the student complain and plead for cessation, the subject-teacher usually turned to the experimenter and asked if he had to go on. The experimenter simply replied that it was his duty to continue: this is what is expected of someone in your role. When the student was finally silent, the subject-teacher inquired if he now must go on or could quit. The experimenter informed him that silence should be assumed to be an error and the shock should be increased for every nonresponse period. In spite of the cries of pain, the pleas to stop, the eventual silence, fully 65 percent of the subjects went all the way to 450 volts.

The experimenter reports the behavior of one of his subject-teachers:

> I observed a mature and initially poised businessman enter the laboratory smiling and confident. Within twenty minutes he was reduced to a twitching, stuttering wreck, who was rapidly approaching a point of nervous collapse . . . and yet he continued to respond to every word of the experimenter, and obeyed to the end.[7]

They obeyed as though they had no choice, no freedom to act otherwise. After all, it was their role, their job to be done. Surely then, they acted as machines, rooted to the workbench of their roles, having no freedom of choice.

What is surprising is not the behavior of the subject in these experiments, but rather that anyone should be surprised by the results. Our everyday lives offer continual testimony to this primary quality of our behavior: we routinely conform to role descriptions; we routinely respond with amazement whenever those descriptions are violated. Thus do we ensure the maintenance of the social order in which we live out our daily lives. Our amazement and our responses to deviants function to keep the institutional order intact and stave off threats of chaos and disorder.[8]

The reason we enact our everyday lives in routine and habitual ways lies in our continuing efforts to defend ourselves collectively as well as individually against the sense of dread and terror that chaos would provide. The institutional order, its rules and roles, is maintained to provide security and comfort, even to those for whom relative comfort may seem lacking. If the revolution came and replaced one order with another, all we would find would be a different group maintaining the automatizations of daily living. The transition period during which chaos threatened would be quickly replaced by a new system of orderings; our daily lives would continue in much the same manner as before. To be sure, the once rich and powerful would then be poorer and weaker, but the daily lives of most people, even those dethroned, would quickly take on a mechanical and routinized quality. Man cannot for long endure anything but order. The economy of thinking itself, as Freud noted,[9] demands a kind of continual defensiveness that functions to keep us unaware of much that goes on; to be too aware would take more effort than do blissful ignorance and habit.

People in life and in the lab behave as though they are readily manipulated, passive cogs acting out their roles in some larger drama. In life and in the lab, people behave relatively automatically and routinely in conformity to social rules and shared constructions of reality whose legitimacy they accept without question or awareness. This routinization is an ongoing accomplishment of everyday living[10] that serves to provide psychic security in the midst of potential for disorder and the terror of chaos. To retain some semblance of order, we give up our aspirations to be free and spontaneous.[11]

3

Image, Paradigm, and Policy

Social scientists are in most respects like other people; they are shaped by and shape the universes with which their science deals. Several years ago, Thomas Kuhn[1] introduced the concept of scientific paradigm. The paradigms of science are thought models which direct their holders to pose only certain questions and to utilize only certain methods in search of answers. A paradigm is to a scientist what a set of glasses or a blinder is to the man in the street. Similar things appear different when seen through the filter of a scientific paradigm. To a Ptolemaic scientist, the moon was a planet; the scientist who saw through the Copernican paradigm looked upon the familiar moon entirely differently, as a satellite. The moon is not the same moon.

Others have discussed the concept of scientific paradigm through the metaphor of the fisherman's net.[2] A fisherman dips his net into the water and catches only certain kinds of fish; some are tiny and slip through the net while others are too large to be contained by it. If the fisherman announced that all knowledge about fish could be derived by thoroughly studying the fish he caught, and further announced that this is the only legitimate way of gathering knowledge about fish anyway, he would be deceiving himself and us.

Paradigms in science are like that fisherman's net. They lead us to catch certain things within their webbing while suffering us to ignore or omit others which just don't fit. Unlike the fisherman, the scientist may go about his business blissfully unaware that he is even fishing with a net or a paradigm of a certain type. The typical scientist simply applies the normal, known, and legitimate rules of his discipline's paradigm without realizing that those normal, known, and legitimate rules predetermine the things he catches as much as does the fisherman's net affect his catch.

A scientific paradigm does not simply *reflect* reality as it presumably exists in some pure form; paradigms function importantly *to shape* the very reality they hope to capture and understand. Unlike the mirror that passively reflects the world presented to it, the paradigm helps to create the world on which it focuses, selecting this bit here, that bit there, emphasizing one element and one relationship while deleting another element and another relationship. In this manner, reality is open to many different views; reality is to a great extent determined by the nature of the models of those viewing it. The viewer's paradigmatic lens is important to consider.

There is no realm in which the paradigms of science function so significantly to shape the reality they hope to understand as the social sciences. Atoms and molecules do not care how the paradigm views them. People do. How the social scientist thinks about the fundamental nature of persons not only reflects the existing nature of human social reality but, more importantly, helps shape and thereby determine the very nature of that social reality. The social scientist who thinks of persons as being fundamentally like machines helps to create persons who are in fact much as he thinks them to be. A paradigm in the social sciences has important policy implications that help establish as real the worldview that the paradigm describes.

Rarely through directly conscious collusion or with malicious intent, the social scientist's paradigm affects each of us in ways that soon become an unquestioned part of what we take to be normal, known, and legitimate. What today's social scientists assume to be real and inevitable become tomorrow's practices of child rearing, educational socialization, and public policy. Decisions are made with direct and influential consequences for each of us based upon experts' views regarding our *real* nature. What teachers learn about teaching, for example, is very much influenced by what social scientists have to say about how children learn. The socializing institutions of education put into practice the social scientist's paradigm and thereby help to create the kinds of persons that the paradigm describes. There is a "contamination of 'ought' by 'is' "; the social scientist comes to accept the status quo as the desirable state of affairs and fails to see the abuses his conceptions bring.[3] Today's machine paradigm becomes grist for public policy that establishes what is, the status quo, as what ought to be.

Robert Rosenthal's[4] interesting and provocative work on the self-fulfilling prophecies of classroom teachers reflects this general process on a smaller scale. Rosenthal suggested that the teacher who defined Johnny as a problem child, and related to Johnny as though he were a problem, soon managed to create a problem-Johnny. The teacher's model or paradigm, Johnny-is-bad, thus becomes true, aided and abetted of course by an inadvertent collusion between Johnny and the teacher. A labeled "bad-Johnny," or one who is treated as though he were a bad-Johnny, can readily become in fact the bad person that we all *know* him to be. And all of this usually operates on a level well below that of our critical self-consciousness. As teachers, we think we are acting sincerely and correctly when we treat Johnny with the special care that someone with his obviously bad qualities deserves. And Johnny, any claims he might make to the contrary, senses that he is the bad-Johnny that others see him to be. He learns this lesson more easily than he learns to read.

A prophecy exists in the form of some expectation we have about the future, in particular about how another person (or even ourselves) is likely to behave. A prophecy is self-fulfilling when that expectation leads us to act in some manner to make it true. This process occurs in all forms of human interaction; and as I am suggesting, in the larger arena as well, in which social scientific paradigms become self-fulfilling prophecies, generating validity for the truths they hope to discover about persons. The holder of a paradigm can create the very reality that his paradigm leads him to expect, albeit without conscious intent on his part or on the part of those persons with whom he interacts. The same consequence can derive from the conscious policy decisions that flow from the social scientific paradigm to the institutions of socialization and decision making, and finally to the persons who are socialized and affected by these policy decisions.

We no longer see the ivory-towered social scientist as creating theories of human behavior that have no influence on policies that affect human life. The step from social scientific paradigm to socialization practices and public policy is a relatively short one, thus increasing tremendously the burden of responsibility that falls upon the shoulders of the practicing social scientist. His thoughts about mankind may quickly become influential instruments that help shape mankind in a manner congruent with those thoughts. The more widespread his audience and the more popularized his view—facilitated by the media, the mass move toward higher education (especially in the social sciences), and the increased utilization of social science knowledge by socializing and policy agencies— the more direct and rapid is the impact of the paradigm in our lives.

In school, the theories of learning, teaching, and motivation based on the dominant social scientific paradigm then being preferred directly influence the structure and organization of the classroom, the content taught, how it is taught, when it is taught, and so on. Parents, increasingly sensitive to their role in healthful or disturbed child development and attuned as best they can be to the prevailing models of proper parenthood, build their own practices of discipline, family organization, and child rearing around such models.

As adults, our daily work activities are regulated in many ways that fulfill a social science paradigm of worker needs, worker motivation, techniques of proper management, techniques of decision making, and the like.[5] Social science views influence the nature and form of media presentations; they are especially involved in matters of advertising, which in turn influence consumer attitudes and behavior.

The entire notion of health, disease, and treatment, especially in the area of mental health and illness, is influenced considerably by the prevailing paradigmatic conception. Definitions of who is sick and who is well serve to legitimate certain forms of disorder as proper while others are relegated to the trash bin.[6] Social science paradigms describe and thereby legitimate certain forms of sex-role behavior, sexual practices, and sexual relationships as proper while other forms are defined as deviant or unnatural. Even societal patterns of authority find their way into the social-scientific paradigm's perspective, thereby legitimating some forms (e.g., individualistic and democratic) while casting grave doubts on others (e.g., collectivistic and socialist).[7]

In indicating the variety of ways in which a paradigm can influence socialization practices and public policy, I do not intend to place the full blame upon the shoulders of the social scientists. That would be foolish in the extreme. Rather, I want to suggest the vital role that social science perspectives play in reinforcing, supporting, legitimating, justifying, and motivating particular practices.

The circle has been completed. The scientist finds a reality that is consonant with his paradigm, not because that is the way social reality is in some absolute, fundamental sense, but rather because his theory has served to help shape that reality in one or both of two ways. In the first place, his paradigm serves like colored lenses with blinders attached, shading and coloring the world in particular ways, emphasizing certain elements and omitting others. Second, his paradigm has managed to alter the nature of social reality by influencing those institutions responsible for socialization. Much as the master's ideology (i.e., his paradigm) which tells him that his slaves are lazy is indeed confirmed by the constant and quite understandable laziness of his slaves,[8] much as the teacher's philosophy which tells him that his students are lazy and unmotivated without his taking a firm hand is confirmed by the student's lack of motivation, so too is the social scientist's paradigm confirmed by persons who are in fact as he knows them to be. In all cases, the knower has helped to create the reality that he knows and has then erroneously attributed an existence to it that is independent of his active intervention in creating that reality. In essence, there is no slave character without slave masters to create it; there are no unmotivated students without teachers and settings that create them; there are no social realities without paradigms that make them real. Thus, there are no fully mechanical persons without affirming paradigms.

This circularity of reasoning is potentially disastrous for the growth and development of any scientific discipline, but its harm to mankind can be even greater. The social science discipline will suffer from an unfruitful, self-fulfilling process that screws itself downward upon itself, thwarting progress in knowledge until the scientific revolution of which Kuhn writes eventually arrives. In the interim, however, persons will be shaped to fit the social science paradigm. Who is to say what human potential has been lost thereby?

Ernst Cassirer has commented that "ideas cannot advance a single step without enlarging and even transcending the limits of the actual world."[9] Scientific progress would never have come as far as it has if the great thinkers of the world began and ended their inquiries with the immediately presented, given universe. The scientist who concentrates his efforts on describing and analyzing what predominantly or typically is, loses his chance to move into the realm of possibility and to learn thereby about what might be but is not yet.

For the most part the social sciences have taken it upon themselves to describe and analyze the existing nature of social reality; and in this they have done fairly well. They can tell us a great deal about how the typical person thinks, feels, and acts. But, if the entirety of a science is based only on the present nature of reality, it will never progress beyond an understanding of what *is* rather than what *might be*. A crucial fault in the social sciences is their tendency to adopt the typical and normative as the inevitable and to stop searching further. By maintaining that "what is" is what "ought to be," the social scientist errs by mistaking existing knowledge for the inevitable.[10] He never gives "what might be" or "what rarely is" a chance to take its place in the universe of phenomena he is endeavoring to understand.

Adopting the typical and normative as the inevitable is as damaging to the life of the individual and the society as it is to social science. An incomplete or partial social science helps create and maintain an incomplete or partial person. From the point of view both of progress in scientific theory and of human potential, a social science paradigm that begins and ends with the existing or typical nature of reality is partial, incomplete, and unfortunate.

In an age where science is the new religion and proclamations made in the name of science carry the same weight as those once made in the name of God, the link between a scientific paradigm and a social policy is intimate and vital. The search for an alternative paradigm on the nature of man is motivated by the realization that without this alternative view, a prime stimulus to accomplishing a transformation in the human character and condition will be missing. Insofar as existing paradigms stress the routinized and mechanical side of human life, the liberating alternative lies fallow. A model for human freedom, then, is a prime requisite to its realization.

4

The Perspective of the Natural Standpoint of Everyday Life:

AN OVERVIEW

Insights that have taken the social science investigator so long to demonstrate or document have been part of the common currency of poetic and artistic sensitivity for many years as well as a quality of the life style of millions of the world's non-Westerners. The mechanical state of much of our existence has moved poets and authors to critical comment, to anger, or simply to saddened recognition.

T. S. Eliot's hollow men[1] live out their lives in the cactus land, the dead land; they exist as mere forms marching through the routines of their everyday world without ever really living. It is no wonder, then, that Eliot offers us a picture of the world's ending with a whimper of silence and inaction rather than a lively and vigorous bang. What other way of ending could these automated machines ever manage?

W. H. Auden's[2] tribute to the death of the unknown citizen offers us another statement about the life of the everyday man: he surely must have been happy and free, for if he weren't, we who kept records of all else he did would have known of his sorrow.

Bertolt Brecht's[3] biting commentary on the man of wisdom who lives his life fulfilling no desires but rather avoiding all strife, whose existence is one of complacent and convenient forgetfulness, paints another portrait of our mechanical man, now a man of letters and purported wisdom.

Don Marquis'[4] tale of the moth recounts the mechanical man's encounter with this little creature whose only life's purpose is to be snuffed out in an instant's glorious dive into a candle's flame. Our viewer hesitates but a moment, the thought circling round his ever practical, wise head, "If only there were something I desired as much, for which I would risk frying myself." But we know his practical mind will never find that flame to capture his wish; he too will live out his life never knowing the lesson of the moth.

Colin Wilson's[5] description of the outsider offers us a penetrating perspective on the man who has dared to extend himself beyond the everyday world. While the outsider "sees too deeply and too much," our everyday hero is a sleepwalker who lives in the land of the blind where the distance of the mind's reach goes no farther than the tips of the fingers: everything that is seen and touched is accepted as reality; little is questioned or doubted.

Philosophers, theologians, and social scientists have likewise painted a portrait of this world of everyday life. Alfred Schutz[6] writes of the world known in common but taken for granted: the world of our everyday affairs. Using Husserl's[7] term, *epoché*, an intentional suspension or bracketing of the usual way we have of looking at and thinking about things, Schutz defines what he terms the *epoché* of the natural attitude. In our everyday existence, we suspend our *doubt* concerning the reality of the world as it appears to us:

> . . . man within the natural attitude also uses a specific *epoché*. . . . He does not suspend belief in the outer world and its objects, but on the contrary, he suspends doubt in its existence. What he puts in brackets is the doubt that the world and its objects might be otherwise than it appears to him. We propose to call this *epoché* the *epoché of the natural attitude*.[8]

* * *

Harold Garfinkel[9] has built upon Schutz's ideas to develop the contemporary branch of sociology known as ethnomethodology: the systematic study of this seen but unnoticed background feature of everyday life. Our daily world is one we see but do not attend to; thus it exists for us as a background that is taken for granted. Much as the construction of the language we speak is seen yet unnoticed, while nevertheless guiding and directing our thoughts, so too, are the rules of everyday life. Ethnomethodology seeks to uncover these features of everyday life by making problematical and thereby open to self-conscious scrutiny everything that is taken for granted: doubting the reality of the world as it appears to us. There is no better way, it seems, to uncover the taken-for-granted than to engage in rule-breaking or deviant behavior and witness the amazement, outrage, or rejection that is rapidly forthcoming. Recall some examples in the previous chapter.

The essential perspective of phenomenology which Husserl outlines and which Schutz and others have used involves putting into brackets the natural standpoint of our spatiotemporal existence in order to get at the more fundamental levels of experience. Husserl's position is that in our everyday lives we adopt a particular attitude or standpoint, which he calls the natural standpoint, from which we view all phenomena. The phenomenologist who wishes to get to the roots of all human experience must put this natural standpoint aside, into brackets, in order to experience purely, without the suppositions that these categories of the natural standpoint impose.

Alan Watts'[10] analyses of Eastern thought and religion offer us another version of this same distinction. He refers to the samsara or the routine of everyday living, "the round of birth and death," which itself is wound intricately around the maya or the illusion provided by the thought forms of a culture's social institutions. The maya exists in those symbolic forms that shroud us in the veil through which we confront the world. Watts contrasts these routinizations and illusions of the everyday world with nirvana, a state of liberation wherein seeing and living are again real. Heidegger's[11] distinction between our two worlds of living suggests this same theme: in the impersonal world, man has lost himself in the activities and routine of daily business; in the authentic world of being, man is revealed to himself as he authentically or fundamentally is.

Everyday routines are carried on within the veil, the dream world, the impersonal world of maya, all of which provide us with a sense of personal identity, of historical necessity and meaning. The roots of our being thus lie within the maya of our everyday existence: a sometimes barren and tenuous source of security.[12]

Two sociologists, Berger and Luckman,[13] call it the institutional order rather than the maya; they view this order of our everyday living as the framework which shields us against chaos and terror: "On the level of meaning, the institutional order represents a shield against terror. To be anomic, therefore, means to be deprived of this shield and to be exposed, alone, to the onslaught of nightmare."[14]

Through the ages, wise men, scholars, poets, scientists, philosophers, and theologians have noted man's reality and man's possibility. Whether it be called samsara, the natural standpoint, the seen but unnoticed background, the world known in common but taken for granted, the dead land, cactus land, the insiders' blind land, the institutional order, the maya— it refers to our world of everyday existence, a world characterized by its routine, automatic, and habitual patterns of living and being. It is a world in which more is taken for granted than questioned; where security is sought and granted to those who follow and accept; where the controlling features are kept in the background while the foreground rhetoric talks of freedom and adventurous daring; where illusion is taken to be reality. This is the world of Skinnerism and behaviorism, where men are machines; it is the world of the constructivists where men believe in their freedom while they unknowingly perform routines that are as old as the generations out of which they were derived.

This world of our everyday lives—our day-by-day world of all that we take to be true, valid, and real—is characterized by the existence of a normative, pervasive, and typical attitude which I call the *perspective of the natural standpoint of everyday life*. It is this pervasive, normative perspective we each put on, so to speak, as we venture forth each day, that has so perturbed the poets and men of literature. It is this perspective that has been studied repeatedly by the routine investigations of social science; only recently have some social scientists (e.g., the ethnomethodologists and phenomenologists) sought to undertake a systematic, direct investigation of the perspective itself, its properties, and how it is produced and maintained in our everyday affairs. It is this perspective of the natural standpoint that gives to each of us our generally automatic, mechanical nature.

The perspective of the natural standpoint of everyday life is pervasive in that it is the usual and normatively sanctioned point of view that we put on in our ordinary lives. It is the unquestioned background perspective against which life's dramas are played; it is, as Schutz and Garfinkel noted, the perspective of a world known in common but taken for granted, a world accepted rationally and reasonably. It is a perspective that gives to each of us meaning and identity, a past, a present, and a future. It is an orientation that gives coherence and direction to our lives; it provides the basis for our security and our conviction.

When I say that the perspective of the natural standpoint is one that we *put on*, I do not mean that it is put on and removed much as one would an overcoat. Rather, it is an entire worldview that we each assume every day, all day; it is a guiding set of knowledges and dim awarenesses, directives, and controlling guidelines. It is the foundation of our lives and the explanation of our deaths. It is our society, our institutional order, our blanket of security. Even our major experiences of insecurity are framed within its purview. It is so much a part of us that we are truly unaware of its existence or of the processes by which it is maintained. It is like the air we breathe, always there, always vital, but usually not problematical or part of our foreground except under very specific, usually rare circumstances. It is like a light that illuminates the scenes of our everyday lives, without which we would be in the dark; and yet it is a light that, in being taken for granted, passes by unnoticed. The perspective of the natural standpoint is our samsara, our daily routine of living, breathing, working, relating, being, and doing.

Before we can hope to transcend the world of everyday reality, we must first come to understand its dimensions; we must root out the qualities of the interpersonal world in which we live each day. The perspective of the natural standpoint establishes this context within which we all live; it is the interpersonal sea around us, the social air we breathe.

Fundamental personal (i.e., human) and cultural themes combine with contemporary societal preoccupations to create this background within which we presently live. The perspective of the natural standpoint always reflects the world-as-now-given as well as certain more fundamental qualities that lie at the root core of human existence, growth, and development. When we put on the natural perspective, we wear a cloak woven from the history of all mankind, yet richly textured as well by the momentary preoccupations, demands, and themes of the contemporary moment. In all that we do and all that we know, we have one foot firmly rooted in what has gone before and the other in the instant of today. Our goal now is to sketch in the dimensions of the interpersonal world of our everyday lives, to reveal this background within which we live with ourselves and others.

As we conduct our examination of the perspective of the natural standpoint, we have the entire body of social scientific investigation to call upon as a rich source of material. Although few have sought systematically to investigate the perspective itself, most of the work that has been done nevertheless reveals its attributes. The subject-teacher who dutifully shocked the student into apparent unconscious silence and the persons who sought to convert the deviant to their point of view[15] offer us a glimpse into the perspective of the natural standpoint.

Those who have sought to describe the character of the

entire society or of an entire era offer us another rich source of material concerning the characteristics of this perspective of our everyday life. David Riesman's[16] analysis is especially helpful in this regard. More recently, several efforts to study the perspective directly have come forth. The work of Garfinkel[17] is important, as is some work by Chris Argyris,[18] the approaches of the encounter and sensitivity-movement people,[19] and some of my own research.[20]

The routines and habits of the natural perspective are hard-won human achievements, neither to be taken lightly nor dismissed simply because they may sound unappealing. The perspective of everyday life is no idle matter, no cloak to put on and take off at whim; the roots of our collective survival are revealed within this perspective. To study the interpersonal world of everyday life, then, is to study an accomplished human creation, nurtured and nourished daily for its maintenance, which is inevitably the maintenance of the human social order itself.

5

The Stranger Within:
The Interpersonal World of
Everyday Life:

DIMENSION I

R. D. Laing's analysis of the divided self[1] describes a fundamental property of our everyday human existence. Our daily life separates the inner world of our fantasies, wishes, dreams, feelings, and emotions from the external world with its hard-core reality. Antoine de Saint-Exupéry's Little Prince[2] said it well in describing adults as those who *know* another person only after they have discovered his name, his address, how much money he paid for his house, how old he is, how much he weighs, and so forth; the Little Prince, by contrast, wonders only whether the person likes butterflies. The house is beautiful to the adult only when he is informed that it costs $40,000; to the child its beauty lies in the doves that nest up on its roof and the pheasants that roam around its yard. How different are the worlds within which children and adults live!

The young child learns in school, albeit slowly and often painfully, to limit the range of his feelings and emotions, to search for *reasons* for his behavior, to eliminate the role that wishes and dreams and fantasy play in his life. A teacher said recently, "I learn a great deal from watching the children work in groups. You see those who want to do it this way and who offer good reasons why; others just say, 'Let's do it this way because I want it this way or because it's fun.' They'll never get on well."

Early in life we learn to create rational, legitimate, and socially acceptable bases for our wants. Those wishes without the proper degree of rationality are not permitted to emerge. Soon we limit not only the expression of our inner world, but even our personal awareness that we have an ongoing, rich inner life. In pursuit of reason and logic, we forget our dreams and conceal our feelings.

The split and the separation go deeply. We learn to quash our inner experiences. Not only do we learn to deny our inner world a literal representation in our outer life—it does not seem to fit into the practical demands of everyday existence—but we also learn that it is evil, dirty, frightening, forbidden; soon we learn to eliminate a major part of ourselves even from our own view.

At night in our dreams a life takes over that is in most respects alien to us in our waking world.[3] Some people take pleasure in the fantastic creations they weave at night; others fear them so much that they never recall them. Most of us never fully accept this alien within ourselves as a part of ourselves for which we should be held accountable: "It isn't me— I was just carried away." Yet at night we each wander through a world of our inner creation, a world of fantasy, of wishes fulfilled, of characters fading in and out, of associations unbounded by time or space or day-logic. All that might be is; all that ever was is. Past lives with present and future in equal freshness. Nothing is too wild or strange to appear. We drive alone at one instant and at the next find a companion in our car which now is a chariot, next a parachute. We run but cannot move; our legs are filled with lead. Then we are free again, roaming on a great mountain peak. Or is it a snow-covered plain? All that might be is in that world of our night.

With the alarm clock the world of our inner life is cast aside, a curtain drawn over, covering it tightly, hiding its secrets and fantasies from expression to others we now meet "in reality." Our inner world is hidden even from ourselves. A split occurs within each of us; at least two minds, two processes, two worlds, two lives. The daytime one is rational, logical, problem solving, consistent, reasoned, and reasonable. We know in this daytime existence what is real and what is not; we know what is past, what is present, and what has not yet happened. We know people; they have time and spatial boundaries, even as we do. We are in one place at one time and are aware of how we move from that place to another. Things do not blend and melt into one another with the ease they show in our night lives. We are alone *or* with someone, not both simultaneously. Our feelings remain within boundaries as well, defined in terms of shared cultural categories, fitting roughly the proper circumstances for their expression, or at least for our awareness of them. We are closed off in our day life from all that exists at night; in our night life, our day world is vividly represented.

When the inner life of our dream world threatens to venture forth into our day life, we defend against it with great vigor. We manage our affairs so as to keep that other world present only dimly, if at all. We deny our feelings to others and to ourselves, lest their emergence might usher in the rest of those ugly monsters that our waking ego senses lie just beyond the tightly shut gates. We cut ourselves off from ourselves, dwelling in a split-level existence, divided eternally as two living in one body, one using it for eight evening hours, the other calling upon its forms for the remainder of the time.

I have used this model of the dream world vs. the waking world as a basic paradigm for the split quality of human existence. It need not only be in night dreams or waking life that we note the split between feelings, impulses, wishes, or fantasies on the one hand and reasoned, practical thinking on the other, between the nonaccountable alien and the consciously known. In any number of routine ways, the inner life of our feelings is shunted aside and given a back seat in our everyday affairs. This does not mean, of course, that feelings and emotions do not play a part in the transactions of every day. Rather, it points up the ways our steadfast refusal to come to grips with our inner world leads us actively to control, to channel, or to deny the presence of this other part of ourselves. We are not in touch with our feelings; we neither court them openly nor do we own up to those that emerge. Yet in split-off segregation, this inner world may rule even as we deny it a legitimate place in our lives.

A group of persons I recently studied through depth interviews[4] spent much of their time attempting to keep their inner world under careful control. They were so fearful that the inner life would seep through their unconsciously erected defensive barriers that they were *denying* realities in every other breath. In expounding on his patriotism and "anger" at those who would engage in war protests, one of this group, Robert M.,[5] said, "When that guy jeered at our flag, he got me so angry that I almost cold-cocked him. Of course, it really doesn't matter to me what someone else thinks or does. I don't get angry very easily; I'm easygoing." In the same breath, we have both the expression of that surging anger from the inner world and the denial of the anger. Robert M. says, "I hate" and "No, I don't hate," as though the slight vision of himself hating brought about enough fear of his own feelings that he sought their denial in an instant, lest more come out and he lose control.

Robert M. was not unusual in this regard. He was but one example of many who repeatedly told me just how few feelings they actually had, how coldly rational, how reasonable, and how reasoned they were. In the next moment they revealed a portrait of one struggling to keep in control of the bubbling inner world of feelings—especially anger. A private world even unto themselves; they never owned up to that part of them. On weekends, this group would bomb themselves into mental oblivion on beer, quashing even more the threatened emergence of that inner world which they sought to keep private from everyone and from themselves.

But the inner world will come out, even among those who deny its existence. I asked these persons to make up stories to Thematic Apperception Test pictures. One picture had a father and son talking together. Most of the stories described the two as arguing—the son wanting something the father would not grant and in the end, having lost the battle, dutifully complying with the father's wishes. No anger, no feelings, no resentment, just bland compliance.

The next picture showed an operation scene, a boy standing in front of an operating table. It was fascinating to note how many of the stories involved a son who had intentionally shot and killed his father and was watching the operation that was being performed to save his father's life. These are the same persons who lost the battle to their father in their fantasy stories. Yet they are quite unaware of this impulse to get even and to destroy as an expression of their anger. They have split themselves off from this part of themselves and reveal it only as some alien piece of material told in a story.

It is as though the feeling from the inner world is faintly represented to the waking, conscious ego, producing great anxiety that more will come and that the person will be engulfed by his inner world; this results in a rapid defensive denial of the existence of that feeling or any other aspect of the inner world. Or it may be that the feelings are so threatening to begin with that they never even make it into the light of conscious day; they are denied before the waking, conscious ego senses them. In either case, the person lives his life split in two.

This state of being, this self divided, is a dominant attribute of our everyday lives. This is the mode of existence that is most consistently reinforced, praised, and appreciated. In general it is the most practical method for getting by in our everyday reality. For were the inner world to gain expression for too long or too often—as it does in some forms of mental illness—the person would find it an unfruitful or disruptive episode, not helpful in getting him around his everyday world. We split ourselves off from ourselves in order to live in the world of practical affairs, as men of relative logic and reason. And we thereby lose contact with a part of ourselves.

6

On Risk-Taking and Security:

DIMENSION II

The pursuit of the safe way, the conservative way, the orderly way, the way involving the least change and least risk, describes a second characteristic of the interpersonal world of our everyday natural perspective. Once we have found a safe base, a spot on which to stand or to call our own, we venture forth only minimally and then without much conviction. It is safer and less disruptive, for example, to assume without doubt, until further notice, that what we see, touch, and know is the only true reality, that everything else is fiction; it is safer and far easier in getting about every day to assume that what I see and know about our common situation and what you see and know are much the same and that if we changed places, the facts of our shared everyday life would in no way be altered.[1] It is safer to stick to what we have always stuck to; to keep things much as they have always been. Even the symptoms of madness involve efforts to play it conservatively by perpetuating the known over the unknown: at least the known horror is familiar.

The horror of Camus' Caligula[2] was not that he killed and destroyed, but rather that he did so with a senseless absurdity that in and of itself threatened everyone's stability and inner security. It was not the murderous world he created but the topsy-turvy one that caused his associates to turn on him.

Human history is living testimony to the fact that we tolerate killing better than ambiguity and insecurity.[3]

The couple who have been married many years and who have found their every interaction fraught with pain, argument, and anger, remain together; after all, this known hell of one's mate is far better than the unknown hell of trying someone new. There are those, of course, who appear to venture forth boldly and take a new partner. But do they really? Rarely. They seek a new partner who will help them maintain their old ways. At the moment's bloom of its inception all seems different; but that is short-lived as each manages to re-create the old and familiar patterns that marked their first relationship. To experiment with a new pattern is more threatening than to keep the old albeit distressful modes.

I have seen numerous people come to sensitivity groups to try on a new role, to create a self unlike the one they say they no longer like. Soon, however, they slip slowly but relentlessly back into their old patterns, throwing off the possibility for the new, exchanging risk-taking for the security of the familiar.

Our everyday world is constantly re-created as we automatically reenact old dramas, creating history over again in unconscious preference to creating a new form, a new way. No wonder, then, that possibilities for change derive mainly from the young who have not yet fully acquired the existing forms and thus are less resistant to change.[4] But even they may quickly form a pattern which they then refuse steadfastly to abandon even as their mouths talk of a utopian newness. If the role of the young is to be agents of change, to open up to question everything that exists, regardless of what it may be, this too can soon become a pattern, a way of life that interferes with venturing forth and trying out something new. For as soon as that something new is tried, it becomes the very item to be criticized. One can become as rooted to a conserving pattern by talking incessantly about radical change as by refusing to budge from a secure place. It contributes as much to security and non-risk-taking to put on the old garb in the new setting as to compulsively keep putting on new garb after new garb after new garb. Both can become routinized, automated roles. The rebel is as much a compulsive conformist as is the traditional compulsive conformist.[5] Both find their security in exactly the same mode of relatedness to others. And both establish definite patterns which work against their experimenting with new possibilities.

Much of the stability of any social system derives from the resistance of persons to taking risks, to trying out new ways of thinking and doing. In the everyday world of practical affairs, it is more useful and adaptive to keep to the known paths and not to venture forth too far or too widely.

Robert M. and his group once again reveal this conserving characteristic of the natural standpoint. With considerable boasting, Robert and his associates indicated to me that at age twenty-one they had achieved a fully formed, definite structure to their character; that they were not likely to change much in the years ahead and that this achievement pleased them. I had the impression that for Robert and the others, risk-taking, experimenting with new possibilities for growth and development, had been written off as undesirable and unlikely. Perhaps Robert was more honest than most of us in stating what is a general fact of life. In fact, most of us settle ourselves as quickly as possible into some routine, some pattern, some role, some manner or style of life that we find comfortable, even in its moments of discomfort, and then cease to want to experiment or to risk-take. While our rhetoric may not be as honest as Robert's in expressing satisfaction with the facts of our present life, we nevertheless manage ourselves each new day in much the way we did on the previous day. This provides continuity to our selves. We are who we are, known as we are known, by virtue of this consistency. Thus a fundamental component of our everyday interpersonal world is our effort to minimize the surprise value of life,[6] to minimize risk-taking, to re-create anew each day our previous ways of being.

7

On Secrecy and Vulnerability:

DIMENSION III

In the world of the natural standpoint the issue of trust—both of self and of others—is complex. We have already seen a distrust of self based on the separation of our inner from our outer world (Chapter 5). Our fear that our inner world will break through and swamp our everyday world of hard-core reality speaks to a distrust of self. Distrust of the self does not offer a firm foundation on which to build trust of others.

Interpersonal trust involves vulnerability. Our ego is concerned not only with losing itself on the floodtide of its own inner world, but is also worried lest others who witness this inner life use their knowledge to control or manipulate us.[1] When others have access to our inner thoughts, motives, dreams, wishes, fantasies—our mysteries and secrets[2]—we are vulnerable to them. We believe that if others were to know us deep down ("If they really knew me"), they would be able to hurt, insult, or embarrass us; they could control or manipulate us. Hence, to reveal our inner world is to make ourselves vulnerable to mastery by others.

In an insightful essay, sociologist George Simmel[3] notes that in contemporary society secrecy serves the same vital function as did spatial distancing in earlier social systems. Now that we live close together spatially, privacy, once facilitated by physical separation, becomes based on secrecy, which helps us maintain autonomy in an otherwise intrusive world.

In psychotherapy, for example, even the client who seems most eager to share his innermost secrets with the therapist stops at a certain point, resisting efforts to open up *that* much to his own and to the therapist's scrutiny. Working through resistance becomes a major part of the therapeutic process. In social science investigation, too, secrecy plays a major role. The paradox is one which David Bakan[4] suggested several years ago in noting the tensions for the social-psychological investigator between mastering the mysteries of the human condition and keeping humanity shrouded in a veil of secrecy and thereby free from the indignities of scientific manipulation and dehumanization. Even the educational process partakes of this paradoxical mastery-mystery theme. The cry for relevant educational content fades once relevance is defined as revealing the mysteries of the very classroom and persons who are crying most loudly for it. *Relevance* means unraveling the secrets of some other person's life style, but not one's own.

There is more. We not only fear becoming vulnerable to others, but we also fear revelations from others which make them vulnerable to us, and therefore make us responsible for them. Take an example from the animal world: Two dogs begin aggressive displays. Finally, a battle ensues. The smaller dog, sensing his impending doom, lies on his back, legs apart, and offers his jugular vein to his rival. He makes himself vulnerable to total annihilation. This places a burden of responsibility on the rival. Shall he strike to the jugular, thereby defying all "rules" of nature, or shall he accept victory with grace and understanding? In human affairs as well, the vulnerability that lays someone open to our manipulation, insult, embarrassment, and so on, at the same time places an important burden of responsibility upon those of us who have seen through to his hidden depths. Hence a normative veil of secrecy is established whereby persons agree implicitly and automatically to relate to one another as though in blissful ignorance of the other's inner life and qualities.

Thus secrecy and mystery about the inner world serve three

key functions: (1) they help our ego in its battle for its own integrity against those fearsome forces of the night; (2) they help shroud us in mystery and hence minimize our own vulnerability as we engage others in our daily affairs; and finally, (3) they assure that neither we nor others will have to bear the burden of responsibility of someone else's life.

In everyday life, we really do not care to know *that much* about ourselves or others. We act in ways that tread a dangerously thin line between exposure and secrecy, with the pursuit of secrecy and mystery winning hands down. Distrust of self and others becomes a normative part of all social relationships; secrecy and mystery become the implicit norms by which we function.

The all-too-human tendency to tell secrets almost as fast as they are acquired may seem an exception to this general rule. But I do not think it is. Secrets that we reveal about others serve many functions, but perhaps none more important than those involving the themes with which I have been dealing. If I learn a secret about you from you and reveal it to another, I am both commenting on my apparently intimate relationship with you—"Why he even tells me those intimacies about his life"—and showing my mastery over you. In addition to whatever feelings of intimacy I may experience, knowing a secret about you gives me a sense of power over you.

But what about the situation in which I reveal a secret about myself to you? Is this not a violation of the apparent norms regarding secrecy and mystery? Again, I think not. This apparently revealing act has several possible meanings. In the first place, as we already know, my secrets make me vulnerable to you; by making myself vulnerable, I may hope to guarantee that you will not tread on my weaknesses. The vulnerability I offer to you places the burden of responsibility upon you not to tamper with me. Thus my revelations in fact give me mastery over you: knowing this about me, you tend to treat me with special sensitivity and regard. I have seen numerous instances of this sort in sensitivity groups. One member will reveal some deep, dark secret about his inner life, precisely in order to make himself so vulnerable to being hurt by others that everyone simply leaves him alone. That person can then sit back and hit out at others, seeking to delve into their secrets from a position of relative personal security and invulnerability!

In the second place, we all have at our disposal an entire network of personal secrets of the sort we automatically let fall without much thought, as though we were revealing some still-hidden matter in our lives. Of course, off guard, we may inadvertently reveal something we would have preferred to have kept hidden; but it is not unusual to offer up little tidbits of secrets-at-hand from our storehouse. These are hardly real secrets that open up the mystery of ourselves to others or even to ourselves; rather, they are little conversation stoppers and people-pleasers.

Finally, there are those occasions when we reveal something of ourselves to another with the hope of receiving something equally revealing in return.

In spite of all the talk about trust and openness, in our daily lives, secrecy and mystery play a necessary role. Needless to say, those whose rhetoric is most demanding of total honesty in all interpersonal relations tend to participate as fully as the rest of us in supporting the mystery norm of our ego's natural standpoint.

8

Our Other-Directed Character:

DIMENSION IV

To describe the manner by which we obtain our values, beliefs, and attitudes, David Riesman[1] has called ours an era of *other-directedness*. The dominant character type in an other-directed society is the person who attends carefully to the dictates, tastes, fads, and fashions of others in order to determine how he will act and what he will like and dislike. What is "in" and what is "out," what is proper and improper, who is good and who is bad, what music is popular, what beliefs are the right ones—all are determined by reference to what others think, do, and believe.

Other-directedness and its broad consequences compose the fourth key dimension of the perspective of the natural standpoint of everyday life. What Riesman saw as a specific character type, the social psychologist has studied systematically under the rubric of man's social-comparative nature.[2] Social-comparative man is other-directed; he understands what he understands and knows what he knows by reference to what others around him understand and know; his judgments of truth and reality are social judgments based on others' judgments of truth and reality.

Confronted with an ambiguous judgmental problem—e.g., how many dots have just been flashed on the movie screen?—people in a group will offer answers that gravitate toward a judgmental norm based on each person's knowledge of how the others saw the dots.[3] Thus, if initially John says there are 250 dots, Tom, 182, and Bill, 65, each will alter his subsequent estimates toward convergence once he has heard the others' until a norm or judgmental frame of reference is achieved. In fact, what John, Tom, and Bill actually *see* may change as a function of hearing one another's estimates. In time, individuals respond in conformity to judgmental norms, thinking themselves to be acting autonomously, unaware of the shaping influence of others' judgments.

In a classic study of this genre, Asch[4] presented his subjects with one line of, say, 8 inches in length, and three comparison lines of, say, 6 inches, 8 inches, and 6.5 inches. When others in the group, who had been briefed by the experimenter, reported that the 6-inch line was *equal* in length to the 8-inch standard, this "group pressure" had a significant effect in changing the subjects' own judgments: in several cases subjects under such pressure actually *perceived* the 6-inch line as the same length as the 8-inch line. Of course, those who "simply" changed their reports of what they saw in order to fit in better with their group also indicate the potency of our other-directed character even in the controlled confines of the social-psychological laboratory. And, note well, "group pressure" involved only hearing what one's peer said; no direct forms of coercion were applied nor were they necessary.

This convergence process is noted in all group settings; the more ambiguous the task at hand, the more influential will the opinion of others be in changing each individual's view. Other-directed, social-comparative man uses other persons as a framework for making his own assessments about the nature of reality, including his assessments about himself and his own abilities.

I do not know that I am good or bad at something according to an absolute set of standards, but rather by reference to others who are doing the same thing. Likewise, my opinion about some matter is correct or not as a function of its convergence or divergence from the opinion of persons I know, identify with, or accept as credible sources of information. Knowing that someone I like and respect thinks in a particular way about a particular matter sets up a tension within me to think similarly.[5] In fact, if someone I like disagrees with me, that is sufficient cause for the tension to be acted upon—whether by changing my opinion of the other person, or changing my opinion to match his, or trying to influence the other to accept my opinion, or dissociating myself from the other, etc. Of course, if I discover that my view differs from the view of someone I dislike, then all is well; my comparative world is at peace and harmony.

Numerous laboratory and field investigations have validated this view of man's nature.[6] Riesman's other-directed social character is more basic than he imagined; it describes one key component of everyone's everyday perspective, one of those background items we take for granted. We respond reflexively and unconsciously in terms of this other-directed, social-comparative dimension.

Some important implications flow from this basic quality of our everyday character. As we dig further into them we will note the validity of my earlier statement that for all intents and purposes we live out our lives as machines, automatically adopting the perspective of the natural standpoint, rarely glimpsing this background which guides and governs the interpersonal world we create and in which we enact our daily dramas of living.

I have alluded to one consequence of other-directedness in an earlier chapter: our tendency to respond to deviant persons or events with amazement, ridicule, ostracism, or some similar reaction that affirms our need to have our views validated by others who live and act in ways congruent with them. Given that we are all basically other-directed, gaining our sense of self and of social reality by comparing our perspectives with those of others, we are thrown into a state of potential confusion whenever we encounter a discrepant point of view. After all, someone else offers a compellingly different perspective. Who is to say that we are right and he is wrong? By ridding our world of those who deviate, we affirm the validity of our perspective and maintain a state of relative harmony.[7]

Our tendency to resist innovation, change, and difference is deeply rooted in our nature. We are by nature intolerant and untrusting; tolerance and trust demand a self-conscious abandonment of an attitude that forms the foundation of our own sense of personal security. The deviant is not merely an oddity, but a vital threat to our existence. Why trust someone who provides so potent a force for insecurity? Only a fool would be amused by those whose very existence raises grave questions about our existence; and the everyday man of practical affairs is no one's fool. When we object loudly to the presence in our community of persons who represent radically different perspectives on the nature of reality,[8] our intolerance is a clear human reaction of survival and security seeking.

Additional implications of other-directedness need careful examination before we continue. Like the ones we have already discussed, they are so basic to our everyday life that we are rarely aware of them. Yet they are a vital and fundamental aspect of our perspective of the natural standpoint. I shall examine these consequences in two general categories: the first in a further examination of trust and intimacy (Chapter 9); the second in the broader issues of shaming, teasing, and social protest (Chapter 10).

9

Other-Directedness:
Trust and Intimacy

Since what I am is defined primarily by the ways in which others evaluate me, I must be sufficiently pleasing to others to receive positive feedback from them if I am to have a positive opinion of myself. Being pleasing to others is the route to personal self-esteem. In his years of clinical work, Carl Rogers[1] noted how persons distorted their authentic selves in order to receive positive regard from others. We all create these distortions every day; they are not rare occurrences found only in psychiatric patients or in neurotics. Rather, the very soil out of which our everyday lives are lived involves a fundamental impression-management process.[2] It is the observer, of course, who may see this as a distortion; the pursuit of positive feedback is so deeply ingrained that the person himself is simply doing what comes naturally.

If I cannot trust myself independently of others to define right from wrong, good from evil, happy from sad, joy from sorrow, I must turn to others to validate reality for me.[3] But, if I cannot trust myself, how is it that I can trust you? If I am in need of *your* definitions of reality, are not you in need of me and my definitions as well? Everyday life is obviously not a one-way street: you need me every bit as much as I need you. If I do things to please you in order to please myself, surely you must be doing things to please me so that I will give you positive feedback and thereby offer you a pleasing picture of yourself as well. We are engaged in an inevitable exchange, each leaning upon the other for his own validation; truly the blind are leading the blind.

At a rather deep, intuitive level of consciousness we are aware of this state of affairs, and this is one of the bases for the fundamental sense of distrust that obtains between persons. It also contributes to the fundamental sense of insecurity about reality which lies barely hidden beneath the surface of our everyday lives. Society itself is founded upon this sense of personal insecurity about the nature and meaning of life and reality. In no way does this mean that we spend our everyday lives tormented by the agony of mistrust of our fellow man or focused intently on these basic matters of our insecurity. It does mean, however, that every day we act in ways that reflect these themes and that reveal our constant pursuit of a stronger, more stable sense of security about the nature and meaning of our lives and of reality.

Social institutions are geared to prevent these feelings of insecurity from taking over.[4] They provide the shield against the terror of ontological insecurity which lurks just beyond the faint fringe of lights shining out from the city limits at night.

We have a paradox, one of many on which our lives are founded and which motivate our daily affairs. On the one hand, as other-directed creatures, we are each sorely dependent upon others. On the other hand, we know that others are equally dependent on us. I cannot be trusted "to know" independently of you; you cannot be trusted independently of me. Together we stand in a somewhat precarious void, each defining the shadows on the wall as real, and each wondering at rare moments just who can be trusted and what is really real.

With little to put our faith in, we have created gods, spirits, devils, fads, fashions, and the consumer marketplace to define and give meaning to life. Gods have a distinct advantage over the marketplace of ever-changing values; in the deity we can at least discover enduring values and enduring definitions. But if God is dead or never really existed, then what is there but the ever-changing "truths" packaged and ready to be sold in the consumer's marketplace of today's values or fads and yesterday's nostalgia?

I am always looking at others for self-validation, and they at me. We watch each other rather carefully for cues that will inform us about what is appropriate, proper, real, and good. Watching and being watched. Are these not a basic part of the true paranoid's sense of his life and his world? Indeed they are. But they are also a fundamental background feature of our own everyday interpersonal world and life.

"Being on" is more than a term that describes the life of the actor;[5] it is descriptive of our own lives, as we seek that proper cloak in which to present ourselves to others who we sense are even now presenting themselves to us. That we are "on" or at times "off" is itself a surface reflection of this more basic, *natural social paranoia:* watching and being watched. Whereas the true paranoid spins out rather elaborate tales concerning his own situation of personal persecution, natural social paranoia builds upon socially shared, institutionalized, and legitimated modes. Watching and being watched are part of the normal, expected, and thereby unnoticed background feature of everyday life.

The experience of normal people under psychotomimetic drugs often casts this daily background into the foreground. The effect is attributed to the temporary consequence of the drug, and thereby the illusion is preserved. For what the true paranoid experiences vividly and the drug taker sees in a moment's highlight exists for each of us every day in one form or another as part of the routines of everyday life. Rarely to be called into question, we manage our self-presentations daily, however, in order to assure that the routines of watching and being watched are conducted properly.[6]

Given this routine background, however, it becomes important for each of us to package our *product* (i.e., ourselves) carefully so that what is presented to the watchers is a protected, projected image, not the "inner" us of which even we are hardly aware. We are especially concerned not to show the various blemishes, pimples, and odors that would reveal us in our "off" pose, or at least to show them only at rare moments and then only to a highly select audience of more trusted intimates. Others serve as the mirrors we use to know ourselves, just as we serve as their mirrors to reveal themselves to them. We want the mirror to reflect the best of us, our "on" selves, not the selves we encounter at night when the package is removed and our bloated, naked bodies fart and shit.

Both consciously manipulative as well as the more usual non-manipulative efforts to conceal the blemishes of our human existence—amply facilitated by the advertisers who help us become definitely unnatural in our smells, colors, and appearances—produce a *defensiveness* that separates people. Defensiveness is the key word and the key concept: defensiveness that distances, shields, and conceals, even as we seem most revealing.

To Europeans, most Americans seem extremely, often excessively, open and honest, blurting out with abandon and to perfect strangers the most intimate facts and details of their lives. Yet, though this surface comes across as *trés intime*, once the seal is broken and the package entered, true intimacy is rare. Kurt Lewin[7] saw the American as having a surface region of great openness and apparent intimacy with a deeply concealed inner core, hidden perhaps from everyone, and the European as having a heavily guarded outer surface which few managed to penetrate, but which, once broken, revealed inner regions of true intimacy.

Packaged sincerity, openness, and intimacy sit upon the surface, conveying the proper image that one ought to have today. Defensiveness, however, remains fundamental. We approach one another with the fear of being discovered, of being revealed, of having the contours of our self-presentations and personal packaging cut open. We fear to appear stupid, naive, empty, human, confused, unclean. We live a distanced life, founded upon a basic superficiality of relationships.

Our patterns of communication and the recent wave of group cures for social ills reveal both our defensiveness and our superficiality.[8] In talking with others, we use language to shield and distance more than to reveal and share. We talk, but hardly listen; we attach our own thoughts as riders onto others' conversations, moving the talk in ways we want. We act as though we really don't want to know about them, to hear, to understand; nor do we want them to see or know us. Our relationships become superficial—friendly, but vacuous.

Under these conditions, even our sexual relationships become routine and automated, lacking depth of feeling. Rollo May[9] commented that persons today seem to want to have sex without falling in love whereas the Victorians sought to fall in love but have no sex. I am not certain to what extent things have changed or whether it is just an exaggeration of a human theme. Persons have always had problems with matters of intimacy; this is a fundamental part of human existence.

Defensiveness and distancing produce a depersonalized interpersonal world, a world in which, in Martin Buber's[10] terms, I-it or It-it relationships prevail. We relate to others and soon even to ourselves as objects, not as persons; as "Its," not as "Thous." In the very process of relating, as an "I" to a depersonalized "It," we necessarily change our view of ourselves. We too become "Its," thereby completing the depersonalized circle and founding a world of "It-it" bonds. Machines linked hand in hand, smiles etched firmly on robotlike faces, marching without joy down the street together.

Depersonalization,[11] a useful mechanism of defense to all of us at times, overwhelms when it becomes a way of life. The surgeon must depersonalize the individual he cuts into, must think of him as a patient rather than a human being. The social scientist who examines the victims of war and disaster must depersonalize them and think of them as subjects or respondents, lest he become overwhelmed by their misery and be unable to function in his role as scientist.[12] The soldier who must shoot and kill finds it far easier to act if he depersonalizes his opponents—calling them "the enemy," "gook," or whatever term is then in vogue. It is far easier to kill nonpersons than to kill persons.

When the psychological defense of depersonalization becomes a living part of our everyday reality, our relationships with others become based on roles rather than persons.

Instead of people, we become victims, oppressors, blacks, whites, Chicanos, men, women, chauvinists, or whatever term is used to describe the role in which we are cast.[13] Thus depersonalized, we can readily hate but not as readily love, except as one loves a soul sister: a personally unknown spiritual ancestor. Thus depersonalized, we can come together as basically good people and destroy others; we put on our role as professor and call them students and then systematically rid ourselves of their foul breed by denying their individuality and personal dignity. They put on their role as students and see us as professors and thereby work to undermine us just as we retaliate. Together in the categories of everday life, we depersonalized nonpersons try to relate but find little that is personal and human. Thou is lost in a sea of it.

This interpersonal story is not yet over. Depersonalized relationships, so superficial, defensive, and protective, produce a state of mutual nonconcern and noncaring. We fail to see the potentials for empathy that exist between *thous* but which are alien to *its*. If you are a black and I am a white, how can I really know you, your life, and its concerns? As black and white, as victim and oppressor, we have no hope of relating as caring persons with empathy; we can only intellectually attempt to bridge a self-imposed gap. It is only as persons that you and I can join in bonds of mutual caring.

Watch the TV footage of wartime bombing. Do you see your mother and your child in the mother and child separated by war? Do you know her plight as a woman, a mother with a dead child held in her arms? Or is it only another slant-eyed alien who sits cross-legged in the ditch rocking and holding her dead baby? Her baby is my baby is our baby? No.

How can I care for depersonalized objects? How can they care for me, yet another object among many? Better to withdraw into caring for no one but myself. Better to face off against the world alone and lonely. Better to keep distance and be uninvolved. Better to let things happen and not be too concerned. Better to keep our packages apart.

The interpersonal world that is created and sustained by

our other-directed social-comparative character nurtures a disease with severe implications for our survival and well-being. This disease involves a basic inability to form or maintain an intimate relationship with another human being. In our normal everyday work lives, intimacy of relationships is usually inappropriate;[14] yet, when such intimacy is absent in our everyday personal lives, we are diseased. Let us look more closely at this interpersonal disease as it exists in especially heightened form in contemporary Western society.[15]

Doubting ourselves and trusting in no other, we seek to be entirely self-contained, to be the complete person, needing no one to achieve satisfaction. What does this complete, self-contained person look like? To draw upon a sexual *metaphor*, the complete person is both male and female, has both penis and vagina.

Human relationships of true intimacy are founded on a vital *trust* in the other to achieve the completion of the self. Metaphorically, if not literally, the male is completed by the female; the female by the male. We who would be self-contained, however, a male and female combined, distrust any other person to complete us; thus we avoid all persons or enter into only superficial bonds with others. To establish true intimacy with another demands that we trust the other to be there, to be involved, to care, to be concerned, to complete that part of our self which needs completion through him or her.

This notion of intimacy implies that no self is complete or fulfilled until it merges with another self. It is this very fear of merging with and losing the self which, when coupled with the lack of trust in others, drives most of us in our everyday lives to move apart from true intimacy and toward self-contained isolation without others.

Two separate but related ideas are embedded in this view. The first is the ever-present human fear that merging with another person means losing the self. The child experiences this early in life,[16] as does the adult in issues involving individual desire vs. group need. The issue is most salient, however, at those moments when a potential merger is in the offing. At that time, the fear of being swallowed up, taken in, submerged, losing individuality becomes so strong that it drives persons apart.

The second aspect is the fundamental distrust at the root of all human existence. Intimacy requires trust that our vulnerability will not be mishandled and that our completion will be accomplished through an enduring bond with the other. But if distrust keeps us from intimacy, we are in a trap: we need air to breathe but do not trust the air around us.

This disease of human relationships provides a never-ending dilemma for most of us for most of our lives. We reject others in order to be distant, removed, and self-contained; we change partners nightly in order to search but never find, in order to avoid the issue. We pursue over-intimacy, an engulfing involvement with someone in order to avoid a mutual involvement. We push for total acceptance of everyone so as to avoid being rejected by them.[17]

These problems have their roots in malformed independent identities. If we are not certain of our own identity, how much more difficult it is to merge our identity with that of another person. Given the basically other-directed nature of our social character, we are not independent of others and not sure of who we really are. How much more difficult it is, then, to trust others in the ways true intimacy demands.

We can trace existing problems with intimacy to earlier problems with issues of identity. This will become more relevant when we consider the societal conditions that have produced and serve to maintain the perspective of the natural standpoint and in particular the interpersonal world which it characterizes.

As is often the case, we can view these societal dilemmas more readily as they are highlighted in the life of smaller social systems, for example, small groups. In small groups (in particular, sensitivity groups), we find persons groping for intimacy without ever having found trust. So they grope for trust. But since they have never found a personal identity apart from the group, they do not find trust either. A vicious circle evolves; the group's interpersonal world is founded upon dependence or counterdependence, each of which thwarts the development of true intimacy.[18] We repeat the old stories over and over, like a repetition compulsion, a spiraling circle, a web in which we trap ourselves. The spider who gets caught in his own web may complain, but it is his web.

10

Other-Directedness: Shaming, Teasing, and Social Protest

Protest during the 1960s and early '70s revealed another facet of other-directedness—the fear of being shamed. Anthropologists have differentiated between fear-, guilt-, and shame-based cultures.[1] A culture founded on fear is one in which behavior is managed by implied or realized threats of punishment. The possibility of being caught and punished serves as the mechanism of social control. A guilt-based culture, of which our own partakes in rather full measure, is one in which persons have internalized the cultural dos and don'ts in the form of an inner voice, a superego or conscience, which speaks out with jabbing pangs of guilt when the transgression is committed or even anticipated. Freud[2] wrote extensively about the mechanism of guilt and how it maintains a hold on our impulsive id-world. Normally, when we think of conscience, we think common-sensically of that inner voice that warns us: "Don't do that, don't think this." Unlike a culture based on fear, in which punishing agents of social control must be in evidence—much as a policeman must be visible—a culture based on guilt has little need for the visible presence of agents of control. After years of proper socialization have inculcated persons with the culture's conscience, they become their own agents of control, their own cops, heeding the "wisdom" of the inner voice.

In contrast to either fear or guilt, shame calls upon exposure to the glare of public ridicule or scorn. It is the feeling we have on being exposed to public scrutiny, to being revealed with all our blemishes and odors; when the audience sees us, the performer, "off" and in our natural pose.

No culture bases all its mechanisms of social control on only one of this terrible trio; rather, all cultures have heavy mixings of fear, guilt, and shame. Nevertheless, it is possible to note the dominance of one form or the other in a given culture or in a given point in culture's own historical development. The totalitarian state governs and controls man's behavior by fear, rarely trusting persons enough to place much weight on either guilt or shame. Yet, even here, socialization practices teach persons to internalize a proper conscience and thus to experience guilt when transgressing the dictatorial demands made on them. Likewise, shaming rituals form a part of such cultures, as for example, when the person's head is shaved or in some other way deviant misadventures are brought into public view where they may be properly ridiculed and shamed.

Likewise, the culture that hopes to base its control on guilt nevertheless has punishment waiting in the wings, in case guilt fails and unacceptable behavior pops out. Most democratic societies operate in this manner, using guilt-type techniques but reserving the iron fist of naked police power when they fail. When the appeals to honor thy country, thy president, thy flag, thy school, thy pentagon, all fall upon deaf ears, tweaking no consciences but those of the elders, one finds the police and troops called out to quell the riot and restore order.[3]

We would expect that the use of shame as a mechanism of social control would be especially characteristic of a culture that is other-directed. What could be worse than the embarrassment of being shamed in public, of being seen for the person we really are? All societies utilize shame. When a society reaches a point at which persons fundamentally serve as mirrors for others, however, being shamed becomes a potent mechanism for social control. The threat of being shamed may take the form of "what will the neighbors say or think?" In such a society, the person knows that his outrages will be revealed for all to see; he will be ridiculed; he will be the object of community scorn.[4] Recall Asch's[5] laboratory demonstration of the impact of shame: persons even distort their actual perceptions in order not to be exposed to the ridicule of looking different to their peers.

In an other-directed society, shame can be utilized not only for social control but also for social change. The same mechanism that can keep behavior in line can be employed to change it. Thus, while fear of being punished, for example, may keep us walking the narrow path, it can also be used by those who wish to change the society. Threats and counter-threats by revolutionary groups fill out this picture all too clearly. In like manner, shame can be employed as a mechanism for attempting to induce change in a society.

Since others serve as mirrors to reflect our life to us, if what they reflect through their actions and behavior reveals a portrait of our inner life—impulses and longings that are carefully kept under wraps and of which we are only dimly aware—in looking at them, we see a part of us we wish never to see portrayed. Their shameful acts, their public outrages, while shaming them, does much more. It shames us, it embarrasses us, for we see ourselves revealed in their mirrors.

At a San Francisco repertory performance of Genet's *The Balcony*, the director placed three huge mirrors on the stage, so angled that the audience could see itself reflected in them. The performance on stage thereby became more personally revealing to the audience, which was not simply viewing actors engaged in outrageous behavior, but at the same time seeing itself.

The mirror thus reveals and exposes; the mirror-holder, while revealing himself, also reveals those who do not wish to be defrocked in public. Shame can be utilized to effect social change by raising the person's consciousness concerning heretofore denied, neglected, or unconscious parts of life. If all the pimples and blemishes of the society were to rise up in one brash moment and declare, "Look at me," everyone would try to hush them up; after all they spoil the packaged image. At the same time, everyone would become painfully aware that what the blemishes reveal is real. He who raises up the mirror to our blemishes is more likely to be crucified as outrageous, shameful, deviant, an agent of the devil, than to be considered worthy of concern or esteem. But at least he has planted a seed before his demise.

It is useful to examine several aspects of protest in the 1960s in this context of shame and other-directedness. In particular, the counterculture's life style, its forms of dress and demeanor, was shameful to the established society in that it held up a blemish-revealing mirror—a mirror that revealed the superficiality of relationships, the cool but inhuman efficiency of the rationalized bureaucratic structures, and so on. Likewise, the protest of Third World groups revealed the painful blemish of inequality and injustice that had existed for so long but had been carefully denied by the American ideal of equality for all. Predictably, the response to seeing these blemishes revealed was an attempt to do away with those who dared to expose this shameful side of our lives.

The child of rich parents who wears tattered hand-me-downs or at times nothing at all, running naked through the streets, his long hair flowing, is engaging in a potent shaming ritual. We know that we are not to run naked in public; we know that men are not to wear hair so long that it confuses them with women. We can almost hear his mother pleading, "Tommy, what will the neighbors say when they see you running around naked or in tattered clothing?" We know what the neighbors will say: "What's wrong, can't they afford a barber?" "What's wrong, can't they buy him better clothes?" "What's wrong?" That is what they will say. And much more. Neighbors do talk, especially when an outrage is being perpetrated.

Tommy is shaming himself and his family by running naked through the streets. But he is doing more. In revealing himself, he is at the same time holding up a mirror and revealing societal blemishes. He is showing those who are upset by his nakedness but not by the deaths caused by taxpayer-supported bombs just where their real values lie. He is telling *his* parents and *all* parents that their efforts to give him everything material in the form of clothing, haircuts, a good home, and so forth have not been sufficient; he doesn't want more products to add to an already heavily cluttered list. His nakedness, his long hair, or his tattered clothing are a comment about each of us as much as they are a comment about him. And our response reveals more about us and our situation than about him. The mirror-holder, and this is what little naked Tommy is, shows his audience their faces and their lives. We live through his reflection of us.

But that is only part of the picture. The audience rarely receives such images quietly and thoughtfully. The threat of the naked Tommy, the tattered Tommy, the long-haired Tommy, the bearded Tommy, the black Tommy, the Chicano Tommy, the angry Tommy, is that his very presence tells us too much about us, reveals too much about things we cover over and keep hidden even from ourselves. His actions make us liable to being embarrassed and shamed as well.

The man who sees Tommy run naked through the streets may see himself longing after the boy; he resents the boy for revealing such an embarrassing, shameful idea to him and surely to those who can read his lecherous mind. "Get the boy clothed!" thus becomes a means of reducing the impulsive discharge within one's self. During the early civil-rights demonstrations in the U.S. South, many well-meaning towns-folk urged that the marches not be held because they served to bring out the bad element in town. In effect, they said, "Stop your marches and there won't be any trouble; have your marches and the bad people in town will come out and hurt you." "If you don't reveal my hidden impulses, we'll all be better off. So blemish, please go away and remain concealed."

There is more. While shaming his culture, Tommy is also a member of that culture. He simultaneously holds up a mirror to society and to himself. He now has a dual victory with which to deal. As he runs naked through the streets, engaging in this embarrassing outrage, even he feels that he should be caught and punished for his shameful activities. This does not mean that Tommy is aware that his shame must inevitably be punished. It does mean, however, that given his own embeddedness in the society he is trying to change, he is dimly aware that the story he is telling through his behavior is not complete until he is caught and punished. He, too, senses that deviance is to be punished; then, and only then, can the story end.

Thus Tommy cannot be fully satisfied until he is caught and punished. And at that moment, his second victory occurs. For once caught and punished for indecent exposure (I am using this example both as a real case in point and as a metaphor for all such instances of shaming behavior), he can now express moral outrage at a society that punishes him for being naked while it wages wars and keeps persons frozen in poverty and hunger at home.

So glorious a victory for one small young person to have! In being caught he can be doubly fulfilled. On the one hand, his capture validates the system which he has opened to question; he satisfies even himself as a person who is intimately embedded in that system. On the other hand, by being caught and punished for so ridiculous an act, he has forced another mirror revelation on the true nature of the society.

As complex as this picture now is, it grows even more complicated by the further implications of other-directedness. A society that is other-directed is not only responsive to being ridiculed by shameful acts, but in addition is responsive to the changing images these acts represent. The mirror-holder both shames the other-directed society and at the same time begins to represent an attractive alternative system of values, fads, and fashions that we might all entertain adopting. The innovator or prophet may be killed but at the same time may leave behind a legacy of social change when the followers adopt his innovation and make it their own.

The preceding pattern clearly emerged during the 1960s, ranging from the adoption of the protest modality itself through the adoption of ethnic and other category-based group formations (e.g., woman's liberation, gay liberation, Jewish Defense League), to various countercultural life styles.

Out of innovation, rejection, and adoption there emerges an escalating cycle which leads to depressive despair. The shaming innovator, holding up the mirror, declaring all to be bankrupt, notes that he may actually have created a bandwagon effect. Other-directed societies are quick to gobble up all new things in their ever-moving search for new fads to conquer, new thrills to experience, new values, new fashions. Our innovator is gobbled up and destroyed by his very act of innovation. His life style, which meant something and was a social commentary and analysis at its inception, is gobbled up and spit out by the masses. Love-burgers are sold in Haight-Ashbury; beards, beads, and long hair appear on Madison Avenue and Wall Street: yesterday's innovation becomes today's "in" thing and tomorrow's old hat.

Motivated still to shame and thereby to effect real change, the dedicated protestor must now be committed to an ever-increasing escalation of his shameful outrages. In an other-directed society that mass-markets a thing the day after it appears, to be outrageous requires that one escalate the outrages. The question the social teaser must ask himself is, "What can I do next that will be outrageous?" If what was outrageous on Monday becomes the dominant other-directed cultural norm on Wednesday, then by Friday, I must think creatively in order to push the monster just a bit further.

And so the protestors sought to push things more and more to new boundaries of outrage. Yet the other-directed gobbler became increasingly capable of absorbing every new outrage, adopting that latest madness as its own ideal. No one really intended that persons adopt the maddest fringe ideas and life styles as their own; rather these were life styles that sought to mirror the societal blemishes and thereby to effect a change in them by raising levels of self-consciousness. But the monster didn't know that; it only knew that the avant-garde had found a new thing that we all simply had to try on and try out. So the most ridiculous and foolish manners of living were to become an integral part—at least for a day—of the culture. Finally exhausted, filled with despair, or at minimum, having moved about as far to the fringes as one could ever go, the innovators stopped. They abandoned us, left us wandering about, wondering, waiting for that new Messiah of pop culture to come along and drag us on but one more journey. Maybe this will be the right one; or is there ever a right one?

The vanguard innovators whose shame turned into the very norm they sought to reveal cut their hair, trimmed their beards, went into isolation, cynical, despairing. They had failed. They hoped that through shame they would create change; instead they served only to feed the monster what it wanted, never revealing the true shape of the beast. It is as though the Zen master, knowing that the basic truth is that there is no basic truth, nevertheless sought to teach his students this as a fact which they would then adopt dutifully, thereby missing the main point of his lesson. It would be like the psychotherapist who sought to help his patient become free and autonomous by hypnotizing him and then declaring him autonomous. So too with the protesting vanguard of the 1960s who misread the tarot cards and fueled the attributes they had hoped to modify. When you do battle with a bowl of soft jello, one that absorbs whatever you put into it, you must remember that with every step forward your followers are there for the wrong reasons.

11

On Responsibility and Apathy:

DIMENSION V

Of the various dimensions of the natural perspective and the interpersonal world it generates, none is as crucial as that concerning the entire concept of individual responsibility. Earlier, I suggested that role theory successfully describes a key aspect of our interpersonal world. In that view, societies are organized into positions or roles, rather than persons. We can conduct an analysis of how roles function within a group, an organization, or a society without much consideration for the unique contribution of the person who is enacting that role. As the analysis suggests, within certain broad limits it matters little who becomes the President of the United States; for in that role, even the most liberal man will necessarily have to enact more conservative policies, just as the most conservative will necessarily be liberalized.

Awareness of this influence of roles on our behavior has led both to innovations in psychotherapy and to a reconsideration of the phenomena of brainwashing and thought reform. If it is true that a person's behavior is affected by the roles he takes on, this fact provides a potent technique for those interested in producing behavior change. Psychodrama[1] utilizes role playing in much this manner. By enacting the various roles that have influenced his life, the patient gains perspective on himself and uncovers areas of hidden conflict which can be worked through under the guidance of an able psycho-drama therapist. The use of role playing in intergroup conflict and in industrial training is another effort to use role taking to change an individual's outlook and behavior. Brainwashing and thought-reform techniques[2] place the prisoner in a dependent role—much as do prisons and mental hospitals—and thereby manage a change in his entire outlook on life. Being placed in the position of a dependent child can have potent effects on the once-adult who now must turn to others to have his every need satisfied. Bettelheim[3] comments on this factor in the Nazi concentration camps, in which the prisoners had to get permission for everything they did, even going to the toilet.

One of the cornerstones of this theory, and thus of our everyday life, is the careful differentiation made between the person and his role. On the one side we have the ego, the self, the person; and on the other, the role, the societal position that the person takes. In the language of role theory, much as in the language of everyday life, we enact roles, put on roles, play roles, perform roles, etc. In other words, our ego is not the role, but rather is presumed to exist somewhere beyond the role or apart from it.

For example, in common parlance we say, "*I* wish *I* didn't have to do that, but as a parent I must; as a teacher, I must; as a juror, I must; as an *X*, I must." (Fill in your own *X*.) In these simple, everyday declarations, we manifest the intuitive, background social analysis by which our behavior is governed and which declares that our ego is separate from the obligations required by our social roles. To extend this analysis a bit further, we note that our everyday life almost always involves role contexts in which we enact roles that we feel to a certain degree are not us. Most of the time we are involved in part-activities, where the part is never the whole of us.

The preceding state of affairs gives many of us a sense of personal alienation. We are never wholly engaged in our role performances; there is always a degree of separation between ourselves and our role's obligations. The teacher proclaims,

"*I* don't want to flunk you, but the teacher must." From all around we listen to the proclamations of a society of persons who are not responsible, never responsible, who would have acted otherwise, if only they could.

We listen to the subject in Milgram's study.[4] He asks the experimenter to take responsibility for his behavior. The experimenter agrees. The subject, recognizing the obligations of his role, says "*I* don't want to continue, but I must, and since you've taken responsibility from me, I can now act in better conscience." He applies devastating electric shocks to another person. But in his view, *he* is not the one who applied those shocks; it was the experimenter, the system, the others: never me, the subject, the ego, I.

Recent formulations of the attribution process are relevant to this analysis.[5] The issue is how we use the behaviors of another person (or even ourselves) as the basis for attributing motives and personality traits to them. For example, how is it that I conclude that you are a happy person or angry or courageous or responsible? Research on the attribution process has suggested support for the position I have taken regarding the typically nonresponsible quality of our everyday life. As long as a person behaves in a manner consistent with the demands of his role, observers who view his actions conclude that he should not be personally held responsible for what he does: after all, he was simply following orders, responding to external pressure. It is only when a person's behavior deviates from what is expected according to his roles that we observers reach conclusions about his motives, personality, or responsibility: about him as an ego, an I. As long as you do what any reasonable person in your role would do, we conclude very little about you personally or about your responsibility for what has been done; however, as soon as you deviate from the usual, then we begin to attribute qualities to you as an individual.[6]

These conclusions from the systematic social-psychological laboratory are especially important; they indicate the dominance of the perspective of everyday life as revealed even within laboratory contexts. They demonstrate that the manner by which we infer or attribute qualities to another—qualities such as "he is personally responsible for his actions"—follows the role-theory process as outlined.

This research also enlightens us further; it suggests that not only do our inferences about others function in this manner, but so do our inferences about ourselves. If my behavior falls within the proper confines of my roles, I do not hold myself personally responsible for what I have done. I was merely following orders, just as you were. To the extent that our or others' behaviors can be attributed to external pressures—e.g., roles, institutional demands—to that extent do we refuse to hold ourselves or others personally responsible for the consequences.

What would we do without the external pressures, the roles, the others to take the burden of responsibility from us and thereby provide an everyday perspective that is built upon a background of personal nonresponsibility? Obviously, without those differentiations, we would always be personally involved and personally responsible for others in whatever actions we took. How distressing!

One goal of sensitivity training is to help persons *own up* to their responsibility both for their own feelings and behaviors and for the group's.[7] This turns out to be a difficult task indeed, since the cultural attitudinal system has a built-in, almost "instinctive" mechanism for taking the copout: "Don't blame me"; "I'm not responsible"; "What do you expect of me? I'm just playing a role"; "They did it, he did it, my role did it, not me."

An expression often heard in such groups is a variant on this role copout: the psychiatric copout. The person, his face wracked with the painful anxiety of a past memory now brought to present life, mumbles, "I couldn't help it, I didn't want to say that, I didn't want to hurt you, but you see it was because . . ." He launches into a lengthy psychoanalytic story of a mother who did this to him, a father who did that, and on and on and on. He can now proudly say that "I" didn't want to; it was that bad me, the past me, that forced me to act in this nasty way. Hardly different from the role version in which we say that we were only doing our duty, following orders. This psychiatric version has the orders coming from a past-determined role.

In each case, the *I* is left off the hook and *They* take over responsibility. How convenient *They* are. We use *Them* to explain the woes of the entire universe. *They* are the forces of evil affecting our past and shaping our present. *They* are ever-present, ubiquitous monsters preventing the real *I* from coming forth and doing what good needs to be done.

I am talking about a crucial dimension of the total perspective of the natural standpoint, one which we each put on unconsciously and routinely every day in our relationships with life. We do not have to think twice about this matter, for it exists as a commonplace, accepted background understanding.

The alternative perspective is especially difficult to take; it demands that we own up to the personal responsibility for our own actions, regardless of circumstances and conditions. This alternative requires that we not differentiate between actor and role but rather be aware of the presence of the actor in every act taken, including those which conform to role demands and those which deviate from role demands. We are only too eager to take personal responsibility when we defy convention and stand up for our rights; then the *I* is vitally present and held aloft as a responsible force. It is only when we seem to be pushed against our wills that the natural perspective permits us to get off the hook. The alternative is not as kind; it requires a presence of *us* in all that we say or do, in the mundane and cowardly as well as the heroic.

Nonresponsibility serves as a potent mechanism of social control. Ideal social control is achieved when the persons within a system are so properly socialized that they come to *want* to do what they have to do in order to maintain the system.[8] Any system of either punishment or reward would otherwise require more surveillance than would be feasible in a large society. Thus it is especially useful for persons to acquire an inner valuation of conforming to expectations and requirements.[9]

Roles provide a representation of social organization that limits the range of legitimate individual behavior and helps place us in contexts in which we are naturally doing what we are supposed to do. Every time we put ourselves into a role, whatever that role may be, we also place ourselves in an entire network of expectations and requirements that are well beyond our own individual peculiarities. In the role, we act in a manner that suits system requirements, much as an actor in a play portrays a character that fits the playwright's requirements.

A professional actor who thinks of himself as kind and gentle may accept a part in which he is required to act cruel and evil, and he does not worry that he, the person, the ego, is in fact the role. Much the same thing happens in everyday life: we put on a role and perform its requirements as part of the societal drama's demands without feeling that we *are* in fact that role. Thus, we can *act* cruel and evil without having to *be* cruel and evil. The society's needs are met and we are able to preserve whatever self-image we wish, at least within the limits offered by others' responses to our performance.

Just as the audience grants to the actor his right to be whatever he really is without confusing him with his role, so too does the societal audience let us play our roles without feeling that we really are that way. Eichmann's friends and associates can praise him for doing a good job and for being a good person, thereby helping to reinforce his picture of himself as a good person whose role asks him to do bad things.[10]

Without the kind of split just outlined, it would be difficult indeed for a social system to function; for in such cases, it would have to police everyone (and where would the police come from?) while training them to perform roles that might otherwise not be compatible with their wants or desires. A system that splits person from role, one that is reinforced every day in our relationships with others, permits us to be recruited to roles that accomplish socially essential things while not engaging us personally. Thus control over the performance is had without necessarily having to change our basic nature or our desire to think well of ourselves and be thought well of by others.

If we are all merely actors playing roles, then we may safely do all sorts of things and not change our beliefs in ourselves. The functions served by this sense of personal nonresponsibility thus are served both for the individual and for the social system. Both are maintained without as much disruption as would occur were we *to be* the role rather than to *take it on*, or were others to insist that we are what we do rather than being something more than what we do. The teacher who says, "I would like to help you, but as a teacher I cannot do that," can continue to think well of himself as a helpful person who is just doing a job properly; this conclusion is aided and abetted by all those with whom the teacher comes into contact who express the same kind of sentiment: "Yes, it is too bad that you as a teacher couldn't do otherwise, but don't worry too much, you had no choice, you had to act as you did." Thus reinforced, we can continue doing our job well. And the job itself, as part of the network of jobs and roles within the social system, gets done and on we go.

There is more. The same system of everyday life that creates personal nonresponsibility also creates personal apathy. If I am not to be held responsible for my actions or their consequences, then why should I care? Why should I get involved? Why should I be active? The rhetoric of the day lauds involvement and caring, but any society would in fact suffer terribly if all its citizens were to become equally interested and involved in its affairs. Apathy serves a vital function to any social system.

An organism that did not selectively process the huge array of stimuli that confronted it every moment would soon become immobilized. Selectivity of responsiveness is necessary to organismic survival.[11] Imagine trying to think about something while noting with equal concern the total array of stimuli now coming in: the feeling of the pants on your legs, the ringing in your ears, the taste in your mouth, the breaths you are taking, the blinking of your eyes, the smells in your nose, etc., etc., etc. A society that did not have the selective engagement of its members would be as overwhelmed and unable to function as the unselecting organism. Apathy serves this vital selective function.

Picture the situation that would exist if all the citizens in a community wished to participate equally in the processes of government and decision making. Nothing would ever get done; services would come to a halt; everything would be in chaos and confusion. Finally, the system would die like a dinosaur from its own weight. While a certain level of citizen interest and involvement is necessary, that level never requires full participation, and in fact, depends upon citizen apathy and unconcern in order to succeed at all.

Apathy is a frequently, albeit implicitly, reinforced dimension of the perspective of everyday life. Apathy, as a societal selector mechanism, permits more to be done for more persons than would otherwise be possible. A system that builds upon apathy to maintain itself, of course, must assure that the needs of its apathetic members are met, lest their apathy turn into activity and threaten to overwhelm the survival capabilities of the entire system. As long as reasonable services are provided, the normal citizen will be more than willing to maintain himself routinely and automatically (i.e., without awareness) in apathy, as an uncaring cog in the machinery that requires him to be apathetic.

12

The Developmental Thesis: The Production and Maintenance of the Natural Standpoint:

ARGUMENT I

To this point, I have argued that the behaviorist's and the constructivist's views of persons are both generally correct; that for most practical purposes these two seemingly opposed theories are more alike than different; that we commonly and routinely end up after our years of socialization with a shared orientation or perspective, which I have termed the natural standpoint of everyday life; that we thereby create an interpersonal world of relationships which we pass through daily in a more or less mechanical, habitual, and routinized manner; that for better or worse, in our everyday lives, we are like highly complex, sophisticated machines rather than the glamorous image the poets and wishful thinkers of social science have imagined or hoped.

But why? What are the conditions, both psychological and sociological, that *produce* and *maintain* the perspective of the natural standpoint and the kind of interpersonal world which it brings into existence? There are three major arguments for the existence and maintenance of this perspective: (1) the developmental argument; (2) the functional argument; (3) the population-technology argument.

* * *

Developmentally, society *precedes* the individual; the individual is from birth a creature of his society, a realization of social forces. Society precedes self; collectivity precedes individuality. Our very concept of self develops on the basis of those reflections we receive from others.[1] Before any individuality can be carved out, if at all, we are first and foremost a collective being, a "me." (See Chapter 19 for details on this view.)

The society in which we live creates the mind we evolve, including our concept of who we are and where we fit into the entire picture. While a naive position maintains that mind creates society—that the person's mind functions to create a conception of society—a long line of sociological, psychological, and philosophical thinkers have taken the opposite view: society creates mind. From birth, we are utterly dependent on others for our own sense of external reality; in this developmental sense, we are all other-directed, social-comparative creatures.

Marx's analysis[2] of individual consciousness maintains that mind develops from the person's relationship to the means of production. The worker develops a mind, a consciousness, a self-concept, very different from the owner. In the Marxist analysis, the material social order of economic class precedes the individual's psychological order of mind and forms the basis out of which individual mind develops.

In his analyses of the symbolic systems of cultures, Ernst Cassirer[3] has noted that in the myth, the discovery of a purely individual self, an I, occurs not at the beginning but at the end of the process. The I emerges and is known only as an outcome, a product of interactive relationships with a thou, another person or character.

We can see how, from life as a whole, from its undifferentiated totality . . . one's own being . . . rises up and separates out only very slowly—and how within this being the reality of the genus and the species always precedes that of the individual.[4]

* * *

To paraphrase Cassirer's position, we can say that individual consciousness arises from the stream of cultural consciousness that exists before it and continues to live after the individual mind has ceased its own existence.

To borrow the term used by psychoanalyst Ernest Schachtel,[5] the growth of individuality is characterized by an emergence from "embeddedness"—in the womb in which life begins, in sociological webs of mother, family, play group, community, and eventually the entire society: all are ongoing contexts in which we are embedded and from which our individuality slowly emerges.

From several different theoretical perspectives, therefore, it is clear that mind, self, or consciousness could not emerge without the existence of an ongoing social process out of which this reflection of individuality stands forth and grows. Once having arisen, of course, mind then becomes another constitutive element that influences the very social process which was its origin. Though individuality derives from collectivity, once individuality emerges, it becomes a new part of the collectivity to which it and other individualities must now respond. As with most things social *and* psychological, there is both a *reflective* and a *shaping* process involved. The mirror that reflects also shapes.

Sartre's *No Exit*[6] includes a striking scene in which the incessantly primping Estelle, without her usual mirror, asks Inez to be her mirror. Inez reflects a pimple on Estelle's otherwise perfect and attractive face. In agony over this apparent blemish, Estelle seeks its eradication, only to be rebuffed by her very human mirror. But it turns out to be a joke; there is no pimple, only a lark mirror, reflecting in order to entrap.

In much this manner, but perhaps more benignly in most cases, our concept of ourselves, our "me," emerges from a social web within which we become reflections of others' views. Who we are arises in interaction with others, is sustained in this interaction, and ceases only when we cease to exist. Our social selves, this "me" that grows within, carries the message of our life history and our ongoing experiences. From our inception, we are socially rooted beings.

While some authorities view this developmental process as passive, in that we receive but do little to shape,[7] those of a more psychological persuasion, especially within the constructivist paradigm, speak of two complementary processes involved in all development: assimilation and accommodation.[8] The initially vague inner organizing tendencies of the person, which Piaget has termed *schema*, exist from birth, shaping while being shaped by encounters with the surrounding world of persons and social institutions. Schema transform raw experiences by assimilating them into an existing, ongoing mental organization; yet schema are themselves transformed through their accommodation to these newly emerging experiences. Assimilation works to achieve consistency over time by modifying the moment to fit our existing state; accommodation works to achieve change, growth, and development by modifying our existing state as a function of new experiences.

In this developmental view, we both transform the social order that exists independently of our consciousness (i.e., assimilation) and are transformed by that order (i.e., accommodation). The outcome of this interactive encounter is mind and self, anchored both within our schema and within social reality.

Obviously it would be possible to enlarge the list of philosophers and social scientists who have adopted this developmental position. The point, however, is not to provide a burdensome listing of like-minded analysts, but rather to point out what to me seems a simple but important truth. If our very mind, our consciousness, our sense of self, emerges as an outcome of a social and interactive process, we are then developmentally from our beginnings rooted in and dependent on other persons and social institutions. From our origins, we are fundamentally other-directed and socially comparative; our consciousness itself arises from other-directedness.

In this view then, all persons, everywhere, regardless of the nature of their social system, are basically other-directed characters. This fundamental aspect is important to understand when we puzzle over why persons seem to follow routinely and mechanically the norms of groups, their roles and social institutions. If our origins are within society, then our present everyday existence must certainly reflect this fundamental fact of our life. It could not be otherwise.

The real puzzle, then, is not how we fit in and live out our lives routinely within the perspective of the natural standpoint, but how some persons manage to move beyond the routine into the exceptional; how this fundamental developmental fact is ever transcended.

13

The Functional Thesis:

ARGUMENT II

For the survival both of the individual and of society, it is necessary for people to adopt and live by the perspective of the natural standpoint. But a thing that is functional[1] to the survival of a social system may be detrimental or dysfunctional to the survival of an individual part of that system. In time of famine, for example, it may be functional to the survival of the larger community for certain persons to die, e.g., the elderly, the sick, and the weak; some groups that live in an environment of extreme scarcity do indeed abandon the very elderly or kill newborns so that the collectivity may survive.[2] We who live in a society of plenty shudder at such a practice, yet species survival overrules apparent individual need. On the other hand, something that is functional to the individual, contributing to his personal survival, may not be functional to the collectivity: e.g., criminal behavior, or for that matter, any individualistic action that benefits oneself at others' expense, such as cutting in front of others and pushing to the head of the line. The production and maintenance of the perspective of the natural standpoint, however, is functional *both* to the individual *and* the larger social system.

A functional analysis should demonstrate how the interpersonal world of everyday life serves to maintain individual and collective survival and therefore suggest why it is so difficult for each of us to transcend the natural perspective. The seen but unnoticed interpersonal world of everyday life is a human accomplishment that serves a vital purpose; resistance to its modification is understandable once we understand the functions its maintenance serves.

In several previous chapters I have examined the specific functions served by the various aspects of the everyday perspective. But its function *fundamentally* revolves about the theme of *mastery*, including mastery over self, over others, and over the environment.[3] Without mastery, there is neither collective nor individual survival. The growth of the ego is testimony to the individual's persistent pursuit of competence, control, and mastery. Culture itself is a construction which seeks to conquer chaos, to offer a shelter that permits the human species and its individual members to survive. For every angry arrow we sling at the culture we have created and at times find oppressive, we also reserve a quiet rose of thanks and appreciation for its service to us in enabling us to escape from the jungle. Cultural perfection has never existed, but the unknown offers only a fearful and risky alternative. Few of us are ready to open the doors, let alone pass through them to venture into whatever void lies just beyond the warmth of the hearth.

Mastery over self, others, and life demands a sensibility, a reasonableness, and an orderliness about us, about them, about things in general. We gladly sacrifice adventure for this order. The potent pressures that others bring to bear upon us to "shape up and fit in" are met about equally with the pressures we bring upon ourselves not to extend too far beyond the limits of the known and the sanctioned. The perspective of the natural standpoint is an achievement not only of others' demands upon us; we also passionately strive to find the straight-and-narrow, and when we have, we tread it with dutiful pleasure.

But mastery is a tenuous accomplishment in need of constant surveillance and defense. Once attained, it is not an achievement that rests easy; like the freedom we love and which it gives, it must be eternally and vigilantly guarded. The inner world of passions threatens to burst forth and flood upon the surrounding scene. Strong feelings in ourselves and others are troublesome; they introduce too much nonpredictability and noncontrol into life. Passions threaten to master us; we want to keep them in control.

Time itself moves relentlessly forward, introducing changes we once could hardly imagine, presenting alternatives that beckon even as they frighten.[4] We find conflict between choices that we wish had never been possible; options thrust us this way and that, moving us about too loosely for our pleasures long to endure. In their very diversity, other persons make claims of doubt upon our own perspective on reality. Their refusal to fit into our scheme of things threatens our own pleasant party.

Along with about thirty others, I was invited to a Halloween party given by a colleague of mine. Our instructions were to come fully disguised, "so that no one would ever know who you were." I felt it a great idea and took the instruction literally, arriving in a loud leap over the garden wall onto the terrace dressed in full disguise as a monster. People were properly amused. The evening wore on. I continued in my disguise. Others had already emerged from theirs. There was Tom, and Marjorie. As soon as the disguise came down and the person was identified, each of us cheered within ourselves, for now we knew how to relate to this otherwise mysterious thing. But I never revealed my identity. I remained anonymous. Was I treated with joy as the night wore on? Hardly. I was seen increasingly as a foreign element, an alien, an intruder. I was something no longer to be laughed at, but rather to be questioned. Who was I? People poked me, pushed me, probed to find out. I never yielded to these pressures and finally I was rejected. No one wanted to deal with me now that the game had worn on far beyond their limits.

A person concealed within a black bag enters the classroom and takes a seat. All laugh. Teacher lectures. All laugh. "Why doesn't he notice the bag?" Tomorrow arrives; the bag is still there. More laughter, but more nervous than previously. Tomorrow again. Bag there. Laughter subsides, replaced by anger. Days pass and soon intolerance becomes the norm. Get rid of that bag. Who is the bag?[5] We tolerate little that intrudes onto our scene; we tolerate little that threatens our mastery over it.

Knowledge provides one avenue to mastery; so too does conformity: Ours and Yours. Ignorance is bliss as long as you and I act in expected ways. Our fundamental anxiety is not fear of death; for in death all need for mastery has passed away. Our anxiety is in living. Conquering life drives us more than worry about death does. Suicide reflects a final running away from the puzzling commitments that claim us in our lives.

Coming of age involves learning ways to be competent in one's culture, to minimize its confusion, to gain mastery, to control. The ego is open and curious, wondering; yet at the same time we hope the puzzle will be solved and order restored. We walk a line between the pursuit of a novelty that whets our appetites and our passionate need to have everything known and predictable, well within the bounds of our control or at least someone's control.

Moreover, we care more that there be control than we care about who or what exerts it. When confusion mounts, we cry out for help, for guidance. Give us a tyrant who will give us order, who will set the limits of our freedom. We differ in how much disarray we can tolerate, but fundamentally, we would all grab for anyone's mastery over pure anarchy.

To lose control is to lose our self, our identity as a person, an individual with a past and an anticipated future. We waken and dread the day before us; its path is too well known. We claim boredom; it is dull. But awaken one day and know not where you are, who you are, where you have come from, where you are going. Exciting? Don Marquis' philosophical moth[6] plunges into fiery death, shoots his wad for one pure moment; we civilized folk give up beauty and excitement just to live a bit longer routinely, even in boredom.[7] The pain we feel gives comfort; better to be in pain here and now than in doubt somewhere unknown.

By mastery we seek to reduce surprises in everyday living.

Routines that reduce surprise, that help us fit in, get by, adapt, are reinforced by us and Them. We reinforce Them for acting in nonsurprising, reassuring ways; we are reinforced by Them for behaving in minimally surprising and disruptive ways.

All of us are fundamentally conservative; we resist change. None of us really wants to venture too far beyond the lighted boundaries of our particular life. Those who appear most hell-bent on creating change are as resistant to change as those in whom they wish to induce change. The battle rages over which changes will prevail, over whose circle of light will encompass whom.

Our friends validate us; our enemies threaten.[8] They introduce doubt, cause surprise, confuse. Gather round me men who think not too much. We want our freedom within the sandbox; outside is too free,[9] too vague: ill-defined boundaries, few limits to offer guidance and control, to light the way. All is darkness; culture's everyday routines light the way. Damn the light! Praise the light! Where is the light?

Does this mean that to question or to doubt is dysfunctional? Doubt is the vehicle to tomorrow that also keeps us here today. Too much doubt and we return home again, opting for the security of the known over the questions of tomorrow. The line is so thin, so delicate; even in our roughness we are fragile. We want to know what lies beyond but do not really want to pay the price such knowledge would bring. Help us get through today; give us this day our daily bread and tempt us not. That is our want, deeply and fundamentally. *We* control, *we* master, or you, Lord, control, master, define the limits and keep us within them. It is not only children who ask for limits to help them maintain self-control even as they rebuff those who offer them these limits; in this respect we are all children, God's children.

14

The Population-Technology Thesis:

ARGUMENT III

Until now, I have argued that mind, self, and consciousness are emergents of social interaction; thus, the other-directed quality of our everyday perspective and its consequences are fundamental to all human life. I have further argued that the natural perspective serves important functions to the individual and society and is therefore continually reinforced and validated in everyday interaction. We come now to a final basis for the production and the maintenance of the natural standpoint. Population growth coupled with technological development has created and maintains a typical societal character type whose predominant perspective is describable as the natural standpoint.

Roger Barker,[1] a pioneer in research on psychological ecology, relates certain stable features of man's environment to several psychological consequences. He introduces the concept of behavior setting to refer to the ecological locations in which we carry out our daily living: e.g., a drugstore, a classroom, a bowling alley, a restaurant, a baseball team, a school play, a picnic. Barker maintains that although men create behavior settings, once these settings are established, they follow a logic that is not dependent on individual psychological factors as much as on economic and technical ones. Similarly, Ellul's concept of technology is of a development that extends beyond the scope of the individual's psyche, that leads a life of its own and drags persons into its web.[2] As in the Frankenstein story, man creates a monster which sweeps its creator up into its own dynamic. The master-creator soon becomes the victim-pawn.

According to Barker, about 95 percent of our behavior can be explained by reference to the behavior setting in which it occurs.[3] Once we know the setting in which the person is located, we can fairly well predict what the person will do: if a man is in a bowling alley, this very fact narrows the range of options available to him and thereby increases our ability to make accurate predictions about his behavior.

Barker next maintains that of all the features of which behavior settings are composed, persons are both the most indispensable and the most malleable. In one of his studies, Barker and his colleague Gump[4] examined the difference in the impact on the individual of being a student in a small school or a large one. In the large school, there were many persons to staff each of the several behavior settings that existed—football team, band, school play, classrooms, etc.— whereas in the small school, while the same number of settings existed, fewer individuals were available to man each one. The effect was to make the individuals in the smaller setting more *needed* and *individually valuable* than those in the larger or overpopulated setting. In an overpopulated environment there are enough persons to staff all the settings that are available; each person is more or less *superfluous*. But in a smaller setting, each person's work performance is vital.

Barker extended his analysis to the study of two communities, one in the United States and one in England.[5] For his purposes, the key difference between these two communities was their ratio of population-to-setting. The U.S. setting was underpopulated, having too few persons; the British, by contrast, was overpopulated and thus people were superfluous.

Barker noted the implication of this difference on the communities' philosophies of education. In the U.S. town, where every community member's services were vital to keep the system functioning, each person's school life was integrated with his or her community life. The philosophy of education maintained that schoolchildren should be involved in the community's activities; this was an essential part of their educational experience. We need only think of a farming community at harvest time to appreciate this sense of individual value. By contrast, in the overpopulated English community, where each person was superfluous, the educational ideology maintained that children should be kept away at school, that there should be only minimal involvement of school-age children in the adult affairs of the community. Barker noted that if one were to take an American child and put him into an English setting, and take an English youngster and put him into an American setting, each would soon adapt to the different prevailing philosophies and psychological concomitants. The transferred American would soon learn that his involvement in the community was not wanted and that he had better stick to the books and let the adults govern; the transplanted Britisher would learn that his isolated ivory-towerism was not desirable; his active involvement was vital.

Barker takes us one step further. He notes that in overpopulated settings, *what* we do (i.e., our performances) is not relevant to our definition either in the eyes of others or in our own eyes; therefore, we become highly sensitive to non-performance, *qualitative* bases for differentiating and evaluating others. To put this another way, if you are superfluous, both others' definitions of you and your own self-definition cannot be meaningfully based on what work you do. What you do is not essential to the community; there are many more at home like you. But, what you are, how you live, what you look like—all kinds of qualitative distinctions—become salient points for defining self and others.

Is this not the essence of the other-directed society in which persons become highly sensitized to others, not for what they do but for what they are like?[6] Indeed. Barker has taken us on a slightly different theoretical tour to end up at much the same point.

In comparing Israel with the United States, we note that persons in overpopulated America are more superfluous than in underpopulated Israel and thus that the other-directed quality of the natural standpoint is reinforced more in the United States than in Israel. Americans who emigrate to Israel find themselves no longer superfluous, but wanted rather for what they can do, not for who they are. In such a context, the interpersonal consequences of the perspective of the natural standpoint are attenuated. Of course, there are other-directed characters in Israel. In daily encounters, however, alternative modes are more likely to be reinforced; therefore the circle can be broken.

In the United States, where superfluity has become synonymous with being, there is little chance for the pattern to be broken or for nonreinforcement of the natural standpoint to occur. We are so intent on being recognized and appreciated for our unique life style that even those who loudly proclaim their liberation from the routines of everyday living soon become a parody of what they want to be. They cannot break the circle. Developmental, functional, and population-technology factors all combine to reinforce one dominant perspective; it is indeed difficult to remove one's self from its purview. In the context of superfluity, even liberation efforts become vehicles to evaluate the worth of new-found life styles. Every move soon brings the hordes of other-directed followers to gobble up, engulf, and transform even liberation itself into a false quality by which one is known to be "in" or "good" or "chic."

There is still another theoretical link relating objective societal factors (i.e., population and technology) to a pattern that reinforces the interpersonal world of the natural standpoint. As Eric Fromm[7] noted, the use of technology to control the forces of both nature and man has deposed God; technology and other men replace Him as our harsh master. As long as God existed in the minds of men to account for the misfortunes of life, we had at our disposal a relatively impersonal force to explain whatever fate befell us. No use blaming the man next door if it was God's will.[8] But as scientific advances created a technology that could control the once unknown forces of nature, misfortunes could more readily be attributed to evil men than to an impersonal God. Man and man's creations, not God, became man's harsh master.

Under God, if I lose, it is God's will. Under man, if I lose, it must be some other man's will. Thus, I become especially sensitive to other persons, to what they are out to get and to do. Not only does this transformation help reinforce our natural bent toward other-directedness, it also reinforces our tendencies toward mutual mistrust and paranoia. For if my fate is determined by human forces beyond my control, why should I trust other persons? What results is a strong sense of personal manipulation and exploitation which, when combined with the social paranoia of other-directedness, produces an uptight, defensive interpersonal world. When God was pulling the strings, I could at least be assured of as fair a shake as the next guy; but when persons pull them, just how am I to know if justice will prevail? God is not out to manipulate and exploit me for His benefit; I have little doubt, however, that other men are.

We mistrust all authority and have good evidence to support our claims. The sense of being manipulated and exploited runs like a theme through contemporary society. We hear people complain about the way they are being pushed about by the designs of others. Deep down, we are convinced that we are being exploited; our efforts are really being expended only so that someone—somewhere else and in power—will reap the benefits.

This sense exists at all levels of the social system, among those who are at the top and presumed to be in control, and among those at the bottom who feel themselves the victims of someone's gain. This prevalent feeling cannot be understood simply through its correspondence with actual manipulation and real exploitation. The notion of a secret group of really powerful manipulators, even if occasionally validated, is too simplistic.

Each of us is caught in a stream of psychological, social, and historical events; we move in accordance with rhythms of which we are personally unaware, and toward which we may even be negatively disposed. Yet we are caught in a pattern that we both reflect in our everyday behavior and which through our reflection we serve to reinforce.[9] We enact our parts in a drama that we helped create and now manage; having created it, we enter into it as passive but willing pawns. We are both caused and cause.

The limits of freedom are social facts, dictated before we ever arrived upon the scene; our self-consciousness and reflectivity is but another part of this same drama, from which it is difficult to extricate ourselves. We are born into a perspective, live within its routine, and die within its purview; we have tasted otherwise, we have sought otherwise, but we have never been able to make it beyond.

15

The Perspective of Transcendence:

AN OVERVIEW

Standing in apparent opposition to the perspective of the natural standpoint is another perspective, the transcendent. While this perspective is an important aspect of Eastern thought and existence, it seems at first to be rarely observed in the everyday affairs of contemporary Western man. Yet the overwhelming evidence from numerous sources, both East and West, argues that this perspective remains a vital part of our contemporary Western existence at some moments and a part of some people's lives at many moments. That social scientists have generally ignored or played down its importance reflects the Westernization of social science with its consequent concern in understanding the typical and normative (defined by the Western cultural context) rather than the atypical, the exceptional. Nevertheless, by not studying the exceptional within each of us as well as the exceptional person in our midst, the science has suffered from a nagging incompleteness. Moreover, persons have suffered by not receiving a supportive climate to facilitate the emergence of this alternative transcendent perspective.

Much that has been written about transcendence and the quest for higher or different levels of consciousness is associated with an excessively utopian literature that has failed to give proper due to the vital conditions that create and reinforce the normative perspective of the natural standpoint. Both perspectives, the natural and the transcendent, occupy a place in each of our lives. While we are machinelike and routinized in much that we do every day, we are *more* than this; the "extra" holds the key to our fundamental freedom. Our search for man's freedom is motivated by the possibilities for blending this something more of transcendence into our everyday life in ways that deny neither aspect of the dualist unity that makes up our fundamental nature.

A review of several fields of reference to this "other side" of man's existence reveals two interrelated themes. The first, focusing on a primitive and childlike form of experiencing, is found especially in the writings of mystics,[1] developmental psychologists,[2] anthropologists,[3] students of the creative process,[4] and men such as Abraham Maslow[5] who have uncovered levels of consciousness beyond the everyday. The second theme, characteristic of those with a more existential bent,[6] stresses the independent, autonomous, often lonely and courageous quality that self-transcendent man possesses: such a person has become the author of his own life's story rather than the character in another's.

These two themes are interrelated; each carries us out of and beyond our everyday mode of relatedness to our world and into a world of our unique and spontaneous creation—a world of wonder wherein the everyday is seen for the marvel it can be. The path to transcendence as self-authorship (theme 2) is gained through achieving contact with this primitive, child-like mode of experiencing (theme 1). To see with wonder, to break free from the often necessary bondage that the natural perspective demands, to author our own stories, all require a form of knowing we once possessed as children, but which in the name and for the purpose of growing up we have lost.

The world of the child, long forgotten or beyond the grasp of most adults, reveals qualities of experiencing that differ radically from the socialized vehicles by which the natural standpoint is conveyed and in which we confront ourselves, others, and our world every day. Though he worked principally with adults, Maslow's[7] pioneering studies provide an important guide into this world of primary experiencing. Maslow maintains that a hierarchy of basic human needs exists which must be satisfied before we can hope to achieve the transcendent state of self-actualization and perceive our world in what he called the *peak experience*. Until our basic physiological and safety needs are met, for example, we cannot move toward the realization of those potentials that lie waiting within ourselves. In the peak experience, we transcend the immediate givens and move into a realm in which our experiencing has much in common with primitive, primary, and childlike forms.

The world of the peak experience differs radically from the world of our everyday attitude. In our everyday perspective, perceptions tend to be differentiated and organized into figure and background; we see objects and persons within frames of reference. We experience ourselves as standing apart from the world of objects and other persons that are lying somewhere out there beyond our personal bodily boundaries. In the peak experience, by contrast, perception captures our total attention; we become absorbed within it, poorly differentiating figure from background or ourselves as existing apart from others. All becomes timeless; a moment extends infinitely; the next moment and the last exist with equal intensity in the expanded present.

Within the peak experience we are open, passive, and receptive to the world around us; unlike our typical perceptions, those of the peak experience are nondemanding and less insistent about shaping reality to fit existing categories. We do not fight against it or seek to contain reality within known and familiar boundaries; rather, we submit to experience and experience with wonderment and delight. Whereas our everyday perceptions are goal-directed, seeking to attain an end for some purpose, the peak experience is an end in itself. In the alternative world that Maslow describes, there is no requirement that we achieve anything, go anywhere: the goal is the state of being we then-and-there experience. We do not see in the service of any other need than to see; we do not smell things, touch things, hear things, know things, sense things, feel things for any purpose beyond those of the experiencing itself.

Perception within the peak experience is an absolute: it is noncomparative, not relative to any social context. We do not compare ourselves with others or our mode of experiencing with others' modes; we simply experience. Maslow describes a world apart from our everyday reality, a perspective that is a radical departure from the way in which we confront our lives each day in conducting our practical affairs. He describes a primitive world of experiencing.

It should come as no surprise to learn that the world of the adult's peak experience qualitatively parallels the primitive forms of mentality which Heinz Werner[8] has described and which both Piaget and Freud[9] emphasize in their writings about child development. Werner's analysis of primitive mentality, characteristic of each of us in our early years and of some adult experiences, both normal and pathological, stresses several important qualities. Primitive mentality tends to be more vivid and sensuous, more absorbed in and with objects than our everyday forms of thought. It is *syncretic*, a term that indicates the mixing of sense modalities in perception. Syncretic experiencing occurs when we feel a light, smell a sound, see the music we are listening to, and so on. Primitive mentality is physiognomic and metaphorical: objects are life-like; symbols (e.g., words) are what they represent. The rock that rolls, for example, is seen to be acting intentionally; the word we utter or hear does not simply represent an object, but actually *is* the object. Thus, for example, to utter the name of the Devil is to bring his presence upon us, for the name does not merely represent the thing, but rather is the thing itself.

Ernst Cassirer notes the survival of this primitive expressive and physiognomic value in all words, "even in those of a highly developed language,"[10] but especially in forms of myth and art. Yet, even in the more abstract and more highly purified realm of scientific discourse, in which words are generally representative rather than expressive and physiognomic, Cassirer notes the possibility of continuing to regard phenomena in a physiognomic manner. He cites the example of a line. If we merge ourselves into our experience of the line,

> . . . we become aware of a distinct physiognomic character in it. A peculiar mood is expressed in the purely spatial determination: the up and down of the lines in space embraces an inner mobility, a dynamic rise and fall, a psychic life and being. And here we do not merely read our own inner states subjectively and arbitrarily into the spatial form; rather, the form gives itself to us as an animated totality, an independent manifestation of life. It may glide quietly along or break off suddenly; it may be rounded and self-contained or jagged and jerky; it may be hard or soft. . . . But these qualities recede and vanish as soon as we take the line in another sense—as soon as we understand it as a mathematic structure, a geometrical figure. Now it becomes a mere scheme, a means of representing a universal geometric law . . . what merely appears as an individual factor in the line, now becomes utterly insignificant.[11]

Primitive mentality is dedifferentiated; boundaries between objects or between self and object blur and blend together. Thus, the primitive experience is one of fusion and unity, wherein things that formerly existed apart and separately now appear together, joined as one. We are not over here, separate from the universe out there; rather, our boundaries fuse and join us with all there is; there is a merging sense of Oneness.

As we shall later see, Piaget's view of the development of adult thinking from its primitive beginnings and Freud's analysis of primary process thinking likewise emphasize qualities similar to this alternative perspective. Developmentally, we begin our lives by experiencing an undifferentiated, timeless, fused, homogeneous world; our history is marked by the stages of our growth within society, wherein we learn to make those differentiations that are valued by our culture. We learn to see and to experience in known and familiar ways and thereby miss the wonders that await those who can see anew with childlike, primitive awe.

To see with a fresh vision and to view the wonder and the significance of the everyday, the seemingly mundane, and the familiar, are not only the hallmarks of this primitive mentality, they are also characteristic of the creative process. The essence of creativity is to see the old in a new way, to see with a vision that conveys a sense of awe, wonder, surprise.[12] What most of us take to be a simple scene of children playing in Central Park, the painter sees in an entirely different manner; the poet uses oversocialized and familiar word-vehicles to convey new images; the scientist gains fresh insights in the simple structure of a molecule. As Erikson[13] noted in his essay on Gandhi, the creative and charismatic political leader finds a universal meaning and significance in even the most minor and petty of circumstances. In all instances, the person's mode of relating to his everyday and familiar world is shattered when contact with this primitive, transcendent realm is achieved.

Whether achieved through drugs, meditation, or via some other systematic manner by which we disengage ourselves from the everyday mode of our experiencing, the world of the mystic also reveals this primitive mentality of transcendence. The mystic's world is experienced with an intensity and vividness that is absent from our everyday world; there is a unity and fusion, an ineffability that words cannot describe; a transsensate extension of knowledge beyond those modalities by which we typically experience ourselves and others.

Arthur Deikman[14] sought to study systematically the fresh vision that meditation and mystical experiences are said to provide. He invited subjects into the controlled setting of his laboratory and asked them to concentrate all their attention upon a blue vase on the opposite side of the room. They were instructed to avoid taking an analytic attitude toward the vase, to avoid looking at its parts or thinking specifically about its details.[15] Rather, they were to look at the vase-in-itself, to let its perception fill their entire mind, just as the mystic focuses his totality upon one item or one thought, thereby eliminating all competing elements of concentration, in order to be swept into the whole. Similar instructions are given to those in Zen training, for example, who use breathing exercises to relocate the seat of their consciousness from its sensed presence in their head or eyes, downward into their stomach.

Deikman's subjects spent twelve meditation sessions over a period of some three weeks, the sessions varying from five minutes to a half hour or more. The reports of their experiences form the basis of his data; they reveal the return to a primitive mentality here as a function of what on the surface seems to be so simple an exercise: concentrating over time upon a blue vase. Several specific findings are of interest:

1. Some subjects report their new vision under meditation to be more intense and vivid than their everyday experiences; in some cases, the blueness of the experience is so intense that the vase seems to come to life, to undulate, almost as a fluid stream of blue motion.

2. The everyday sense of time was radically modified during the meditative exercise; most persons felt that time had shortened: that less time had passed than "actually" had.

3. The ineffability of the experience was striking; subjects found it difficult to put their feelings and sensations into words. It was as though words were not adequate vehicles to contain the quality of these new experiences. As Cassirer has noted and Zen experts contend, the physiognomic experience is always far richer and full-bodied than the mere words which seek to represent it.

4. A merging experience was mentioned by several subjects. One reported, for example, how she began to feel "almost as though the blue vase and I were perhaps merging. . . . It was as though everything was sort of merging and I was somehow losing my sense of consciousness almost." In later sessions, this same subject said, "It felt . . . as though the vase were in my head rather than out there . . . it seemed . . . it were almost a part of me." The subject and others reported a near-total

merging experience in which they were enveloped in a misty film of blue, a sea which engulfed them.

5. Several of Deikman's subjects reported the kind of dedifferentiation that characterizes primitive forms of thinking. One, for example, removed his focus from the vase to look out the window; but rather than seeing the everyday world of objects his experience was of a scattering:

> Things look scattered all over the lot, not hung together in any way. When I look at the background there is much in the foreground . . . drawing my attention . . . clamoring for my attention . . . [there is] no way of looking at the whole or any individual part of it.

In another session, this same subject, more fully dedifferentiated than previously, comments:

> The view didn't organize itself in any way. For a long time it resisted my attempt to organize it so I could talk about it. There were no planes, one behind the other. There was no response to certain patterns. Everything was working at the same intensity. . . . I didn't see the order to it, or the patterning to it or anything and I couldn't impose it, it resisted my imposition of pattern.

As Deikman notes, unlike experiences in our differentiated everyday world, this classic dedifferentiated experience was characterized (a) by the resistance of the stimuli to any kind of organization, i.e., any differentiation and integration into coherent units; (b) by the equality in intensity of all parts of the total perceptual field; and finally, (c) by the equal demand of all parts of the field for attention.

It is clear that the experiential outcomes which Deikman reports for his subjects parallel those Werner describes for primitive mentality, those Maslow uncovered for the peak experience, and those associated with the creative process. In all cases, the normal worldview stops dominating; we come to see old and familiar scenes with a fresh vision; we become aware of relationships we had ignored; we experience qualities that seem alien to our practical-minded world of daily experience. The patterns have been broken; the automizations and routinizations that have made the familiar scenes so familiar that we notice little within them anymore have become de-automized, revealing the wonders that lurk just behind the familiar. The creative, artistic view takes over.

In what may at first seem to be an entirely different realm, sociologist Harold Garfinkel[16] has systematically sought to uncover the qualities that make familiar scenes familiar by breaking the implicit rules and social norms, and thereby making "the familiar" problematical and unfamiliar. Garfinkel involves his teams of student-workers in deviance techniques, asking them, for example, to bargain over the cost of merchandise in a drugstore or to pretend that they are guests in their own homes for dinner. In each case, the deviant behavior causes the participants, including the student-deviator, to take a new look, to experience differently what was heretofore a familiar, routinized, and automated social scene. We enter the store to purchase some aspirin. The price is 98 cents. We offer to pay 49 cents. The familiar scene is now broken apart, de-automized; what would have been simple, routine, taken-for-granted, and unproblematical is now opened to a fresh look; it is now something problematical and puzzling. The student enters his home for dinner by ringing the doorbell, acting like a guest. The familiar routine is broken, forcing a new look upon this once-familiar scene.

An excellent account of the worldview of primary experiencing is found in Carlos Castaneda's[17] writings about the mystic don Juan. Don Juan's world is one of primitive mentality, a world apart from the everyday, a reality separate from our own yet attainable. Don Juan experienced things with his total body; syncretic perception was the norm, not the exception, for him: his eyes did not simply see, nor his hands touch, nor his ears hear; he knew through all his senses and his body in its totality. His world was a unity, a fusion of self with objects, of objects with other objects. His was a world of metaphor, wherein physiognomic perceptions were typical rather than exceptional forms. Each action both represented and *was* something more than what it seemed to be. As with Gandhi,[18] even the most trivial event was significant: it represented both itself and qualities well beyond itself.

A child talks to animals, knows meaning in the wind-sounds, soars with the birds; it is not surprising, then, that the world of don Juan and the world of the child are so similar. Don Juan's world is our own childhood world, seemingly lost as we venture into our socialized maturity; it is as well the everyday adult world of primitive groups that have been studied by cultural anthropologists. Dorothy Lee's reanalysis of Malinowski's[19] original studies of the Trobriand Islanders reveals to us again, but now in typical, everyday, adult form, a world that is an alternative to our own.

Our worldview is lineal: it may be compared to a line that connects points in reality, like a road joining points and regions; a line that moves from the present backward into the past and forward into the future. This is a developmental line, in which the causes of the present are understood to lie in the past; a climactic line, in which events are arranged in orderly succession, each leading to some goal or end state. Our ideas of happiness and misery, of success and failure, are embedded in this lineal way of viewing the world. Happiness is reaching the goal at the end of this line; failure and sorrow occur as the goal is not achieved. Our concept of freedom is tied to this same view; we are free as long as our progress along this linear route is accomplished without interference; as long as the end we intended is achievable.

The Trobrianders' worldview, by contrast, is nonlineal: activities are not arranged into an orderly progression leading from here to there; there is no ordering of events into means and ends, into activities undertaken now in order to achieve this end-state at some later point in time; there is no causal sequence in which things from the past shape the destiny of the future; there is no analysis of motivations or causes behind the acts which we see now-present. The Trobrianders did not seek to explain to Malinowski the motivational causes for their behavior in terms that would be familiar to Westerners, and he therefore found their answers to his questions confusing and contradictory.

Dorothy Lee notes as an example that while the Trobrianders consider intercourse an important preliminary condition to conception, they do not consider it the *cause* of conception. The entire pattern of procreation is a complex one, in which intercourse plays its part; but it is indeed only that, a part of an entire pattern that does not lie on a linear or sequential plane.

When Westerners tell stories, including stories designed to explain or justify our own or others' behaviors, our accounts are linear and climactic. The Trobrianders' stories, on the other hand, are a collection of seemingly unrelated and disconnected anecdotes, beginning in no special place and heading toward no particular climactic ending. Trobriander stories have no plot, no development, no climax, no direction in which they are going, nor any place from which they have come.

When we interrupt someone who is trying to tell us something, we are generally met by annoyance: we have interfered with an event that is going in a direction and toward some end-point. On the other hand, Trobrianders show no annoyance if they are interrupted while telling a story. Since it is not headed in a lineal direction, there is no continuity to be disrupted by someone's intervention in the middle: there is no middle, since there is no beginning or end, and therefore there is no sense in which it can be interrupted.

In terms of the themes I've been developing, the Trobrianders' typical worldview is more like the adult Westerner's atypical, yet attainable worldview of childlike, primitive mentality: the view seen by the adult Westerner in moments of meditation or the peak experience, those moments during which the everyday patterns are broken and an alternative manner of conception is experienced.

In his work on transcendence, the late Alan Watts[20] turned his attention to other cultures. Eastern thought says that we see the world in which we live through a curtain, a veil, a maya, and that these institutionalized forms of comprehending life must be transcended for true enlightenment to be achieved. The enlightened man of the East transcends the illusions and thought-forms of his given culture by becoming aware of them sufficiently to see through; thus he is no longer the victim of the ways of the maya, but rather makes them work in his service. We see here the themes of "new perception" and self-authorship combined. The man of enlightenment becomes the master of his own fate, the author of his own life story in that he can acquire control over his manner of seeing and experiencing his world. Insofar as he rules the curtain of the maya rather than being ruled by it, he can take charge of his own life. To engage the primitive, primary mentality that resides within each of us, then, is to break through the automated blindness of the familiar everyday scenes and to approach them with a new look, a fresh vision.

This Eastern mystical view seems less alien when we realize that its analysis is similar in structure to that of Marx and Marcuse.[21] False consciousness is a concept dear to their hearts; this false consciousness is the maya of social and economic institutions that lead persons to be victims of society rather than its masters. The everyday realities of the worker, for example, things that he takes to be inevitable truths, are carved out of the nature of his relationship to the economic system in which he is embedded, including his relation to those who own the means of production: this relation sets the conditions of his consciousness. His consciousness, shaped by these economic forces, is false insofar as he is oblivious to its economic underpinnings and comes to think wholly within its terms. Consciousness-raising parallels the Eastern efforts to see through the illusions of the maya, to take a fresh look at what one has taken for granted and blindly accepted.

The Protestant work ethic, as Max Weber[22] so aptly noted, helped pave the way for capitalistic expansion, creating in the mass of potential workers a consciousness that made them hospitable to "being saved" through hard work and the strict control of their hedonistic impulses. To see through this veil of the maya, to see the degree to which this ideological ethic, far from being an inevitability carved in granite by God, is a cultural, class conception shaped by economic factors, gives the individual an opportunity to look upon his everyday work with a fresh perspective. The worker, for example, may more readily come to see who it is who gains pleasure and capital from his self-denials. Consciousness-raising, this effort to provide a different way of looking at familiar scenes, is the first step toward individual autonomy, toward breaking free from stereotyped (and in this case, economically rooted) patterns of thinking.

East and West, mystic and politician, meet. Carlos Castaneda and don Juan on the mystic side and an avowed Marxist British University professor[23] on the political side offer much the same description of their personal efforts to avoid being captured by the institutional maya of their social systems. Castaneda comments how it is important for him to "create a fog" around himself, never permitting anyone to know him, to identify him, to capture him by their categories of experience and thereby diminish his personal freedom. Castaneda goes so far as to reject being photographed or tape-recorded at lectures, the better to maintain himself as a person of mystery and hence of freedom. The Marxist professor, in a paper outlining his decision to resign from academic life and take up a position as an unskilled worker, notes how he systematically sought to avoid making friendships with his colleagues, to avoid getting to know or to be known personally by anyone: "Once you form any kind of social ties with people of that kind [i.e., academic colleagues], there arise all sorts of psychological difficulties in opposing them when it is politically important to do so." By keeping people ignorant of him, keeping himself in an interpersonal fog, so to speak, this professor experienced the kind of personal freedom he needed for his political activities. As I noted earlier, mystery of self thwarts others' efforts to control and master. As these cases make clear, it also thwarts one's own impulses to be seduced by the categorizations and analyses of the prevailing social forms.

* * *

The transcendent person sees through and beyond the maya of cultural categories and is thereby better able to act with inner guidance. This often uncomfortable man of mystery is Colin Wilson's[24] outsider who has awakened to chaos yet feels that truth must be told at all costs: "he sees too deeply and too much," an interesting phrase that captures the essence of the transcendent perspective and suggests the fate awaiting this person. How difficult it must be, as indeed it is, to seek, let alone to reveal the truth at all costs; to see through false consciousness, the maya, the illusions, the institutions; to see too deeply and too much. How much more comfortable to accept the maya and dwell within its secure folds.

It must be as Paul Tillich[25] tells us: an act of courage is required. Tillich's courageous person is one who affirms himself *in spite of*. This is the key phrase in Tillich's analysis of courage. Most of us live out our everyday lives avoiding those encounters that would lead us to see and to act *in spite of*. We see and act primarily *because of*. The perspective of the natural standpoint leads us to act as we do *because of* this social force, that event in our personal history, that manner of thinking, that fear of being shamed, of looking different. In the natural standpoint, we are always acting because of, not in spite of. In the transcendent mode, we act courageously *in spite of* all these harsh realities of our past history and our present context; we act *in spite of* the pain and anxiety, the shame and the doubt; we act to affirm ourselves and our values.

At first blush, it may appear that transcendence involves a negation or denial, a nay-saying. It is as though the transcendent person must see, think, and act *in spite of* the demands of the concrete present, in defiance of the conventions, the maya, the familiar routines of everyday life. It appears to require an act of great faith[26] and courage even to glimpse this realm beyond the threshold of the ego's immediate now. Whereas attainment of this "vision" may demand faith, courage, and negation, the transcendent perspective itself is more of an affirmation than a denial. As Tillich notes, to be courageous is to affirm the self by acting in spite of the anxieties and doubts that keep us by the warmth of the hearth, denying the self in the name of security and safety. In negation there is affirmation.

The paradoxical pairing of negation with affirmation is a major developmental concept.[27] In our developmental history, the initial and tentative emergence of independence is not coincidently simultaneous with our utterance of "no." "No" is our first major step toward self-affirmation and autonomy; in saying "no" we declare ourselves an entity apart from those who would have us move in their directions. "No" is the first expression of our will; a positive affirmation of self, though framed within the context of an angry negation. As Sartre[28] noted, choice, freedom, and self-authorship are related to the ability to resist external influences; therefore the seed to positive self-affirmation and growth lies in our nay-saying.

In psychoanalytic theory, nay-saying is likewise a crucial first step in the development of thought and the emergence from our concrete embeddedness in the immediate surround. Nay-saying permits the growing child to withhold his immediate response to the stimuli that constantly impinge on him. By saying "no" to some things and *selectively* dealing with others, he is released from having to deal with everything. In this almost reflexive gesture, so vital to survival, negation is at once a declaration, an affirmation.

Piaget's work on the concept of conservation demonstrates this point.[29] A child is presented with a short, squat bottle filled with water; the water is then poured into a tall, thin bottle. While we adults know that the amount of the water in the two bottles is the same, the young child does not. Seeing that the level is higher in the tall, thin bottle, it appears to him that it contains more water. With development comes conservation. The child's ability to "say no" to the *shape* of the bottle permits him to affirm and "say yes" to the equality of the amounts of water in the two bottles.

This kind of nay-saying parallels Descartes' use of "doubt" to transcend the givens of reality and thereby to discover more fundamental truths; it is also akin to Husserl's concept of *epoché*, a suspension or bracketing-in of the natural stand-point, so that the more fundamental layers of reality may be uncovered.[30] In the pursuit of basic truth, we are urged to step outside the realm of the everyday by doubting the reality of all we know (Descartes) or by putting it into brackets (Husserl). Through such actions, we will encounter truth more readily, to see more clearly through lenses now cleansed of our everyday assumptions. In our developmental history, we engage in much the same endeavor as we emerge from our surroundings by negating the totality and selecting those aspects of reality with which to have commerce.

One of the basic avenues toward the transcendent perspective is not only a method which some philosophical approaches urge upon their students but, equally important, a fundamental aspect of our own developmental history. As each of us develops, we do so by participating in self-affirmation through negation. We were all capable of adopting the perspective of transcendence at one point in our lives; that we may have lost the capacity through lack of exercise or will or fear is an understandable feature of our developmental history. For the sake of fitting in, of knowing and living with some certainty and security, we exchange the negation that works in the service of self-affirmation for an acceptance. To develop at all, we had to have courage given through negation; to survive, however, we have abandoned that courage and neither negate nor affirm.

The child that lives within each of us, however, manages to reveal himself from time to time, giving us once again a moment's glimpse into what we were once and perhaps what we might still be again. Yet the fear of returning to the non-being that existed before childhood drives most of us neither to negate nor affirm in our everyday lives; rather, we act mechanically and routinely, driven along in another's drama rather than writing and living our own.

A person may be a character in a drama written by some-one else; his life is the vehicle for working out a part that has already been written. Some of us spend our lives searching for the dramatist so that we may know our parts better, may see where we are heading. Others care little to search or question, but adopt fully the natural standpoint, and carry out roles without much thought. Still others, sensing that the part they are playing is not to their liking, search about for another author who might rewrite the part for them.

But all such persons remain part of another's drama. Their performances are shaped and guided by others' dictates, by forces out there over which they have little control or knowledge. They are the victim, the pawn, the passive tool used this way and that by those who manage the show. They are not responsible for themselves or for others, but lie waiting for the next chapter to be written. The transcendent perspective stresses our authorship of our own drama and thus our responsibility for all that happens; it places the burden upon our shoulders and refuses to give us any way out of the prison we have made for ourselves. If you are the author of your own drama, then surely you are responsible for the characters within it.

The outcome of negation-and-affirmation is self-authorship. Through negation we not only affirm ourselves but characterize ourselves as actors, not reactors. But negation by itself is more reactive than active; the rebel is as dependent on others as is the conformist. The rebel's negation reveals his *counter*-dependence, his efforts to break free from external authority. Negation in the service of self-affirmation, however, is an autonomous act characteristic of independence rather than dependence or counter-dependence. The person who negates in the name of himself evolves a self-directed, personal authorship. The counter-dependent, however, forever remains tied into a system of external authority.

We have here the clue as to why negation, so important to autonomous development and self-authorship, usually results in an intensification of the natural standpoint rather than of transcendence: why negation, which should produce self-authorship, produces persons who take their place as characters in another's novel. The first breath of negation taken by the developing child, his first ventures into the realm of nay-saying, are his efforts to place firm boundaries around himself; they are declarations and affirmations even in their negativism. But all does not fare as well as one might imagine.

Difficulty arises from several sources including our evolving self. The emergence from embeddedness frightens even as it pleases. It is indeed frightening to step forth from the comforts of passivity and attempt to take our own place among others, in control, with responsibility. There are benefits to passivity and dependence of which the developing nay-sayer is aware. In fact, we should like it both ways: to be ourselves when it pleases us and to be dependent and taken care of when it pleases us. That we cannot have it both ways is soon obvious. The familial and school worlds are not always helpful in reinforcing our nay-saying in the service of self-affirmation. What often is reinforced is nay-saying for its own sake, thus producing a dependent rebel or a passively dependent conformist.

It is not difficult to see why we characteristically opt for the natural standpoint over transcendence. Even the developing child is aware of the problems that face the outsider who experiences uniquely and who would be his own author. Shame, ridicule, pressure, ostracism, rejection—all await the person who would affirm himself. *Because of* factors are more potent than *in spite of* factors, especially to the growing child who searches as much for security and safety as for real independence. When independence and autonomy also mean isolation, outsiderness, loneliness, and insecurity, only the fool would move toward self-authorship. The summation of factors within us and within the social system conspires to reinforce our fitting in.

16

Into a Different World

Our preliminary search for the other face of man has taken us far, but not far enough. We have uncovered only the tip of the iceberg. Below is an earlier, more fundamental process, one that functions before the development of the ego and thus exists prior to the emergence of the natural perspective itself.

This process lies at the most fundamental level of human conscious development. It is rooted in action and pure experience, and continues without influence from external factors or its own developmental history. It is a world of the absolute, the unchanging, the forever, a realm that the ego does not control, but rather to which the ego submits itself.[1]

Imagine, if you will, two worlds in process living side by side, the one encompassing the other while remaining alien and unknown to it. We live in two worlds simultaneously while remaining firmly embedded in the one—the world of the ego's everyday perspective. Glimpses of the other world are so foreign that they must be translated before we can understand them. And even then, we treat them as foolishness, insanity, a lapse of awareness, or perhaps, as creativity or religious ecstasy.[2]

Relativity theory in physics maintains that systems appear differently as a function of the framework within which the viewer himself is located. Our framework typically is that of the ego in its everyday perspective; thus we view any other system within the ego's terms. So dominant, in fact, is our ego's framework, that even descriptions of that other system, let alone direct experiences of it, are understood only by immediate translation into the ego's terms. Suppose, for example, that the transcendent perspective does not embody the self and object differentiations that are part of the ego's perspective: that it does not produce a differential experience of self and not-self. But this differentiation is so fundamental that even entertaining the other possibility is extremely difficult, perhaps impossible. What to one system is normal and routine may be illogical, or impossible, to another.

We know with self-evident validity that there is always an ego, a viewer who exists separately from the world of objects and persons that surround him. We find it impossible to imagine a process within which our self, other selves, and objects are one and the same thing, merged and undifferentiated. If there is no ego, no self apart from the world, then *who* sees and experiences the world? Even the questions we ask betray the framework within which we examine the matter.

In relativity theory, no framework is said to have priority or superiority over any other in an absolute sense. What is taken to be foreign, alien, odd, or insane is so only from one nonprivileged perspective. In our everyday lives, however, we commonly and routinely adopt the ego's perspective of the natural standpoint as having privileged status, and thus evaluate anything and everything within its terms. Sense and nonsense derive by reference to our ego's perspective—all things, that is, but the ego's framework itself.

Let us take the kind of imaginative journey that the relativity theorist demands of us, placing ourselves into that other perspective—as if we were riding on its rails. From this perspective, the ego's everyday world seems as unusual, alien, odd, or nonsensical as this other world appears to the ego. Imagine yourself a little child seeing the adult world as the child sees it. The child's developing ego faces an adult perspective that often makes little sense. We adults, framed in our own ego's perspective, argue sense into the little tykes, but they fail to grasp our message; we live in different worlds. Our logic and our reason make little sense to them; nor does theirs to us. We design ways to transform them so that they become members of our world, and we usually succeed. But we have little appreciation for their world's perspective; we think it immature, strange, silly. To them, our world is as foolish.[3]

The child, for example, acts with total involvement of his entire being. His words, his feelings, his thoughts, and his body fuse into one undifferentiated totality.[4] When he is frustrated and angry, his entire being is filled with anger, from the tips of his toes to the top of his head. When he hates mommy, he hates mommy with a full, total, and passionate hate. We sophisticated adults, on the other hand, usually have a more differentiated perspective; we hate in a more piecemeal manner. Of course, the child may hate totally one moment and love with equal intensity the next; we highly differentiated adults do not manage our loves and hates with comparable facility. From our perspective, the child's all-consuming hate is alien, foreign, immature (another ego word); with maturity, we know the child will come to see things our way. We, of course, have great difficulty in seeing things his way; his world is not taken to be the standard framework for evaluating practical reality.

Take this example to its extreme; after all, the child's ego is already developing and so his perception is already tainted by a mixture of perspectives; he does not see purely anymore. But at its extreme, this example begins to communicate a sense of the difference between two world views.

I emphasize this point because it is a major hurdle that we face in our efforts to understand the transcendent perspective on *its* terms rather than on ours. Unconsciously, we adopt the ego's framework as an absolute and judge all else according to its standards. To stop this in order to better view and understand the transcendent requires a vast effort of mind and being, more demanding in fact than the "doubt" which Descartes urged or even the *epoché* of which Husserl spoke.

Everyday reality and our ego itself undergo radical challenge once we enter the realm of the transcendent. In that world our ego no longer lives as master but sits off to the side, as a spectator to an ongoing flow of experience. It is a world at once familiar and again infinitely foreign, frightening, strange, insane. It is a perspective, however, into which we must extend our search if we are ever to find the roots of our dual nature and the fundamental basis of our human freedom.

We can never rest satisfied with a freedom that is completely tied to our ego's processes or to concepts of transcendence based upon the ego's acts. As important as these processes are to our everyday lives and well-being, as important as conscious awareness and ego mastery are to successfully freeing ourselves from much that is mechanistic and limiting, our ego and its world remain forever the outcome of interpersonal social events and thus can never be entirely free of a given perspective. We are in search of a process that lies beyond the world of the ego, however, a process that lies at the root of our most fundamental freedom.

To get to these roots, we must abandon our ego's world and its forms of reality; we must seek a framework that is within itself an absolute, the psychological speed of light against which all else can be measured and expressed. This will take us on a strange journey, puzzling even as it is revealing. But it is a journey on which we must go, if only to understand better what we have given up in the name of civilization and the practical affairs of everyday life.

17

The Reconstitution of Experience
in the Ego's World

The world of our ego's common awareness, the world we know and take for granted each day is a reconstituted world, a reflection of the moment that has just passed by. The stream of our experience is an undifferentiated and continuous flow that begins with life and does not end until death. Although this stream *is* the root of our being, we are usually not aware of it until *after* it has flowed by. But while our ego's perspective is actually post-experiential and reflective, we think of it in our everyday awareness as directly experiential: as happening right here and now. The fresh vision of transcendence involves the wonder of seeing this world unfolding.

The stream of our experience flows forth, an *unbroken becoming,* to use Alfred Schutz's[1] term. Experience enters our ego's everyday conscious awareness as some aspects of it are grasped by the ego and reconstituted into the ego's world, shaped by the ego's categories of time, space, sequence, and so on. The ego is much like a cone of light that "illuminates already elapsed individual phases of that stream, rendering them bright and sharply defined."[2] Our ego faces backward and in a "reflective glance singles out an elapsed lived experience and constitutes it as meaningful."[3]

G. H. Mead's[4] insightful analysis refers to this emerging experiential aspect of which we are *directly unaware* as the *I*; he reserves the object term, *me*, to refer to that part of us of which we are aware as a *reflected* social object. The *I* enters our experience "as a historical figure. It is what you were a second ago that is the 'I' of the 'me.' "[5] Within the perspective of our ego's everyday world, we are not aware of our emerging self, our transcendent experiential stream, our *I*, except as it is reflected back to us as a *me* or as a memory of *I*. The *I* engages in actions which flow forth with spontaneity, unhampered by the conventions and demands imposed by the ego. Creativity and novelty, the unknown and unknowable part of man, lie in this world of the *I*.

As egos, we are aware of our experience only after our experience has emerged, not before. "It is only after we have said the word we are saying that we recognize ourselves as the person that has said it."[6] The actual present remains just beyond our ego's grasp, an ever-emerging stream; yet the reconstituted world in which our ego lives is known in our everyday perspective as the given, immediate Now. The experience that we as egos take to be the present is in fact a reconstituted, just-emerged past. Our ego's everyday perspective does not assume that its world is a reflected glance or a cone of light illuminating an already-lived experience, but rather that its world is a living experience, present now.

There is a transformation by which our ego reconstitutes its historical reflections into an existing and living presence. Thus, what is over and done is phenomenally and experientially taken to be happening now. We do not usually experience our *I* as a historical entry into our awareness. We experience our *I* as acting right here and now: *I* act, *I* see, *I* know, *I* understand, etc. We do not usually experience our ego as grasping its behavior reflectively and thereby giving meaning to it; we experience meaning as directly given here and now. "An action can be evaluated immediately after its performance—so immediate that it feels subjectively as if evaluation and action occurred simultaneously."[7] The linguistic and social act of our ego that constitutes meaning is concealed from our everyday perspective; within the transcendent mode, however, we are in touch with the as yet unmeaningful, unconstituted fundamental world that, moments hence, will see the light of the ego's day.

The notion of a stream of pure experience[8] has its roots in a concept of life itself as a stream ever in flux and change.[9] The stability of our daily experience is realized as we grow up within a given society and learn its symbolic systems and cultural routines: the terrain of our culture. It is as though our life were an underground river, with only certain portions emerging into the full light of day where we, as egos, become aware of them. The processes of socialization produce a vital transformation, taking the unbroken becoming of our experiential stream, a nonlinear emergent, and reconstituting it into a differentiated, linear worldview.

The ego's cone of light that illuminates the already-lived experience does not simply shine upon it but actively reconstitutes it into a linear model of thought. If our ego were merely to glance at its experiential stream, it would experience the undifferentiated, nonlinear world of our primary existence: the world of our primitive mentality. But our ego's linear world is rooted in categories of space and time. The duration of a moment's experience requires the act of an ego to transform the undifferentiated flow of time into units that cohere and last, that yield a past and anticipate a future. Without the presence of an ego within the natural standpoint, time would flow but it would have neither duration nor a structure of succession with a clearly marked before (cause) and after (effect).[10]

The linear model of thinking to which we are routinely socialized and which is continually reinforced governs our everyday lives; it forms the basis of cooperative action and social control. The ego's perspective is at the root of our capacity for civilization. Linearity assumes that there is *in fact* and in some absolute sense a before and after, a sequence of cause and effect and of time, with a past, the present moment, and a future yet to come. Everything is joined into one in the nonlinearity of our experiential stream; there is a through-and-through connectedness;[11] there is neither subject nor object, neither before nor after, neither cause nor effect. There is process in constant flow, emerging; all ego times are vividly present, "incessantly interweaving,"[12] flowing backward and forward; there is "a *coexistent interrelation of future, past and present.*"[13] T. S. Eliot has expressed this conception of time: "Time past and time future . . . point to one end, which is always present."[14]

Civilization requires cooperation and social control built upon our human capacity to anticipate action and its consequences. For me to coordinate my life with yours, I must be able to anticipate your reactions to my deeds and modify my acts so that we can get along. Our ego's reconstitution of the experiential stream into a linear framework permits such anticipatory monitoring.

Once again we turn to Mead's[15] analysis. Language permits each of us to enter the other's world and reflect back upon our selves as an object seen through the other's eyes. The *me* of which Mead spoke is just such a reflected object; it lies at the root of our ego's capacity to anticipate action before acting. If our ego can see itself as another might, then action can be monitored and vital cooperation can result.

Thinking as a *me* precedes and guides action; it involves an inner "conversation of gestures."[16] We respond to ourselves as others respond to us; we become objects, me's-unto-ourselves; we take part in our own conversation with others; we take their attitudes toward us and thereby anticipate and monitor our own behavior in the light of the social process.

We are never directly in the presence of our emerging *I*, this experiential stream of our becoming. We are aware only of the *me*, the reflected object derived through the role-taking possibilities that language permits. We are aware of *I* only after it has emerged and returned, so to speak, in the form of a mirrored reflection, a *me*. The *me* is our ego's reconstitution of the lived experience of the *I*; it is our social being, built upon language which permits me to take your role and see myself through your eyes as an object, a me-unto-you; it is our *looking-glass self*.[17]

Language permits role taking with or without the immediate living presence of the other person. The terms of a symbolic system contain within them the categories whereby experience is shaped. Language permits us to abstract from specific others to an ever-present generalized other that permeates our ego's entire perspective. The self with whom we converse is a social self, a reflection of the complete social process, a generalized other from whose standpoint we view ourselves within this process.

An example will help clarify Mead's analysis. Peter and Otto are interacting. Peter's ability to know in advance what Otto's responses will be to his gestures permits the two men to engage in joint interactions. It is Otto's response that gives meaning to Peter's gestures and hence gives Peter knowledge of himself as a *me*. Thus, when Peter says, "Please pass me the butter," he is able to represent to himself Otto's response of passing it. Peter and Otto view themselves and their situation from the same perspective; each is able to understand the meanings of the other's gestures because each has learned to see from the other's standpoint. Imagine how puzzling it would be, for example, if in response to Peter's request, Otto picked up the telephone and began to make a phone call. That Otto is likely to pass the butter in response to Peter's request, and that both Peter and Otto know this (i.e., have it represented within themselves before it occurs), provides the fundamental basis for their joint interaction.

Most of Goffman's[18] work on impression management is based upon this Meadian-type analysis of social behavior. P's ability to indicate (i.e., represent) to himself O's responses permits P to use those responses to create the kind of self-impression he would like to possess. If P and O did not evaluate each other's behaviors within the same framework and from the same standpoint, then P's efforts at impression management would be futile. Thus, it is precisely because P believes that O will infer "P is an intellectual" if he carries a well-worn paperback copy of Kierkegaard in the back pocket of his jeans, that P can attempt to manage others' impressions of himself. Naturally, O's actual response must affirm P's belief for the impression management to succeed. But because P can generally "read" O's likely response to his gestures, P can hope to get the kind of feedback about himself that he would like.

When we speak of P's *me*, we are speaking of that part of P's self that is reflected to him through O's standpoint. It is the social self that P experiences, the self that has already acted and been responded to. This point is important. The self of which P is aware is the *me*, a self that has acted and is endowed with meaning by virtue of being responded to by O. O's response to P endows P's acts and thus P's self-as-me with its meaning. And since P can represent O's likely response to his actions within himself *before* acting, he can monitor himself in advance; it is this anticipatory capacity to take the role of the other that makes the entire social system possible. Thus, P can symbolically act in thought and experience himself as a *me*, as an object through O's perspective.

This social process need not involve overt actions which are then reflected back to P. In fact, the entire process of thinking before acting, as Mead notes, is an internal conversation of gestures which nevertheless involves P's viewing himself from O's perspective and thereby seeing and knowing himself as a *me*. Whether P acts overtly and notes O's actual response or acts covertly in thought and anticipates O's response, P is aware of himself as a *me*, as an object that is endowed with meaning by virtue of O's response. And O need not be another person; O can be the symbolic representation of what Mead terms the *generalized other*, the entire community of others whose point of view we take in judging and knowing ourselves. The important point is that P's self-concept, his knowledge of who he is, his identity, his awareness of himself, his evaluations and judgments of himself, are all socially *situated* and reflective: they are viewed through the mirrored image of the social process. Thus is P's freedom and spontaneity contained and limited. Even as P imagines himself to be acting freely of others' evaluations, the very process of formulating his action-alternatives involves a conversation of gestures, which requires that P see himself as a *me* from the standpoint of others.

> . . . the existence of private or "subjective" contents of experience does not alter the fact that self-consciousness involves the individual's becoming an object to himself by taking the attitudes of other individuals toward himself within an organized setting of social relationships, and that unless the individual had thus become an object to himself he would not be self-conscious or have a self at all . . . for in order to become aware of himself as such he must, to repeat, become an object to himself . . . by taking the attitudes of others toward himself.[19]

Although our ego's world is a reconstituted reflection of our already-lived experience, it is taken by each of us to be the primary world of our existence, given to us right now as it happens. The mediation involved in the very act of reconstitution is rarely noted; we routinely believe that we are in direct contact with our experience as it occurs.[20] We are not aware that we are a constructed self; we do not note the intervening steps involved. It is like reading fluently without being aware of the media through which reading is possible: without being aware of the letters that compose the words, the words that compose the sentences, and so on.

There are some interesting moments in our everyday lives, however, in which the mediating process is revealed. In these moments the experiential stream emerges so clearly prior to our ego's awareness that we find it difficult not to notice the actual ordering of events in our lives. In many of our everyday encounters with others, we are personally unaware of our own moods or emotional states until after they have emerged and others have either commented to us about them or have acted in such a way as to indicate much the same message.

When Marya is anxious, her face muscles tighten and her lips become stiff and narrow. I note this before she is even aware of her anxiety. She is anxious before her ego's cone of light has illuminated this part of her already-lived experience: before her *I*'s emerging anxiety, facilitated by my comment, has been reflected back as a *me*. The emerging experience precedes awareness of it and comes to her awareness either when I directly comment to her about it, thereby setting her to thinking about whether she is anxious, what she might be anxious about, and so forth; or when I act in some special way toward her that leads her to a conscious awareness of her already-present anxiety. Her ego becomes aware (a) of an experience that has already emerged and (b) of the fact that it has already been noted by another. In the routine circumstances of everyday life, we are not usually aware of this process. We are unaware that our knowledge of ourselves, our *me*, is a reflection of an action or experience present prior to our awareness of it.[21]

This position is similar to William James' argument about our awareness of our own emotional states.[22] Do we feel afraid of the bear and then begin to run, or is it in running that we come to experience fear? In the view I have taken, the experiential stream flows forth before we are aware of its presence; as we run we become aware of our fear. In a sense, our *I* begins to run-in-fear before we reflect back as a *me* upon the action-which-is-underway, and as a *me* within the ego's perspective have our conscious experience of fear.

In much the same way, Marya, for example, could have looked into the mirror and seen the expression on her face. Then her experience of anxiety would have been present as though immediately given; the mirror, however, would have served the function of making her anxiety an object of which she could then become aware. Our earlier discussion of the social-comparison process is based upon this same conception of self-consciousness as rooted in other-consciousness.

An interesting implication of this view suggests how our behavior-in-progress can modify our personal states of conscious awareness. The anxious person who begins to fidget nervously not only becomes more clearly aware of his anxiety state but, in addition, manages through his behavior to increase the intensity of that state. It is as though he had noted this very fidgety person and became even more anxious. We have much this same experience in the presence of someone whose behavior makes us so nervous that we ask him to please stop fidgeting. Moreover, just as we can increase our experience of anxiety by increasing our behavioral manifestations of it, so we can decrease it as we decrease its behavioral manifestations.

Nondirective psychotherapy,[23] provides another instance of this process. The client sits and talks; the therapist listens and repeats the client's feelings back to him or at times repeats his remarks verbatim. The therapist's repetition of the client's unfolding experiential stream casts it before the client as an object, a *me*, as something he can now examine with awareness. The therapist functions to reflect the experiential stream as it emerges and thereby to provide the client with a glimpse into his own occluded experiential world.

It is not unusual for the client, on hearing something he has just said reflected back to him, to imagine that the therapist has provided a new interpretative insight, and he may receive the material he himself generated as though it were an exciting new idea. In this case, it is not the therapist who has uncovered the secrets of the client's inner world; it is the client himself.

The therapist makes a systematic effort to provide the person with direct and relatively immediate contact with his own experiential stream as it is emerging; furthermore, this effort is directed toward keeping as much noise out of the feedback system as is humanly possible. Direct feedback of what the patient is doing is undoubtedly one of the most important ways of conducting the entire therapeutic process. And, not too surprisingly, one of the most direct and least noiseful modes of offering feedback involves listening!

Children's play behavior offers another illustration of this process. Children frequently find it important for their parents to witness their play. The parent's presence reflects the child's activity back to him and serves to objectify or validate it as something real. In a very important sense the behavior is not real until it has been reflected back through another's eyes.

How often do we find it necessary to create the presence of that other by standing in front of a mirror to view our-

selves in a new outfit, or by saying something out loud in order
to hear it, or by working it through first in order to see what
it really means? A careful analysis of this kind of behavior
reveals the frequency with which we actively seek to establish self-awareness by calling upon an imagined other to reflect
our emerging selves back to us. In this manner we gain a
better sense of us, including a control or mastery over ourselves. Saying something out loud in private offers us a way of
gaining access to ourselves. It is likewise a means of gaining
self-control or ego mastery. We hear us as the significant
others might, and thereby come into conscious awareness of
ourselves. This indeed is an out-loud version of Mead's often
silent conversation of gestures.

Alfred Schutz[24] has noted that although you become aware
of your own stream only after it has emerged and is reconstituted into your ego's perspective, I am in direct contact with
your emerging experiential stream at the moment of its emergence. Of course, the reverse is also true; you are in *direct*
contact with a part of me with which I am only secondarily
aware. We each thereby grasp parts of the other that have not
yet entered into their ego's awareness. We have a preview, so
to speak, of their coming knowledges. We typically relate to
each other so as to help validate these previews. I reflect to
you and you to me what we each understand is now ready to
be constituted into the other's perspective.

Our ego is just moments behind the experience that is
unfolding. Consciousness follows rather than precedes experience.[25] We typically are not aware of how we become aware;
as Gilbert Ryle[26] puts it, we cannot point our index fingers
at ourselves. In trying to grasp the process whereby our
awareness is constituted, our ego transforms what it is trying
to grasp and thus creates a new order of things beyond its
grasp. In other words, our ego cannot grasp itself grasping; it
cannot pick itself up. And the harder we try, the less headway
we make.

Even if the process itself cannot be, the outcomes of our
ego's reconstitution of its experiential stream are available to

our awareness. Marya can become aware of her anxiety when I point it out to her; she can also become aware of the fact that the anxiety preceded her awareness of it. But her ego cannot become aware of itself constituting that experience into itself. The ego cannot be aware of itself in action until after the action has occurred and there has been an experienced outcome. After the anxiety has been pointed out, it can be known by the ego; but the ego cannot know of its own reflected nature until that nature has been reflected.

Clearly, we have here the transcendent process and man's essential freedom. The unfolding experiential stream can never be known until after it has emerged and has been reconstituted into the ego's perspective of the natural standpoint of everyday life. It is a process about which we know only *after*, never before its occurrence. Thus it is a process unbounded by convention, by social concern, by reference to anything beyond itself; for there is nothing beyond itself to which it may refer. The *I* is the root of all novelty.[27] Though the ego's world is linear and permits us to anticipate our actions in advance, within this other perspective, knowledge and awareness do not arise until after the emergence of action. The artful quality of our ego is its capacity to render coherent and meaningful the experiential stream and thereby to manage our everyday affairs with some measure of success.

18

A Step into the Future?

We are approaching a threshold to a new world—ours, yet alien to our everyday awareness. Fascinating experiences and possibilities await us as we move beyond the ego's world into the transcendent perspective of our unfolding experiential stream.

Our ego's natural perspective dwells in three time zones, each of which is a reconstitution of experiences already lived or a projection of experiences yet to come.[1] There is the reconstituted present which is our ego's natural perspective; our ego's reconstruction of a past in the form of memories; finally, our ego's projected future of things anticipated, still to be done.

These vital everyday realities are not part of the unfolding transcendent perspective, yet our embeddedness in the time-bound zones of past, present, and future constrains our understanding of this alternative point of view. Within this alternative mode, all times are Now; was, is, and will-be interpenetrate. Each instant contains an infinity of thoughts, tumbling one upon the others. The ego's world sees us grappling with the past and preparing for the future. In the alternative perspective, we cannot speak of an actor who is preparing himself to act. Action emerges.

There is no organism that sees sights, hears sounds, prepares to move down this road or that; seeing, hearing, and deciding are processes that join organism and life into a unity.[2] There is no self that sees; seeing is the very process of this communion. There is no ego that lives and prepares itself for tomorrow; living is the entire process. Separation in space and time exist within our ego's natural perspective, not within the emerging transcendent mode.

These are difficult points to understand, even intuitively. We live within a world that so thoroughly saturates our view that any alternative appears to be beyond understanding. Part of the problem, of course, lies with language that compels us to use everyday concepts to describe something that goes beyond the everyday. Sentences in English, for example, demand there to be an actor who acts.[3] Even when we talk about rain, we must say, "It's raining!" But what is the actor, "it"? Raining occurs, yet we must provide an actor. Our language compels a descriptive usage that makes the transcendent alternative seem mysterious and difficult to understand. Yet it is this very difficulty that reveals the problems encountered in trying to move into the transcendent perspective.

Our ego's perspective is a reconstitution of an already-lived experience. What would things be like if we could for a moment experience our unfolding stream as it came forth? Yielding our ego's perspective to the transcendent, leaning forward to reach just beyond our constructed Now to touch this other realm, would give us a sense of looking into the future!

An example will help. I take it from a personal drug experience, not because that is the main or the only way of meeting the transcendent mode, but rather because the example clearly demonstrates and clarifies the seemingly futuristic nature of the experience itself. Several years ago, I was sitting in the living room of my house with three friends. As was the fashion at that time, we began to smoke some hashish. My previous experience with marijuana and hashish had led me to an interesting finding; by smoking hashish and drinking vodka (why vodka, I have no idea), I reached an extremely exciting "high," and rapidly. The combination pushed me into a world in which I felt some loss of ego control, a world of strange experience.

We sat in the room by candlelight that evening; a recent storm had put out all the electricity. I began puffing my pipe and sipping my vodka. Soon, I was wandering, still seated but "high." I looked about me. These were my friends, yet suddenly they were strangers to me. I grew fearful; I had to escape from them and that room. I got up slowly, deliberately. I walked across the living room, down the dark stairs, into the hallway and to my bedroom. I fell into my bed. I was all alone and it was dark. There were no electric lights, no candles, no light. I trembled in fear. I got up and began to move back toward the light and the people. I consciously sensed the meaning of each movement: torn between the fear of the people and the fear of the lonely dark. I moved slowly up the stairs and toward the light, settling at last on the floor halfway between the fearful dark below and the fearful people upstairs.

Each movement carried with it a clear and definite meaning. I was not only moving about physically in space, from the living room down the hall to the bedroom and then back again toward the living room, but I was aware *at the same moment* of the meaning represented by these moves: people and light on the one hand, alone and dark on the other.

Something more soon came into my conscious experience. I felt myself caught in a drama in which I was being propelled along, willingly but passively; guided by some inner force and revealed in my physical movements. I was a character in a play, fascinated with its outcome; I became aware that the play was moving me into a future about which I was eagerly curious. I focused on my actions, trying to read in them the future that awaited me. Was I to move away from the dark and rejoin the people and the light? Would I stay halfway between people and dark? What would I do? I sensed that what I would be doing symbolically reflected my own personal future.

I grew excited as I moved about, for each movement let

me see clearly into the future. As I seemed to be led forward toward the light, I knew that was a step of the future, one with which I would catch up in my conscious mind shortly after it happened. The story unfolded in my movements, revealing the future into which I was heading. I experienced myself following two streams at once; the one represented the future moment of time which in the other I could experience as the present, Now. I felt that I knew the future.

In my excitement, I moved further up the stairs, away from the dark and toward the people who remained seated in the living room. I wanted to share my discovery with them. I lay down on the floor at the far end of the room, visible yet still in the shadows of the dark below. My pose on the floor represented the future, the next moment. I wondered about the future and how it would come out. It was as though I were reading a crystal ball, represented by my actions, that revealed the meaning of the very next instant to me before that next instant actually occurred.

The people on the couch came over one by one and sat on the floor around me. I began to share my exciting discovery, telling them that even as *they* came toward me rather than *my* moving toward them we had just voyaged together into the future moment, the meaning of which I knew moments before it actually occurred. As I talked, I grew more excited, wondering just how much of the future I would understand now, before it actually occurred.

While we lay there, I sensed the two streams coming together, meeting at a point that would return me once again to the present. I experienced a sense of loss, of disappointment; I had been so excited by the prospect of maintaining my ability to understand the future moment before it occurred, to see how the play was to come out just before it came out.

Describing a personal experience to another person, or even to oneself afterward, inevitably omits more than it can include; so much of what we experience cannot be readily translated into words, sentences, or paragraphs. Our ego's world, rich as it may be, is but a poor representation of our experiential stream. So it is with this experience just described. I can, however, offer an analysis of what I think happened, in order to suggest an important quality of the transcendent perspective.

The drug managed to blur the boundary between my ego's typically reconstructed present and the usually unknown unfolding present of my experiential stream. As I came into conscious contact with the stream, even while retaining intermittent flashes of my ego's perspective, I actually believed I was in touch with a future moment, one just about to occur. The experiential stream, of course, is the actual present; however, in our ego's world of the natural standpoint, the actual present is a construction after the fact. When the ego-stream boundary blurs, we begin to believe that we are experiencing the future. What occurs is that our ego loses or experiences a blurring of its reconstructed categories of time and space. Our ego meets the unfolding stream at its actual moment of occurrence. It sees this stream, the actual Now, as though it were the future moment just unfolding. The experience is of jumping successfully on one's own shadow, to use Ryle's metaphor for the elusive quality of our actual present.[4] Thus if we could jump on our own shadow, we would be jumping into the actual, elusive present—and we would experience this as a jump into the future.

This is a difficult concept to understand, rooted as we are in the conventions of language and thought of our ego's everyday world. The transcendent perspective in this experience was one in which I had direct contact with my own stream at its very moment of appearing; however, the blur between my ego's natural standpoint and the transcendent mode waxed and waned, making contact with the stream possible while leading me to interpret it in terms of my ego's usual categories of time and space. It was this which gave the experience its future-quality. Contact with our own experiential stream is experienced as though it were a glimpse into the next or future moment: not the distant future, but rather the future just a moment beyond our usual sense of now. From the perspective of the reconstructed now, the actual now appears to be what *will* occur rather than what *is* actually occurring.

Other important features begin to emerge as we analyze

that experience further. I felt as people do who have described the creative process and the peak experience:[5] I felt myself to be a character in a play, moving along self-consciously (i.e., aware) but passively. I experienced myself as having let go, as submitting myself to myself and following the flow of my actions rather than attempting to intervene and direct them. I was acting spontaneously and freely, aware but nondirective.

This is a vital quality of behavior within the transcendent mode; it is spontaneous; it flows; it moves us along; it carries us; we submit to ourselves rather than doing battle to govern and control ourselves. It is as though we sense that in taking the risk and in submitting to ourselves, all will be well. We are in charge of ourselves by not being demandingly in charge of ourselves. How similar this is to descriptions of the creative process:

> [There is] a sense of mystery which stems from not knowing where one's work is leading. This feeling is so strong that the creator may consider himself passive, as if the solution were not really to come from him. . . . I. B. Singer [author Isaac Bashevis Singer] speaks of an imp that inspires him. . . . Others refer to "something in the back of my mind" that is arranging the material in a particular way.
>
> The element of surprise and mystery in the creative process is not uncommon. Both Simon [playwright Neil Simon] and Singer admit that often they themselves do not know how a piece of writing will end. . . .
>
> A necessary adjunct to this process is the willingness . . . to trust their hunches, to remain open to surprise and accident . . . Franzen [architect Ulrich Franzen] saying, "I wish I could design as if my pen has been slipping all the time."[6]

Another significant quality of this experience is that an understanding of the future is conveyed through action rather than through thinking about action. As I felt myself propelled along, my curiosity was directed toward what I was physically doing in space. To be sure, I was thinking about what I was doing, but my thoughts did not serve to guide my acts. Rather my acts flowed freely while my thoughts were an attempt to find the meaning of this natural, unmediated flow. The flow was monitored, but not controlled by the monitoring; the monitoring was of a more open, wondering, puzzling, amazed, curious sort. It was as though I was viewing a lovely sunset; an appreciative rather than a manipulative mode; open rather than purposive; curious rather than frightened or annoyed.

What I was doing, of course, was moving about from room to room. When we are in direct contact with another's experiential stream, their unfolding present, we are in contact with their actions, not their thoughts; we take their acts as documents or representations of their thoughts.[7] Their stream manifests itself to us in their behaviors: what they say, how they say it, what they do, how they do it, where they locate themselves spatially, what the general context is within which their acts occur, etc.; in other words, an entire range of verbal, nonverbal, and situational cues which carry the other person's presence to us. This is a sizable range of actions, as those who have studied even the nonverbal side of it will attest.[8]

There is more; the clue lies in the notion of action *preceding* awareness of it. In the example, my action flowed forth undirected by my ego's then-unsteady hand; awareness followed rapidly in the form of the meaning of that action as my ego read sense into what I had done. Action flowed independently of the sense, a reversal of the typical mode. Within our ego's world, the emphasis is on action guided by conscious awareness and thinking; within the transcendent perspective, action unfolds naturally and spontaneously and arrives in our ego's awareness for interpretation afterward. When I got up from the sofa and moved into the dark, my ego attributed meaning to those actions. As Schutz has noted, the ego's reconstitution of experience creates a coherent unity out of events that did not actually proceed in such a neatly defined manner. The ego reconstitutes the experience so that it not only has a beginning and an end, but a purpose, a meaning, a direction, a sensibility and a reasonableness about it: "the action, once completed, is a unity from original project to execution, regardless of the multiplicity and complexity of its component phases."[9]

The process is similar to the creative act or to the performances of professionals in sports, drama, dance, art, science, and so on. In these instances, behavior proceeds as though guided by an unseen hand; afterward, what has unfolded can be scrutinized by the ego, meanings attributed to it, reorganizations and reinterpretations undertaken. Self-consciousness, awareness of self-performing, disrupts this being-taken-over-and-acting-without-interpretation. The essence of the professional's performance (and of the creative process) is this quality of action unfolding before our eyes but without our awareness or intervention until it has unfolded and is now before our ego for post hoc analysis. As we shall see, in primary stages of development, thought and action are unified and undifferentiated; with the development of the ego's perspective, thought becomes differentiated from action, and precedes action. Civilization is thereby made possible.

An important implication of the preceding discussion roughly parallels Henri Bergson's[10] analysis of determinism vs. freedom in decision making. Within our ego's linear perspective, a decision is seen in spatial terms; ego is located between two (or more) choice points. Shall ego decide to take route A or route B? Determinism argues that the choice can be predicted prior to action, given our knowledge of the variables that influence human behavior. The free-will position maintains that we can never fully know the choice in advance, for if ego chooses A, he can always say realistically that he could have done otherwise and chosen B.[11]

Within our ego's perspective of everyday life, the linear model makes sense; our ego reconstitutes the experiential stream into a linear, purposive view in which we indeed stand at a choice point. Within the alternative, transcendent perspective, by contrast, action flows forth freely and openly; there is no linear space with an ego at a point of choice between A and B. A and B do not exist until we have already acted. In this view, determinism and free will are both meaningless. After having acted, we reconstruct the situation so that it coheres and makes sense; we take ourselves back to where we were and constitute a meaningful chain of purpose or causes that guided our freely emerging actions. There is greater clarity afterward in reflection than before or during.

For the practical purposes of everyday living, we function linearly, oblivious to the reconstitution that has taken place. Only with an alternative perspective does the ego's knowledge follow rather than precede action. In the drug example, it would be in error to maintain that I decided to get up from the sofa and go downstairs or that I decided to leave the dark and return part-way to the light. I was moved about; afterward my ego knew where I was going and what it meant. It did not guide me beforehand. After we live we know what it all means.

Perhaps it is as Erik Erikson[12] recognized in his description of the developmental dilemma of later life: integrity on the one hand, disgust and despair on the other. As our life moves toward its end and we reflect back on it, do we face someone about whom we feel good? Sure, it was not all a bed of roses, but it was *our* life and we did the best we could. Or do we face someone who is still a stranger, someone we never knew and never want to know? Integrity or despair? Afterward, perhaps we know what it all means. The implication, of course, is that we live with faith,[13] for within the transcendent perspective, sense follows living, it does not precede it.

The transcendent perspective introduces us to a world that is discontinuous and radically unlike the continuity we experience in our ego's everyday perspective. Continuity implies that knowledge about the future of an event is predicated on knowledge of its past. Theories are formulated to link that past to the still-unknown future. Continuity in development, for example, assumes a linear form to growth; later events are founded on earlier ones. The past is the best predictor of the future.

Discontinuity, by contrast, suggests that new things are possible as emergents from a particular past. Discontinuity indicates that knowledge of the future cannot be based on knowledge of the past; historical events combine in unknown ways, in a creative synthesis, to produce a new position, an emergent that is discontinuous with whatever has gone before. Discontinuity does not require that past and future be unrelated, but only that there be neither a simple nor a direct linear relation between them.[14]

In its natural standpoint, our ego grows and lives by a notion of continuity; the transcendent process is discontinuous, unfolding in ways unknown and unknowable. The tomorrow of our ego can be extrapolated from our knowledge of its yesterday; the tomorrow of the transcendent is a discontinuous, ever-emerging new quality; it can never be extrapolated from yesterday's experience.

Our ego houses the continuous, the predictable, the controllable, the social; the transcendent goes beyond and creates. By its submission to the transcendent stream, our ego's continuity yields to the discontinuity of the transcendent process; we are thereby freed from our past and from the routines of the present. A creative synthesis emerges, surprising even the person in whom it is emerging.

If our ego's response to us-unfolding, to this surprise within, is horror, we have returned again to the centrality of its control and hence to the continuity of our life. If our ego's response, however, is of awe, fascination, appreciation, or wonderment, then we have become more truly free and unknown even to ourselves.

19

The Transcendent Origins: In the Beginning Was Not the Word

We search for the origins of the transcendent perspective; we seek a pre-experiential, pre-phenomenal, or as Schutz puts it, a pre-logical "stratum of our experience, within which . . . objects and their qualities are not at all well circumscribed."[1] We search for a perspective within which objects have not yet been selected out from their backgrounds of space or time, a world characterized by its "through and through connectedness"; in which everything has a horizon that extends it into relationships with everything else. We search for a perspective in which present, past, and future coexist.[2] We search for a realm of spontaneity, a perspective that "is what it produces and can be nothing else,"[3] "a sphere of absolute existence . . . pure spontaneities."[4] We search for the world that is ours before our ego reconstituted it into cultural forms.

We find clues to guide us in our quest for the origins of this world from several related sources: Ernst Cassirer's[5] analysis of myth and symbolic forms; Freud's and Piaget's concepts of development.[6]

The Bible tells us that in the beginning was the Word; the word gives the beginning its form, its very being. The word breaks up the flux of experience,[7] gives us concepts, provides our experiences of stability as well as of change; permits us to note similarities and speak of differences; allows us to know identities, to find again the experience that would otherwise be but a fleeting moment. With the word, we can indeed step twice into the same river.[8] "What has been culled from the total sphere of consciousness, does not fade away again when the spoken word has set its seal upon it and given it definite form."[9] In the act of naming every living creature, Adam thereby took "possession of the world both physically and intellectually" and subjected "it to his knowledge and his rule."[10]

But the true beginning was before the word; it was in "expressive experience which lives in the moment and spends itself in the moment."[11] The word was the beginning of man's civilization, his ego, his control over nature, himself, and other men. It was not the true beginning, but the beginning of another beginning. The roots of all our beginnings lie in a "Nameless Presence," a God of ten thousand names, a something without attributes to "limit its pure essence."[12] The true beginning lies in a world of silence beyond language and symbolic forms. This is the world of the Creator who "begets and is not begotten, he bears and is not born, he is Being, the Constant in everything, the Remaining in all."[13] This is a world that was here at the first and remains here when all else passes. Nothing so concrete as that which can be labeled, called, or qualified can be the roots of this beginning of all beginnings, this ever-present Presence. This true beginning "reveals to us a creation *ex nihilo*"; it is a "new existence"; we cannot "conceive of anything *before* it."[14] It is nonpositional consciousness, without contents, "a great emptiness, a wind blowing toward objects."[15]

The usual terms of language stabilize our living and permit us those constancies of thought that allow our civilization to develop. Such terms, however, can never fully capture and represent the full richness of our pre-verbal beginnings. Only the kind of metaphorical thinking that the mythic process reveals can demonstrate that perspective. It is at the cost of the "wealth and fullness of immediate experience"[16] that language can become a vehicle for our thinking, our formulation and communication of concepts.

It has been said that Einstein did not speak until he was three;[17] his world of thought was primarily nonverbal. Even as an adult, his conceptualization was nonverbal; he did not think in the words of language but rather in visual and muscular (i.e. motoric) images. Only secondarily and after much effort was he able to find the words that could communicate his thoughts to others. Was it perhaps his capacity to think experientially and outside the constraining terms and logic of words and language that permitted him to move beyond the world of everyday reality to formulate his revolutionary concepts?

The language of logical discourse differs from the symbolic forms that give rise to mythic thinking. In logical discourse, separate concepts can be joined into a hierarchical relationship in which each retains its own integrity even in union; in mythic thinking, by contrast, "every part of a whole is the whole itself."[18] The neat boundaries that are preserved in normal discourse are lost within metaphorical conception; the fringes of concepts so interpenetrate that one part of the total is the total as well.

Within metaphorical and mythic conception, a part does not merely stand in the place of or represent the union of several elements, but rather it is identical with the whole. If the part *is* the whole, then whoever controls the part controls the whole. Your fingernail does not merely *represent* your body, it *is* your body. In normal discourse, symbols *represent* their referents and are separable from what they represent; in metaphorical or mythic conception, the symbols *are* their referents; they cannot be separated. The elegance of language lies in its capacity to separate symbol from experience so that symbols can be manipulated in ways that experiences cannot be. While we cannot *experience* precisely the same thing ever again, we can attach similar symbols to represent two experiences as being roughly the same.

As Cassirer[19] noted, mythic conception, by contrast, unites elements not by rules of logic but by experiences of feeling. There exists "a fundamental and indelible *solidarity of life* that bridges over the multiplicity and variety of its single forms."[20] Nature and man are one, together in the *society of life*; space and time do not limit either man's or nature's life.

We have come upon a mode of experiencing that differs from the forms within which we pass each day. We are at the roots, the base ground of our experience, upon which our ego's world becomes a vital overlay. We see this base in metaphor, in myth, in pure religious experience. We glimpse a world that is ours to see, if only rarely and then without appreciation or understanding. We have contacted the primitive, the primary, the fundamental, in our personal life history as well as the life history of mankind.

The abiding survival of mythical and metaphorical conceptions, but particularly the surviving vestiges of pure religious experience, bear testimony to the great and enduring permanence of the primary even in our ego's mundane world.[21] Religion does not emanate simply from anxiety or fear of death; these are ego concepts, a cultural overlay. Rather the source of our religious experience lies within the first mode of all our experiencing to which we return to be at one with God, the universe, mankind. Our concepts of God and the Divine, of the Being that began all beings, of the Cause before all causes, is a reflection of the primary and enduring mode of experiencing our world.

The God we sense is our own primal state of experiencing; the God we long for is our own early selves which lie still within. When in our religious experience we merge and join with Him, we have submerged our egos and submitted to our primary mode of experiencing,[22] our transcendent perspective, the fundamental roots of all that comes afterward.

*   *   *

The developmental theories of Piaget and Freud[23] offer further clues to direct our search for the origins of the transcendent process. Each points out that we have experiences long before we are able to formulate them verbally. The initial phases of a child's development place him in an utterly naive relationship with his world—utterly naive in that everything is experienced with equally vivid reality. Dreams are not differentiated from "reality"; wishes, fantasies, and physical needs merge to make their common claim on the child's attention. The child's body does not begin and end with his physical frame, but extends into the space around him. The toe there is his toe, your toe, the world's toe; it is the ash tray and toy bunny as well.

The transcendent experience for an adult has these same features. As we have seen, primitive or metaphorical thinking, for example, does not differentiate between the part and the whole; a part of the body could as well be the entire universe. Lest we scoff at this, pejoratively calling it childlike or primitive, I hasten to note that we have the same blurring of object boundaries in the experience of empathy. In empathy I join in my pain with your pain; I wince when the villain in the film hits the hero. It is as though the nerve endings which carry pain to my cortex extend beyond my body.

It is not only pain we share. Love, joy, laughter: all carry this same primary, undifferentiated, unbounded quality. In love, our bodies merge into one; the boundary blurs and becomes indistinct. We feel and communicate with an intuitive understanding that carries across what might otherwise be a chasm. In empathy, as in the transcendent primary experience itself, we are not fully encapsulated within our own skins; the boundaries extend us beyond and merge us with our surrounding world.

Those who have noted children's pre-verbal behavior comment on its dynamic totality;[24] it is as though the child's entire being participates in everything he does. He does not feel or respond in piecemeal fashion, but rather "seems to be pregnant with and activated by some generalized 'energy' that links together all objects and events.''[25] Joseph Church terms this total organismic involvement *participation*: the person responds directly without distance from the world. While participative functioning characterizes the early periods of childhood, it likewise can characterize adult life in spite of the strong overlay that our ego's contemplative, reflective, or distancing mode brings.

The adult sports fan who leans forward, tensing his muscles, stretching his own body to help the pole vaulter clear the bar, is demonstrating this primitive form of mentality, wherein self and other are minimally differentiated (for that one moment at least) and wherein one's own body literally participates in the other's performance, as though to help him over the bar.

On the basis of his many years of observation and analyses of child behavior, Jean Piaget speaks of a primary, nonrepresentational stage of experiencing which he calls the *sensorimotor*. In this early phase of development, there is no differentiation between acting and thinking; early thought *is* sensorimotor.

Sensorimotor experiencing, characteristic of the first twelve to eighteen months of our life, is a nonpermanent, fleeting moment, a *here-and-now* world of things now-present, then gone; objects do not retain permanence when *not-here* and *not-now*.

The global, participative, sensorimotor patterns gradually yield to representational or ideational forms of thinking, centering in particular around language. Thinking becomes an internalized schema of action. Whereas in the sensorimotor stage, thinking and action are one, in later developmental stages, thinking emerges as separable from action. This contemplative mode, coincident with the beginnings of language, permits the developing child to take distance from his immediate, physical-feeling-filled, undifferentiated universe, and to relate to reality via mediation. He learns to think about it, inspect it, ignore it, fabricate parts of it; all are accomplishments that transform the person and his world, minimizing the influence of the earlier global participative, sensorimotor mode. With the development of language and the representational function it permits, the immediately-given-and-then-gone world of the here and now is transformed into a world of things that may be retained in mind representationally even when they are not-here and not-now. Objects retain a permanency that extends beyond their immediate presence; other persons begin to take on a differentiated and permanent role within the child's life; and soon the child develops the capacity of experiencing himself experiencing, of being a self, differentiated from other selves.

In Piaget's view, the origins of thinking, an ego activity, lie in action: "thought is not the substitute for but the derivative of action."[26] This is too important not to repeat. In our beginnings, we live in a world that is immediately given here and now, without differentiating ourselves from that world. It is not a world filled with objects that last in time, that have similarities with other objects and differences from still others. It is a world that is moments here and then gone. Objects not directly presented do not exist even in imagination; for to imagine objects not present requires a representational scheme that the early child does not yet have. He cannot think in the sense of going beyond the immediate Now, differentiating certain regularities out of the mass of presentations; he cannot imagine in the sense of thinking of things not there, not tied intimately to his actions upon them. The beginnings then, are not verbal, not conceptual, but actions, or in Piaget's terms, sensorimotor actions, out of which thinking as we adults know it emerges.

It is difficult for adults to grasp this world of the child. To us, it would be filled with terror, a sense of disarray and chaos; it would be disorder and madness. But these are terms that our adult egos bring to bear upon an experience that exists prior to the advent of those egos. Chaos, terror, and confusion all suggest an ego's perspective; the child does not yet have an ego, and therefore does not experience this Jamesian "blooming buzzing confusion" as we might.

Within the sensorimotor world, even when language symbols make their first appearance, *ideas* and *words* are only one of several ways in which the child knows his world. Words and things are not separated, but rather "constitute one global unity." The name of a thing belongs to the thing, not to the person who names it. The child puzzles, perhaps, over how we know that the star is called Venus. Did someone venture up there and ask it? In his early, sensorimotor world, names and things are one. He does not yet sense that the name represents the thing rather than being it; this mode parallels the mythic process of our earlier reference.

What is a pencil? A pencil is to write with. What is a ball? A ball is to play with. The notions of things and their names are tied in primarily with actions carried out with those things. Our son recently showed a magic trick to a little child who was visiting us. Our son held a pencil lightly in his hand and waved it about, so that it appeared to be a flexible, waxy rod. The child was fascinated by this trick and kept trying unsuccessfully to copy him. I showed her the trick, using a different pencil and even a table knife. "But, no!" she protested, "the trick can only be done with the magic pencil, not any old pencil." Finally, as she and her parents were ready to leave, she asked if she could keep the magic pencil. I tried to give her one that I assured her would do every bit as well; no, it had to be the magic one. Only that one pencil could do the trick, even though the same effect had been demonstrated to her using other pencils and other implements. A pencil is not a pencil is not a pencil.

According to Freud, the child's world is initially characterized by a diffuse, timeless, fluid quality associated with what he calls *primary process thinking*.[27] Primary process thinking is characterized in several ways. It follows the pleasure principle in contrast to the reality principle; that is, it knows of no delay for its gratification but seeks the release of wishes in action taken right now. The child is hungry and wants the mother's breast or the bottle; he tolerates no delay; it is Now, an immediate, pervading presence demanding action for satisfaction without any sense of the realities of the external world. The hunger and the image of its satisfaction at the breast or bottle are merged and undifferentiated.

The primary process is further characterized by its fluidity and unbounded quality, as in even the adult's dreams, in which ideas stand in for other ideas, parts represent the whole, and vice versa. Displacement and condensation are two major mechanisms within the primary process. In displacement, we substitute ideas, one for the other; in condensation, we freely bring into one new unity parts that have had their own lengthy story to tell.

When adults dream or engage in such other activities as joking (e.g., puns), acts of creativity, or neurotic symptom formation, we are in contact with the primary process. In dreams, nonsense seems to prevail. Things come tumbling out one upon the other in seeming disarray; nothing is impossible. A single dream item can hold within it a story of near-infinite complexity; things fade in and fade out, represent this, then that. Objects have no boundaries but flow fluidly one into the other. What other process could house the source of our creative mind or the often peculiar connections that our neurotic symptoms demand?

The primary process is associated in Freud's writings with the id, that demanding soil out of which later, civilized, ego life develops. When the infant learns to delay gratification, to wait; when motoric phases are overlaid by ideational ones, so we think rather than act, we reach the beginnings of the ego's world, the reality principle, and the secondary process. This latter process, rooted in reality, is necessary to facilitate our gaining *effective* functioning within our everyday world. The world of the id and the primary process care little for delay and for reality; they have no commerce with this daily world but live sheltered within their own undifferentiated, diffuse, global environs. But to survive within the real world, we must develop a way of thinking that encompasses the kinds of differentiations and modes of experiencing that permit us to get on with others. The secondary process, its reality principle, and the ego itself are designed developmentally to manage these more mundane affairs.

With Freud, as with Piaget, we once again note that in the beginning we do not find the word; rather we begin with a pre-verbal action-related phase and process, sensorimotor in the one case, primary in the other. In both cases, this early phase is not adaptive in that it does not make the kinds of differentiations nor tolerate the kinds of ideational delays that serve to manage effective functioning in the everyday world. Sensorimotor experiencing presents the child with a universe that seems to come from nowhere and pass back again into nowhere, having little or no coherence or temporality. The world of the primary process is likewise a world without logic, without memory, without thought, without delay; it is a world without the kinds of fine differentiations and boundaries that permit us to deal effectively with objects and persons or even to manage so simple an act as getting food.

These are pre-verbal, pre-thinking worlds rooted in action, not in thinking about action. These are worlds of the id or some other primitive institution; these are not the worlds of the ego. These are the worlds, however, out of which the ego develops. I can leave aside the variety of disputes[28] concerning the precise manner by which the ego develops from this primitive world process (e.g., independently of it, parallel to it, as a later stage built upon it); it is sufficient to note that we have here the beginnings of our most fundamental mode of existence, described and analyzed in a way that by now should sound familiar. For this is a world of doing, of emergence, unbounded by conventions, by time, by categories of past, present, future; this is a world without objects in the usual sense of the term; a world in which things and actions are united, and in which one thing is everything as well.

* * *

From the Freudian perspective, or for that matter, from the perspective of such post-Freudian ego-theorists as Erik Erikson,[29] bodily modes remain a vital aspect of our primary relatedness to the world. As Erikson noted in his amplification and extension of Freud's writings, certain organ modes offer the primary basis around which our thinking is centered. The functions of the mouth in eating, for example, are an important part of the infant's early activities. He *takes in* food, and *spits out* food; he accepts and incorporates; he rejects and spits out. If thinking and action are a unified and undifferentiated experience, and if these organ modes provide the central focus of the person's early actions, they also provide the focus of his early modes of experiencing.

In other words, the various bodily functions that seem so to fascinate the psychoanalytic writers fascinate them because they are the earliest, intrinsic, and universal bases of the beginnings of all human experience. In all humans, whatever their culture, whatever their social class, wherever and whenever they may have lived, eating, with its actions of taking in and spitting out, provides a fundamental and common denominator for all pre-verbal experience.

The world of our primary sensorimotor experience focuses around actions; of these, the major focal points involve the basic, vital, and *repeated* organismic functions involved with eating and defecating. With growth and maturity, later organ modes enter the arena, e.g., sexuality, forming another focal point around which primary experiencing is constituted. Modes that come into being after the person has become verbal will necessarily reveal a more complex mix of primary experience and secondary cultural overlay.

The cultural overlay of our ego's development transforms all these primary sensorimotor, organ-related experiences into those emergent forms that we encounter in our everyday affairs within society, albeit often in disguised form. Thus all primary organ modes, including those involving eating and defecating as well as the sexual, involve a complex intermingling of primary experiencing with the secondary, ego-rooted overlay. Yet the basic modes themselves remain primary and form the soil out of which secondary or ego growth occurs.

It is now time to introduce a distinction necessary to understand both where we have been and where we are going. In discussing the notion of a primary, primitive process and a secondary, more mature ego process, our temptation is to think in terms of specfic contents rather than of structures and processes; to believe, for example, that in Freudian analysis of dreams the *content* of the dreams *is* the primary process. This is not the case. The contents are within the realm of the ego's world; the *process* is what is of importance to us.

The primary beginnings of which I have been speaking describe a process that is independent of specific contents. It may appear that I have introduced content by speaking of organ modes of action, such as taking in and spitting out. What I have outlined, however, is a process in which action and ideation are unified, in which boundaries between elements are blurred and fluid. Certain action modes that are intrinsic to the human species enter as focal points for this process; but the specific-meaning contents are culturally generated and thereby belong to the secondary or ego processes.

Whenever we speak of our primary beginnings, we necessarily use content words to talk about a process and thereby unfortunately confuse an already difficult matter. Contents, however, derive from the ego's world. Dreams offer us a helpful example to demonstrate this distinction. In analyzing a dream, the clinical analyst may focus on its contents: on what its meaning is to his patient. But to Freud, what was equally fascinating about dreams was to understand the psychic apparatus that must exist in order to produce them.

It is as fascinating to uncover the process that produces the dream as to unravel its specific meaning to the patient. Freud's work *Interpretation of Dreams* does both; but his greatest contribution lies less in his ability to find meaning in dreams (i.e., content) than in his ability to unravel the nature of the psychic process that acts on contents to transform them into dreams. Thus, in Chapter 7 of that book, the process chapter, Freud outlines the nature of the psychic apparatus involved, which has come forward in history as perhaps his greatest accomplishment. Similarly, although specific contents always emerge in Piaget's writing about his observations of children, his greatest achievement lies in his analysis of the psychic process that produces the content.

The primitive beginnings about which I have been talking describe a process of experiencing that *manages* content in a way quite different from the secondary or ego process. And this is an important point. We live our everyday lives and even experience our transcendent moments in terms of specific contents and specific meanings. But those meanings and those experiences were constituted by a process—and it is the process that is of paramount interest to our analysis of everyday reality and its transcendence. Transcendent moments happen within a context of contents, specific meanings, interpretations, and analyses; but these are *not* the process itself.

We are now ready to move one step further in our search and our discovery. What happens to these primitive beginnings once we begin to mature and acquire more refined, linguistic, secondary, ego processes? Do the secondary processes replace the primary or are they an overlay on a beginning that remains forever present and active, albeit rarely known?

Later ego processes do not substitute for this fundamental stratum of our experiencing; rather, they transform early processes and in time become dominant over them. We do not lose our capacity to experience transcendentally; rather, we acquire a process that seems steadfastly to support doing otherwise. We do not lose our sensorimotor modes; rather, we develop formal, logical modes that come to dominate these primitive beginnings. We do not lose our primary process; rather, we acquire secondary modes that remain more dominant in our everyday lives.

Most behavioral analyses, including Freud's and Piaget's, having laid the foundations for what I have termed the *transcendent process*, have in fact dealt with ego processes. Piaget's focus upon developmental stages emphasizes the means whereby the primary, sensorimotor mode is *transformed* through growth experiences into later, formal modes of thinking-and-experiencing. His entire analysis leads us *away* from our primary experiential beginnings and into a world of our ego's everyday reality. The equilibrating processes of assimilation and accommodation outline the means whereby the primary sensorimotor scheme assimilates new experiences to itself, thereby modifying them, while accommodating itself by changing in response to those newly encountered realities of life. Developmental crises mark the movement forward to a new stage of equilibration, when finally the existing schema can no longer assimilate the new experiences but must undergo radical reorganization. We can visualize a spiraling effect in which the earlier stages are reintegrated into a new hierarchical arrangement with the later developing stages. But this is the ego's story, not the one we must find and understand.

In similar fashion, the post-Freudian emphasis upon ego processes has led us away from our primary and continuing roots. Freud's own writings, while maintaining a major focus upon the primary process and its implications for psychoanalytic theory and therapy, confuse the transcendent with the primary. Freud's discussion of the primary process is better seen as an analysis of the *ego's* unconscious world than as a perspective on our transcendent origins. As both Gill and Holt have suggested,[30] the primary process shows more developmental structure and growth than its name suggests. In fact, the primary process itself presupposes an earlier, undifferentiated mode out of which it develops. As such, the primary process, unlike the transcendent, is transformed by social experience; thus, though it may seem primary in the ego's sense, it is *not* the fundamental root that we understand as the transcendent perspective.

A second problem involved in considering the primary process to be truly primary and fundamental in the same sense as the transcendent perspective is that it contains unfulfilled or repressed wishes that find expression in our dreams, slips of the tongue, neurotic symptoms, etc. As Holt[31] has noted, given the conceptual overlap between the id and the primary process, there would have to be an id present at birth for the primary process to be "primary." But the id contains contents, including wishes, that presuppose the beginnings of contact with a social world. It would seem that a wish is a content derived from the ego's world of social experience. To the extent that our unconscious primary process houses unfulfilled and repressed wishes, conflicts, and such, it would seem better to conceptualize this as an aspect of the ego's world rather than of the transcendent perspective. In this view, similar to several neo-Freudian arguments, the ego is derivative from an ego-id base that itself is derivative from an even more fundamental beginning.

Even the dynamic unconscious which forms so central a part of psychoanalytic theory, and which appears to function in primary-process terms, is best understood as an unconscious aspect of our ego's world, derived in part out of the conflicts between social and cultural reality on the one hand and our primary mode of experiencing on the other. Out of these conflicts, an unconscious world is created; however, this is part of our ego's perspective and not of the transcendent mode. The unconscious of which Freud speaks is not the same as the transcendent perspective of which I speak; rather, the unconscious is a derivative of ego processes and remains within its purview, separate from our unfolding experiential stream.

I view the roots of our person to lie within the experiential stream, a pre-verbal, pre-logical realm that is truly primary and fundamental. Out of this beginning, the ego's apparent primary and secondary processes are later differentiated. In this view, the unconscious processes of which the Freudians speak are essentially part of the ego's world, rather than a part of the transcendent perspective. It should be clear by now that in my usage of the term, the *ego's world* includes the id-ego-superego functions that psychoanalytic theory outlines; this world, in turn, is distinguished from the world of the transcendent perspective.

The ego's world, with its conscious and its dynamically unconscious aspects, develops out of the initial world of the transcendent stream. These later aspects develop within the stream's continuing presence. Our ego's world, which comes to occupy our life's everyday center-stage, sits as an island within the middle of a continuously unfolding experiential stream. Our ego's world is a narrowing of this stream, an imposition of its perspective on aspects of that stream.

This view brings quite a different emphasis and focus from Freud's and Piaget's to the entire picture. Within its own perspective, the ego is central. But in the transcendent perspective, it is an island, floating in the midst of our experiential stream. The transcendent process surrounds the ego's world. But it does not function by ego processes. Its aim is not stability or equilibrium; it does not develop, pass through stages of growth or decay. It simply is, always moving onward. The model that emerges then, is of an ego's world that evolves out of primitive beginnings and that contains a conscious and an unconscious aspect with the functions analytic theory has uncovered.

This is not to deny the basic similarity between the unconscious primary process of the ego's world and the parent transcendent process; they share many attributes and thus have been readily confused. For example, the mechanisms of the dream work which Freud discovered reconstitute our ego's world of conscious experience in a manner similar to the way we experience within the transcendent perspective: i.e., object boundaries blur and fade together; time past and present is equally vivid and real; etc. This should come as no surprise, in that the primary process is derivative of the transcendent perspective. Nevertheless, the contents that are reconstituted and the unconscious structures that evolve as we grow up within a given culture speak to our need to recognize the existence of the different process, the transcendent, which remains forever beyond the reach of development.

Where, then, are we? The transcendent perspective begins before the word and lives before the word. It flows forth, an unbroken becoming, an experiential stream, similar to Piaget's sensorimotor operations and Freud's primary process. The transcendent stream is primary and forever; it is rooted in action. It does not undergo any developmental sequence, but rather remains a Presence always as it was in its beginnings. It is a Cause that itself is uncaused other than by the advent of life itself. It is always a process emerging.

Both Freud and Piaget concentrated their efforts in describing processes that belong more properly to the ego's world. This is a perspective that does grow, does develop, does have a history and a future.

All beginnings were at the same point; the departure after that involves the development of a conscious and unconscious overlay. Our egos, though an island within the ever-present experiential stream, take central dominance in our world of thinking and being. Whereas our ego was born from this stream, it grows and develops out of interactions with society; it learns and is modified. The stream itself does not grow out of any interactions or learnings; the transcendent perspective does not learn, does not retain, does not recall, does not know, does not think as we in our ego's perspective can imagine.

The transcendent is a process without content; yet there are themes of content derived from the ego's world, which are shaped by their encounter with this experiential stream. These we now examine.

20

Interpersonal Themes Within the Transcendent World

Our ego's is a world of *either-or*; the transcendent's, of *both-and*. There are no paradoxes of living within the transcendent world. Paradoxes derive from learned cultural categories that differentiate persons and events in ways essential to the maintenance of the existing fabric of the culture. Within the experiential stream, however, cultural differentiations melt together, revealing the fundamental human condition. Fundamentally, we are all the same. Within our everyday lives, we confront choices, different pathways to be followed; we settle for one or the other and live out our lives realizing one way, denying the others. Distinctions so basic to our ego's way of life fade into obscurity in the transcendent perspective.

For example, our ego's world is founded upon neat differentiations between male and female, child and adult, time-now, time-past, time-future, illusion and reality, thinking and doing. These clear distinctions blur and blend within the transcendent view. In every man there is a woman; in every woman lives a man. Sexual distinctions merge; their everyday oppositeness changes into a unity of persons. *I* becomes *thou.*[1] In every adult there lives a child, the *healthy childishness* of which Maslow[2] has so perceptively spoken. The neat boundaries between reality and illusion become fuzzy: all that is illusion is real and all that is real is illusory.

I look at my hi-fi speaker and hear a voice singing. Why should I believe it an illusion to think there is actually a little person inside the 3×3 speaker, but a reality the idea that somewhere across the bay a man in a studio is spinning a plastic disc with grooves that send the sound across the air and into that box?

Within the natural standpoint, for all practical purposes, we are each determined machines, making decisions without significant choice, acting as though we were free, but in fact, as Skinner[3] has correctly noted, simply not seeing the ways by which our lives have been pre-cast and determined. It is only within the transcendent perspective that we may be said to be truly free, unknown, indeterminate, and unpredictable. To be sure, action once taken, even when guided by transcendent spontaneity, is understandable; it is only that we can never say about such action that it could be known before its occurrence. Sensibility and meaning derive from post hoc explanations, not from theories which allow them to be predicted. Action guided by the transcendent mode allows neither prediction nor control; it could always be other than it is; for we and everyone else have no way of even knowing what it will emerge to become. The essence of the transcendent perspective is its disregard for any systematic predictive explanation. It flows along, moves, emerges, becomes. To the extent that we flow along with it, we are carried about in ways that are not truly choices made by a self-conscious ego guided by deterministic factors. We are carried about by Singer's imp, trusting it to lead us.

By manipulating external or internal conditions of their growth, socialization, or present circumstances, we can systematically predict and control the actions of persons within the natural standpoint. But we cannot predict or control actions guided by the transcendent mode.

Our fundamental existence partakes both of the *erklären*, causal, mechanical bonds, dear to the hearts of the physical and most of the behavioral sciences, and the *verstehen*, the subjective, understandable, but not predictable roots, dear to the hearts of some few of the social sciences.[4] We are *both*,[5] always and inevitably; even though one may predominate and does (i.e., the natural standpoint), and even though the other may rarely put in an appearance once we have been properly socialized to function in our everyday lives and world.

Later, I will examine more fully the nature of the mix within us; suffice it to note for now that, being both, we all have untapped resources of personal psychological freedom. And when I say "we all," I mean, in fact, each and every one of us: not the "elite," the "saved," the "good," the "honorable," the "rich," the "educated," or whatever. We differ less in our potential to find the exceptional within ourselves than in the conditions of our living and socialization which have seemingly foreclosed some of the options that nevertheless forever remain alive and healthy.

Those who rebel from the everyday usually show more the taint of duty than the expression of real freedom.[6] Yet, even within our everyday existence, we see glimmerings of the other side, the earlier, untouched primitive. Some of our behaviors are even guided by this transcendent realm, especially our most important decisions.

In making a major decision we often choose from our gut and our heart rather than from our head, our seemingly rational ego. After having chosen, our ego returns to take charge and bring forth good reasons to justify the choices. Sense is the act of an ego seeking to legitimate and justify actions that have been guided from elsewhere.

Our other-directedness evolves from various sources, including the basis by which our self as a "me" was derived. Our inner-direction, fundamental and enduring, awaits within as well. The forces against abandoning the achievements and values of other-directedness are overwhelming; the possibility nevertheless remains for us to get in touch with our transcendent world and thereby gain internal rather than external guidance.

To stand up and apart from the group's definitions of reality; to withstand pressures to conform; to be this, to live and act that way; to avoid shame and embarrassment; to know with certainty what is correct, true, and proper: all require that we be in touch with something within ourselves uncontaminated by social forces, a world within that offers guidance that is fundamentally inner-directed. There are moments in each of our lives when we touch this inner mode, the transcendent perspective, and act courageously *in spite of* what seems to be the costs incurred in our ego's perspective. Most of the time in our everyday lives, of course, we enact the social-comparative, other-directed pattern; we choose the most practical, often least effortful path; we fit in, go along, agree, and thereby avoid the insecurity, fear, rejection, shame, and embarrassment that would derive from acting otherwise.

But there are those moments in which *otherwise* pops up, often as an unwanted intrusion. For a moment, the child sees that he can say "no"; he can refuse to go along. The adult hears deeply within himself a growl of, "No, I won't" emerging, as though controlled by someone or something within. This inner voice, this part of our selves that I have called our transcendent perspective, lies patiently awaiting our arrival. We cannot command it to arrive and guide us; it is there always, however, to guide those who would take the risk and plunge into it. Its message to society is often to be heard as a "no" or as an affirmation of "yes."

College students have frequently spoken to me of the conflict they experience. Caught within their ego's natural attitude, they are never sure whether the things they say, do, or profess are theirs uniquely or something shared, an other-directed fad. We talk briefly about it; I sense they have placed themselves within a true double-bind. They want to say "no," to stand apart, to disagree, to go their own way; yet they see around them others also wanting to say "no," to stand apart and go their own way. If they conform and say "yes," they have lost in their battle for autonomy from external control; if they say "no," they have joined with others and again are not acting autonomously.

This agony of indecision derives from remaining fully

within the natural standpoint and examining this situation as a dilemma which one can never win. Whatever we do, it fits into someone else's scheme,[7] and thus is never truly our own. The dilemma holds forever, of course, if we remain rooted in the natural standpoint, looking always outward and never inward.

But the dilemma disappears the moment we touch the inner realm of the transcendent perspective and act within its guidance, spontaneously, freely, and openly. Within that realm there is no doubt, no confusion, no agony. We then join with the society's majority *or* with its minority, neither saying "yes" in order to conform nor "no" in order to rebel and be different. As our ego defines such situations, there is no autonomous route. Within the transcendent stream, however, there is total autonomy and total conformity. We act; we do; we become; we are. The dilemma fades; the double-bind is gone.

Risk-taking is at the core of the transcendent stream. But things that are experienced as risks in the ego's terms are, from the transcendent perspective, simply spontaneous actions. The ego needs an ordered world, with clear-cut paths and routes marked out *before* the voyage is taken; to it the notion of acting openly, spontaneously, and adventurously is almost unthinkable. "But where will I end up?" "How will I feel?" "How can I know if that's what I want to do?" "Are you sure that's the best way for getting there from here?" So many questions, so many doubts, so many fears, trepidations, worries; so many assurances needed, so little risk possible. From the transcendent perspective, we move forward by *moving* forward. There is no risk because there is only our self unfolding, growing, moving, living.

Within the transcendent, trust of self is fundamental; as must be trust of others as well. Although the terms trust and distrust are the creation of our ego's world and have no meaning as such within the transcendent realm, it is nevertheless possible to speak of the high degree of inner trust that exists when we act spontaneously, openly, and without continuous efforts to monitor, censor, withhold, or guarantee before doing. The nonspontaneous living of our ego speaks all too clearly of the degree to which we trust neither ourselves nor others. We say that passions must be curbed and monitored. Freedom is dangerous. In the name of controlling our unfolding experiential stream, we create systems that manage our lives and prohibit trusting ourselves or anyone else. Why trust those who manage us? Why trust ourselves if we require management?[8]

History reveals the death and destruction that is carried out in the name of our ego's world. It is not that our fundamental nature is inherently destructive and needs to be carefully monitored; rather, our ego's world manages our fates in death-filled ways. Fundamentally, "there is really no alternative to trusting man's nature."[9]

My life is my life, carried out by me. I am living, doing, thinking, acting, being, becoming. I am my roles. Within the transcendent perspective, there exists a unity between person and person, between person and environment. I do not put on roles and take them off with the passing time of day. I am not a collage of faces, costumes, games, façades, or whatever. I am all-in-all; I am me-living. When I act, it is I who acts, not a role, not an alien entity that I claim to have put on for the occasion and which I shall shed as soon as the next role is upon me. I am here, I am over there, I am everywhere. No clear boundaries exist that separate me as an object from other objects; I flow into everything and everything into me. Boundaries blur and become indistinct. I am one and I am all.

Responsibility for what I do is mine; I am what I do. I cannot call upon my duty, my obligation, my social role as though these were things separate from me. These things are me. There is no action, however small, no decision, however trivial, that is not myself acting, choosing. If I sit quietly at home while the fire rages outside, that is myself acting, choosing, deciding. I am responsible, not you, not society, not roles. These do not exist apart from me. I cannot hold to a role analysis and cop-out of my personal implication in everything that I do. My ego handles that end quite well; within the transcendent perspective, however, such options do not exist.

When I act most freely (i.e., guided by transcendence), I am most responsible; when my ego takes charge, I have the least personal responsibility. The freedom from which I may wish to escape[10] is the very freedom that places the burden upon me. Better perhaps to be a machine, a cog, an ego in society's drama than to yield myself to my transcendent stream.

21

The Crisis of Liberation

Two sides of man, two ways, two possibilities. The one dominates our lives as we conduct our practical affairs in the world; the other lurks like an elusive shadow we can never quite grasp (for it is our own),[1] popping up here and there, evident in some persons more than others, spicing and flavoring our lives or threatening to overwhelm us with an alien view. We begin freely; the transcendent mode dominates. Soon we have the growing, ever more encompassing, pragmatic overlay of our ego's natural perspective. Everything converges upon the natural standpoint, making it the only realistically practical direction for our growth. Only a fool or a madman could resist the encompassing fold of this man-made perspective.

In the process of our development, we rush headlong, even joyously, into learning how to become properly socialized creatures of our society; to learn its rules and customs; to use its language; to internalize its ways of seeing, believing, and thinking. The cloak of the everyday standpoint is richly rewarding to the developing youngster who wants to know how to fit in and become a part of this grand, ongoing enterprise known as society. Once the cloak has been wrapped around us, we find the seductive reinforcement of belonging combines with the fearful consequences of standing forth

naked without the cloak, to imprison us within the one dominant mode of our possible existence. To be sure, glimmerings
of other possibilities emerge for everyone at times; but these
usually foreign voices, these moments of exciting and fearful
novelty, are hushed up or placed away in our inner closets,
lest the cloak which seems to be slipping away truly falls to
the ground and leaves us standing naked before the world:
vulnerable, unshielded, in terror and loneliness.

Venturing into this shadow world cannot involve a self-
conscious, insistent trying. The harder we try to command it
into existence, the more we manage to interfere with its arrival.
The passive openness[2] that characterizes the transcendent
mode, the simply letting be, will not hear of command performances. Disheartened perhaps, or relieved, we return again
to the mundane everyday, listening to tales of those who have
made it beyond, or imagining that we too have made it, but
choosing not to call up these inner spirits to public view and
comment.

Inventive souls that we are, we nevertheless at times march
forward boldly, and with an adventuresome spirit seek the
new path for *our* walk through life. Using the tools of our
ancestors to guide us and the rewards of the status quo to
tempt us, our adventures take us but little beyond where we
and others have always been. We may glimpse within, but
fall back all too rapidly into the everyday. And well we
should; for sense dictates, even to the seemingly most senseless
among us, that to do otherwise would be suicide.

The transition from our ego's natural standpoint to the
transcendent, our return back along the highway we took as
growing youngsters, is marked by as much difficulty, if not
more, than the original voyage. And this we too-often forget.
It took us many long, difficult years to become properly socialized: to learn to make those differentiations so vital to our
lives; to build an ego strong enough to control the impulsive
surges that once dominated. The manner by which we learned
to join society has laid foundations of substance; some aspects

of our ego's view are rooted in our very core. The rewards and reinforcements of keeping within the fabric of the social system cannot so readily be abandoned for an adventure into the unknown.

There are those who make a quick buck by offering instant cures to the ills that some experience as they wander about their lives. Sensing a certain emptiness to their everyday lives, some persons fall easy prey to these money merchants or even to well-meaning "miracle workers" who offer them instant comfort and rapid cure: simply follow the way of this fad or that. Touch here, feel there, ring around a circle; swear, curse, strip naked, this drug or that.[3]

We forget how long it took us to get to where we presently are, like it or not. The way back by no means can be so readily or rapidly short-circuited, as though it were simply a marvelous act of will or a game to be played. I give great credit to the psychoanalytically oriented healers who know full well how much time and effort it takes simply to work out the kinks and knots of the past, let alone attempt to restructure the present. I do not mean to be pessimistic about anyone's chances for even momentary contact with the transcendent, but I do want to emphasize the difficulties and the hurdles. Discipline, training, experience, and hard work are required just to reach the level at which one can act spontaneously, transcending the habitual and the routinized.

We enter the world ready to learn, to adapt, to become, to join, to merge even as we separate ourselves from our initial embeddedness within the womb and the family circle. The road forward is fun, exciting, different, fascinating; it is also frightening and new, threatening us even while it tantalizes and tempts. In curiosity and desire we move forward, at times tentatively but forward nevertheless, acquiring the bits and pieces of thread we will use to weave the cloak of our culture. We encounter crises as we move ahead in our natural processes of growth and development. Those we conquer give us a new assurance, a new sense of confidence; after all, *we* did it, *we* made it over the hill, through that crisis. In failure, some retreat; some move to the side; some push on doggedly, hoping to find a smaller hill on which to try out their climbing prowess.

From different ways, along different routes, at different times, we arrive to take on the adult roles of our society. We share much but differ always; our histories have been different. We got to where we got in different ways; many of us are not even at the same place on our arrival. But we are there. We may not even recognize the battle as won; for living is a continuous process, a continuous movement, a continuous development. But we made it; however bad it is, we made it; we're here, *the survivors*. We developed strategies, mostly unconscious, that keep us alive and generally well; strategies that make our life, however miserable it may be, better than the terrors of not knowing what tomorrow will bring. Better to be imprisoned in a miserable world than in one unknown, chaotic, and open-ended. At least in knowledge we can face the pain.

We have developed strategies to fend off crushing disconfirmations of everyday living; personal strategies and shared political gambits keep the new and the threatening at bay or somewhere where we aren't likely to see them or have to deal with them. We have each developed strategies even to fend off ourselves, to dismiss that inner world which is our hope but also our dread. We would rather be cogs in a grand design than choosing actors in a drama of our own making.

Sometimes our strategies break down, flooding us with fear and anxiety; the forbidden world, hidden in shadows, pushes its way through, lunges onstage, taking over the spotlight. Pain, fear, death. Routines save us from ourselves; habituation turns the trick, keeps us busy, occupied. Avoid thinking; avoid meeting those intrusive elements.

It is more difficult to avoid intrusions from within than without.[4] Those external to ourselves can be dealt with personally and politically; we get rid of the bastards. But those within ourselves—they are always there, always present. Forget our dreams at night; drink ourselves blind by day. Dope ourselves up and up beyond any sensibility. Time. Use it up; spend it.

Rushing in the race of the everyday helps keep us from the inner tuggings of our transcendent perspective. If I keep busy, then I can't have time to think; even if I have time, I'm too tired and worn out. Sleep will save me from me. Time in days' routines keeps us from exploring, from moving out into new worlds still there to be visited. Too much to do. The American way is centered around an ego that is busily moving; always moving, always doing. Racing each day just to remain in the same spot. Running; running in circles defined as progress. If you aren't busy doing something, you are un-American, unclean, ungood. Idle hands are the workshop of the devil; busy hands keep hands away from one's self.

Strategies that keep us alive, well, and moving along. We are the survivors, we made it, so why push our luck? A bad thing becomes a good thing. A good thing is a good thing is a good thing: leave well enough alone. It's all right Jack. Strategies that help us move away from liberating experiences, or if perchance we happen upon a proper situation, we avoid believing in it or following it up. Our ego will not easily give up its center, not easily yield to "whim" (its term).

In our developmental history, it must seem as though any change requires abandoning all that has gone before. Indeed, developmental changes invariably demand a breakdown in the old system even as a new system is being incorporated and integrated into the growing person. Though it may appear as though the old is cast out as the new is acquired, in the actual process, the old is incorporated into the new as the new is transformed to fit the old, thereby creating another level or stage of growth in our life history.[5] In each of our developmental stories, crises of growth propel us along to a new level. That level, in turn, offers us a new synthesis that combines where we were with where we are still heading.

The transition between stages within our ego's developmental history proceeds on the basis of crisis and tension. Our existing patterns of dealing with life do not fit as well as they did formerly; we must now think and act differently. Old answers fail us as we now ask new questions. A crisis occurs; the old ways must be reevaluated. New possibilities must be sought. Finally, a new stage emerges and we move along again.

I have described the typical course of ego development, assuming that everyone participates to a certain degree in this developmental program. Of course, some persons do not move as far along the possible sequence of growth as others; they fail to incorporate the new with the old. Tension and crisis can overwhelm as much as they can effect positive growth. Nevertheless, from even this cursory overview of developmental theory, it is apparent that the transition within our everyday life from one level of growth to another requires crisis, tension, and some transformation of the existing us by the newly emerging directions of our growth.

Let me state this matter more pointedly. The transition from the ego's natural standpoint into the realm of the transcendent requires crisis and tension just as does transition within the ego's own developmental history. But *qualitatively*, movement from one realm into the other requires abandoning one for the other. To be more blunt, there must be *major* personal disintegration before there can be any reintegration.[6]

In the first place, movement into the transcendent perspective demands that we pass through and beyond the existing forms of our ego's relationship to everyday reality. This initial step requires that we undergo a disintegrative encounter in which we give up the old simply in order to see the new. A barrier must be reached and much that we value and that is continually reinforced must be sacrificed. The ego cannot remain an ego and still touch its shadow.

But no one would ever make the transition through this barrier if there were no chance thereafter to return to the ego's natural standpoint. The enrichment that derives from encountering the transcendent realm can only be had in a climate of relatively free flowing traffic between it and the ego's world. In other words, to go from A to B, one must abandon A; but only in the service of later regaining a better understanding of *both* A and B.

* * *

The barriers to our move into the transcendent process should by now be apparent. All we know about what we know and all we sense about who we are is rooted in the maintenance of the existing forms of our ego's natural standpoint. The foundations of our existence are invested in a particular bank; if it goes out of business, so do we. Its demise is ours; we cease to be, to know, to exist. Our ego is lost, wandering free, untied to anything known or familiar. We become nothing, an empty floating blob of flesh, without boundaries, without history. We are disintegrated, destroyed, removed; there are no records remaining of our ever having been, or of our being again.

The experiential quality of this descent is akin to the all-encompassing horror of an internal pain beyond belief. There is no place to turn, no place to hide. We carry about within us the seed of our own destruction. It is triggered at the slightest event; even nothing brings it upon us. Sartre described it as the gripping total experience of *nausea*.[7] It covers us as a veil of anxiety, an ocean of feeling, raw and pure, tearing at our guts, wringing us out with drained and lost energy.

We question, and then we doubt that we exist to question. Descartes' doubting ego comes to doubt even its own existence, tumbling the doubter farther into an abyss from which there is no way out. Waves of pure horror swell up and engulf us. We tumble as though caught in a high surf, tossed about and pounded down, down, down; but there is not even the painful comfort of the grating sand to give us solace. We long to touch a concrete reality, even to burn ourselves in scalding pain just to know that we remain. Not even that pleasure awaits us.

We are cast adrift: no sea, no raft, no shore, nothing but adriftness, loss, engulfment in limitless space. Agony floats; we sense it is we who experience this agony, yet find no referent for that we. The underpinnings that kept us in place and propped up have been cut out; we fall, fall, fall, fall until there is only falling, not even a we to whom it is happening.

Soon there is only paining, falling, fearing, losing, despairing, but never any one to whom this is happening. We are everywhere at once and thus nowhere at all. We are with God; we are God. We have nowhere to go, nowhere to be. We have been nowhere and everywhere. We are raw existence, flowing, becoming, emerging, encompassing, joining, merging.

How can so horrible an experience, a nightmare, a nausea, ever be *in the service* of anything? Why let go of the controls our ego keeps to hold us as us and in check? There is pleasure, of course, as well; but pleasure for the moment changes to pure horror as our ego's loss permits us to slip further and further, our ego hanging on, keeping what controls remain, pulling against an irresistible force dragging us on. Irresistible force? Not really. For the forces keeping us in control, though a thin line indeed, remain nevertheless most potent influences prohibiting our movement too far down this path of ego loss and disintegration.

To be reborn, we must first die.[8] Liberation is a process of rebirth. Yet to die is so frightening and so fearful that the pull of looking beyond is forever met by the forces keeping us well within the grasp of our ego's everyday perspective. It is this fear of death that keeps us from living fully.[9] Not fear of our physical death, for that comes and is over and we know little about it. Rather, fear of our living forever in death: untied, unrooted, open, naked, blowing on the winds, never knowing, never being sure or secure.

Fear of psychological death keeps us from the fullness of living, from achieving the transcendent view within each of us. Better to play it safe, keep secure and relatively happy, than to venture forth. In the name of safety, we excommunicate a part of our world to remain forever a hidden shadow from which we are rarely to be enriched. We relegate ourselves to live out our time in the ego's world, relatively happy, relatively secure, but never experiencing the full richness that is ours. Yet even as we would take that step in search of the transcendent, we foreclose our achieving it by our very act of trying so hard. In proper circumstances, the transcendent mode will creep upon us with stealth, by day or night, carrying us upon its currents. But we must let it come, not go seek it.

Cooptation[10] refers to the manner by which an established organization manages its bothersome intruders, buying them off by bringing them into the organization's governing machinery. Cooptation, or regression in the service of reality, occurs to an ego transformed by liberating experiences into a newly constructed way of life. Given the rewards of fitting into the ongoing scheme of things, our ego falls ready prey to rejecting the lessons just learned in favor of belonging happily again to the established fold, even if that fold be one of slavery and submission. At least the slave knows his place. Not knowing is the horror most supreme to the human within the natural standpoint. Bad news is better than no news at all!

Our ego may learn from liberating experiences yet return rapidly to the routines of the natural standpoint seemingly unaffected by this venture. Common among the counterculturists has been the attainment of what are felt to be major insights through drugs, political protests, or whatever, that fade as soon as the press of everyday reality again happens upon them: final exams, parental threats to financial security, arrest, and so on. In despair, they come to hate themselves for not having the courage to live by the insights just gained and to hate the system within which they feel themselves forever trapped.

Lessons of the transcendent are neither easy to come by nor to integrate within our everyday lives. The better socialized we have been into the ways of a given system, the more we achieve our identity by fitting in, the less readily can we gain a foothold upon and integrate the material from the transcendent world; it remains most troublesome and uncooperative when we attempt to put it into practice.

There are ways of living within the everyday world that facilitate the kinds of awareness that put us into closer contact with the transcendent; other ways serve as well to thwart such developments. I previously examined some ways of the everyday world that reinforce our ego's natural standpoint. Here we are searching for those experiences that are *liberating*, that have the potential to open us up to ourselves. *Opening up* involves revealing to our ego in its everyday mode the perspective transcendence offers.

Awareness of this sort, however, can threaten as much as it can open and reveal. Out of the fear which such revelations hold or imply, we may be driven back toward even stronger defenses against further encounters with this alien being within. Yet, only through these revealing meetings at the border crossing are hints of this other perspective slowly revealed to our ego.

Our ego may carry on what amounts to an illicit romance with this part of us that is otherwise concealed from the light of day. Illicitly, the ego finds itself meeting by chance this inner world. With the fascination of a lover seeking new thrills in his affairs, the ego may begin actively to seek out this elusive playmate. But just as the Lorelei's song tempted passing sailors to their destruction, so does the courtship between our ego and this transcendent world hold potent threats to the well-being of the ego. Even as our ego maintains its border trysts with these chance intrusions, it begins to take notions into its framework that cast a shadow upon its once well-lighted surrounding, a shadow of the inner world emerging and covering over the dearly held, well-lighted truths of the ego's everyday reality.

At these crucial moments, the ego faces a crisis, the outcome of which can be at the cost of further encounters with this other perspective. Ego strength is related to adaptability, and adaptability is vital to survival within the world of everyday reality. Part of what the ego learns from its romantic ventures can be useful in these everyday adaptations. Regression in the service of the ego, related especially to creativity,[11] stands as testimony to the potential usefulness to the ego of these intrusions from an alternate process.

But courtship and marriage are two different things. One may court the affections of the transcendent process, but the exigencies of everyday reality demand that the ego always return home to its own world before the relationship has been consummated. One tastes the pleasures and meets the fears, but treads no farther into this realm; to tread farther demands that the ego lose itself. Little can we know that within this new, shadowy realm lies an entirely different form of integration. From the ego's perspective, only *loss* can be seen.

Seeds of doubt are planted in these moments of courtship, perhaps to grow into another crisis in which a full-blown emergence into the transcendent perspective is achieved. The fear, of course, is that once we give in fully to this other perspective, our return to the everyday will not be possible. Images of the raving maniac serve to reinforce this stereotype. Few know what new person would come out of the process to face everyday reality. Perhaps the lessons learned can never be applied in the everyday world. I think they can be, and that they offer more than idle hope to enrich and free the individual caught inextricably in the web of everyday living.

Liberating experiences push our ego into a meeting with the transcendent, casting shadows over the existing forms of the ego's perspective and opening up alternative possibilities. Ego comes to think the unthinkable, to see the unseeable, to do the undoable, to be the unbeable. As meeting after meeting occurs, as the boundary between the natural standpoint and the transcendent blurs, the ego becomes more adept in losing itself, in letting be, in flowing with the moment, confident in the power within to provide more than ample guidance and direction.

The blurred boundary permits new ways to be tried, new possibilities to be explored, new compromises to be reached. New awareness becomes assimilated and forms an enriched inner-guidance system, permitting the ego to withstand or run counter to the prevailing currents of everyday reinforcement. Courageous action *in spite of* becomes the dominant motif for such a person, now freed from the routines of everyday life, while in fact living successfully within an organized social system.

22

Experiences That Disconfirm
and Broaden

The doubting ego, standing on the brink of its apparent destruction, looking through the threshold into the worlds beyond. The strong ego, prepared to face the unknown, ready to move forward in pursuit of something primitive and engaging. A subtle mix of doubt and curiosity.

Our ego grows through crises that cast doubt upon its present while providing fresh perspectives to help guide it past that doubt and into a new realm of security and mastery. Transcendent experiences, while more profoundly disturbing, likewise press our ego with deeply felt doubts, and open its horizon to new vistas. Our search for experiences that liberate, that join ego with transcendent, must consider those encounters that *prepare* the ego for this most disturbing encounter. We shall see that experiences that disconfirm and broaden the ego within a context of ego strength, receptivity, and mastery prepare it to take that more profound step beyond.

Taking as his point of departure the discipline known as the sociology of knowledge, Karl Mannheim[1] offers a helpful concept. He refers to a process he terms "gaining the detached perspective" whereby we come to see the cultural veils through which we gaze out upon the world. Social systems create an inbred form of social reality, concealing to all within the system the sociohistorical uniqueness of their own points of view. Within the natural standpoint we accept basic realities without doubt or question; we never see the properties of the system which remain the unquestioned background. Just as the fish does not know it is in water, man does not know he is in atmosphere unless he can gain distance from the very system of which he is a part; from this distance he can see the relation between what he knows and the view provided by the system in which he is located.

Gaining this detached perspective requires mobility or contact with differences. Contact between different cultures offers us an opportunity to notice the relativity of the belief system of our culture and thus bring into question knowledges we may have assumed to be givens, absolutely true for all persons everywhere. Even moving around within one social system, as when we move from one social class to another, offers us chances to gain perspective on truths formerly taken as absolute. Generational contacts likewise offer us the chance to see the lenses we routinely and unquestionably use. Each new generation must encounter the cultural system of belief and justification that its predecessors take for granted.[2] As Mannheim notes, out of this potential clash of disparate perspectives, the ego is thrown back upon itself and must take a long, hard look at what was held with somnambulistic certainty to be unquestionably true.

Lawrence Kohlberg,[3] in his theory of moral development, introduces *role-taking opportunities* as the vehicle whereby the ego confronts different realities. In the process of coming to terms with different roles and the alternate perspectives they provide, our own horizons can widen and gain depth.

Building upon the framework of G. H. Mead,[4] Kohlberg suggests that a person who is given wide latitude to play a variety of roles will gain widely divergent perspectives on himself and on life. Thus the child who is given important participatory experiences—as leader, follower, initiator, supporter, aggressor, nurturant figure, etc.—gains many points from which to view himself and to experience others, and thus achieves a richer, more extensive conception of both.

As Mead might have said, our initial role taking centers around the mother, the father, and then other members of our family. As we grow older, we take the roles of members of our peer group, seeing both the world in general and ourselves in particular from their perspectives. Later we abstract from these specific others and form a new synthesis, which Mead termed the *generalized other*: taking the role perspective of a given community or society. Kohlberg posits a still-greater audience of role-taking possibilities, as we become capable of seeing even the community and its generalized other within the broader context of all humanity. Within that realm, our role taking now involves synthesizing not only specific persons from our early and later life, not only members of our own community and society, but more importantly, all mankind. From Kohlberg's position, we have now achieved the top level of moral development; likewise from the Meadian point of view, we have indeed taken upon ourselves a pan-human perspective.

We know from analyses of the psychotherapy process that personal growth occurs within a context of ego strength rather than weakness.[5] When the ego is sufficiently strong to maintain or achieve mastery, it can permit formerly forbidden and frightening aspects of its unconscious life to enter conscious awareness. The strong ego, not the weak one, is ready to confront the unpleasant realities of our lives. One author has termed this phenomenon "crying at the happy ending."[6] We feel free to cry at the sadness we experience in the film drama, for example, only when the ending is happy: when our ego is made strong enough by our happiness to deal with sadness. In strength, growth is possible. Likewise, only when the horrible accident is over do we feel sufficiently strengthened to tremble with fear. If we had permitted fear to gain a foothold earlier and overwhelm us, we would not have been able to function effectively during the emergency.

Our ego's preparation for its courtship with the transcendent must occur within a context of ego strength, not weakness; of successful ego mastery, not failure. The disconfirming and perspective-broadening encounters which Mannheim, Mead, and Kohlberg outline are helpful in liberating us from the ego's centrality only when they have prepared the ego for the most profound disconfirmation of all. When experiences that cast doubt upon the ego's validity and point out alternative conceptions of reality have been successfully mastered by the ego, we are better prepared to take the step beyond. In other words, an ego that has already successfully mastered potent disconfirmations and alternative perspectives is ready to experience its own transcendent process; its successful testing in battle gives it the kind of confidence that is requisite to letting itself abandon itself to this alien world within.

In the typical case, confrontations that open up the ego to basic doubt threaten its survival; this offers a guarantee of nothing more than a further retrenchment of the ego into its everyday outlook. The ego will not tolerate a fundamental threat to itself unless it has cleaned up its own house, feels relatively in control of things, and has a successful history of managing otherwise distressing intrusions.

Disconfirming experiences introduce doubt; but rather than doubt necessarily weakening our ego's natural perspective and making it prey to a transcendent encounter, *unmastered doubt* reinforces our ego's defensive system. From the perspective of the ego, anything new has a dual impact. On the one hand, new input fascinates the ego's enduring curiosity, stunted perhaps, but never fully lost by the normal processes of socialization. On the other hand, new input threatens the level of stability the ego has achieved, by introducing doubts, pointing out alternatives, differences, disconfirmations, etc., as well as by threatening to take us over and lead us down a different path. Our life histories demonstrate how the ego's conservative role outshines its openness to the new and different. Perceptions are distorted and experiences denied or recast to fit the ego's ongoing level of functioning. Defenses deny entry to profoundly disturbing experiences. Social processes and institutions evolve to reinforce rather than question existing conceptions of reality. Yet new material is not inevitably met with hostility, distortion, and rejection. We do change and grow.

The requirement that ego mastery be achieved before the profound encounter with transcendence is possible is exemplified in the common cycle noted among persons who are facing death: fear, mastery, surrender.[7] The fear of death becomes a dominant motif threatening to overwhelm the final moments of our life. Our ego struggles actively to master and control the fear so that finally we may relax, permit the experience of death to move in upon us, and gently submit ourselves. The ego, having mastered the fear, surrenders itself to a profoundly meaningful encounter that would otherwise have been lost. This surrender to death has been described as a transcendent experience that gives new meaning to life.

In everyday crises, when our ego is threatened by disconfirming encounters, when doubt permeates our being, we experience anxiety and fear. Our ego struggles for mastery, to regain the upper hand. Experiences are shoved aside, denied, distorted, repressed. We engage in a battle for survival. In the midst of the crisis, we hardly hear, we hardly see; we are not yet ready to surrender ourselves to any new experiences.

Afterward, in quiet moments of reflection, when our ego has become more passive, open, and nondefensive, we can submit and experience what was previously denied or shunted aside. In these moments, a profound experience can be ours; after mastery has been accomplished, our ego can yield itself and hear what, before mastery, was beyond its range.

The transcendent experience softly lies in waiting, not to be called upon by a ringing bell or a loud knock in the heat of battle, but by a whispered, passive openness. We go to the monastery to be trained. We knock, knock, knock at the monastery door; we shout, we plead, we cry out in pain and anguish. Sometimes we glimpse shadowy figures moving within. At times we hear voices whispering. We know that someone is there, but the louder we knock, the more pain we show, the less good it seems to do. They simply will not open the door. Finally, in utter exhaustion and despair, we give up; we simply fall down in a heap on the floor. And just at that moment the door is opened. A prepared ego meets the ever-present transcendent when it least expects to. But an unprepared ego will not enter the open door.

Thus far I have been talking about experiences that disconfirm and broaden as though they occur entirely within the realm of thought. But they also occur in the realm of action. When we act in ways surprising even to us, and later come to reflect upon what we have done, we reflect upon a meeting with the transcendent.

Action is a particularly significant vehicle for gaining insight and moving toward a more facile merging of the natural and the transcendent standpoints. Sometimes we experience in spite of ourselves, in spite of our ego's reticence. We say and do things that we must deal with as a conscious ego afterward. We do something that surprises even us; having done it, we must come to grips with it. Outbursts of emotion are often of this sort; we strike out in anger or bubble over with joy, and later in moments of reflection pause to consider the meaning of what we have done. In these and similar cases, our ego is aware that our behavior has come forth independently of its conscious control and is reflected back to us as something we said or did or felt, and thus as something that our ego must deal with in its own terms.

I am thinking of the person who lets go, for whatever reason, and comes to experience in new ways that can bring a flash of insight to his ego's world. In psychodramatic role playing, for example, the person may become so engrossed in his role that his ego's perspective gets shunted aside. In his performance he may stumble upon a world which gives his ego insights that were heretofore denied it, making connections and associations that reveal the clear hand of transcendent processing.

Traditional social psychology has examined this action-oriented path to personal change in its theory of cognitive dissonance and in models of self-attribution.[8] According to dissonance theory, we change ourselves after we have *voluntarily* acted in ways that are dissonant or discordant with what we say we believe to be the true and proper way to act. The emphasis in the theory is upon actions undertaken voluntarily, i.e., things we have done without apparent external demand. Nevertheless, actions we undertake that are rooted neither in external demands nor in ego processes but which appear to flow forth independently of our typical understanding confront the ego's world with a perspective well beyond that which dissonance reveals. The disconfirmations of dissonance pale when compared with those the ego must face when we act outside its typical world of understanding. When the ego has surrendered itself to the transcendent stream, the actions that flow forth can provide rich material for the ego to integrate later within its everyday framework. We learn a great deal about ourselves by submitting to ourselves and later reflecting back upon what we have done and experienced. The ego that so feared its own death, finally to submit itself to its experiential stream, returns enriched and very much alive.

To the extent that our actions are undertaken at the ego's behest, either driven by external requirements or internal voluntary motives (as in dissonance theory formulations), they have a built-in socialized schema of justification; our elusive "I" is all too quickly captured and placed into a ready framework of social understanding; thus such actions do not provide us with an entirely novel experience with which the ego must reflectively deal. I did that because I *had* to: he had a gun at my back; it was a requirement of my role; I would look foolish or be shamed otherwise; and so on. These are not acts that appear to arise spontaneously and surprise even us. When we act *in spite of* ourselves, rather than because of ourselves, we provide the ego with a rich new source of experiential material and reveal the exceptional that lies dormant within each of us. The ego must surrender itself in order to meet those parts of us that are typically unknown and self-surprising, and thereby hold the key to our freedom.[9]

23

Commitment and the Liberating Experience

Liberating experiences facilitate the transition between the two perspectives within us, providing opportunities for the ego to receive guidance from the transcendent; the freedom, individuality, and spontaneity of our lives is thereby increased. The ego's loss is in the service of a larger gain.

But if the liberating encounter is to provide more than a moment of excitement, it must emerge out of a condition of intense personal commitment. Without commitment, there can be neither the kind of disillusionment that brings about the ego's death and eventual rebirth nor can the individual perform the kinds of deeds that express his being in declarative actions.

The person who remains personally uncommitted never has his roots planted firmly enough in anything to experience the disillusionment and distortion that the liberating encounter demands. To appreciate fully the impact of having the rug pulled out from under our system of knowledge and beliefs, we must first have our feet firmly planted on a rug. The ever wandering, fleet-of-foot person is not likely to have paused anywhere long enough to have gotten a firm foot-grip.

During the many years I worked with small sensitivity groups in university settings, I noted a definite change in the kind of student coming in to "become more sensitive." I characterized the students I dealt with before 1965 as "walls"; those who came after were "windows." The walls were solidly defended; an almost impervious barrier was erected to keep out unwanted intrusions. These people were difficult to reach; but at least I always knew where they stood in their solid defensiveness. The windows, by contrast, were always open to whatever the wind happened to blow in. They were so open, in fact, that no one ever knew precisely where they were or who they were: they were everything and thus nothing; they were everywhere and thus nowhere.

The walls were relatively closed and defensive; they had to be opened up in order to grow. The windows, however, were so open that before they could ever hope to grow they had first to become closed: to make a commitment to a given value position, belief, way of life.

The windows' philosophy was laissez faire: "I have my life and my world; you have your life and your world. Let me do what I want to do and I'll let you do what you want to do. You say that you don't understand me; I say that's O.K. You say that you hate me; I say that's O.K. You cannot reach me, touch me, affect me, influence me; I stand for nothing, I've got nothing to defend, nothing I really care about."

With all their defensiveness, the walls' commitment to a way they actively sought to protect left them more vulnerable than the windows to experiencing disillusionment and doubt. The windows' apparent openness to everything meant that nothing could prove disillusioning; they avoided the crises that were vital to growth not by rolling with the punches, but rather by experiencing no punches. By making no judgments, no evaluations, no discriminations, by permitting everything and anything to come through, they avoided taking courageous stands and acting *in spite of* the personal costs. While imagining themselves to be liberated and free, they were even more imprisoned than the still-reachable walls.

* * *

Relating his experiences in Nazi-occupied France, Sartre[1] perceptively noted how in the midst of this objectively oppressive condition he experienced the greatest degree of freedom. Under the conditions of occupation, even a whispered criticism was a bold act of commitment that carried the threat of death. Viktor Frankl's[2] experiences in a Nazi concentration camp led him to conclude that even with this extreme external control, people nevertheless retained the capacity to choose their attitude and thus to be personally free: this personal freedom could never be taken from the person of courage. Colin Wilson[3] argued that our true freedom appears under conditions of crisis or challenge, when things conspire to limit and restrict us. Then, if we are to be free, it must be through a vital and vigorous expression of the intensity of our will. As Paul Tillich[4] might have stated it, under these conditions we act in spite of the external threats and constraints and thus, in courage, we demonstrate our real freedom and ability to transcend the everyday.

We must make a personal commitment before we can suffer the death and eventual rebirth of merging our ego with the transcendent. In actual crisis, which requires us to screw up our courage and stand forth to face whatever might be, we make the kinds of personal commitments that are potentially liberating. Our acts emerge without our ego's consent, carried by an unseen hand that claims us; our ego trails behind, reflecting upon deeds already done in the name of deeply rooted commitments.

The less demanding the external situation, the less is the potential for the personal commitment that is precursor to the liberating experience. The contemporary acceptance of a laissez faire, do-your-own-thing philosophy is insidious: it systematically thwarts our movements to freedom.[5] In the name of illusory personal freedom, true freedom is lost.

Limits and constraints are vital to individual growth and development. In the family, the *loving fight*[6] between parents and children is essential to the child's as well as the parents' growth and emerging personal freedom. The father who is so permissive that he never expresses his own views and values in restricting or limiting the action of his children fails to provide them with the battleground of love within which their own personal autonomy can be developed. Of course, if the father is insecure in his own position, unsure of what is proper and unwilling to alienate anyone's affection, he uses permissiveness as a tactic to avoid the responsibility of engaging in the loving fight.

To be sure, we can never really know that balance point at which limit-setting loving battles benefit rather than stifle growth. We do know, however, that the refusal to provide *authoritative* guidance of the sort that forces the exercising and testing of wills inevitably thwarts and frustrates more than it benefits. I am not outlining a program of fascism which does not consider the growth of the other person as something to be valued in its own right; rather, I am saying what Erikson[7] and others have said, that the kind of concern that caring authority has for the growth and development of the other person will lead the authority to act in ways that facilitate a decisive act of the other's will.

Hannah Arendt[8] termed the most tyrannical of all authority one in which Nobody rules. The consensus committee system that sends responsibility and irresponsibility scurrying around in search of a body may give us a momentary sense of freedom, but it is a disguised tyranny. Whom do we call out in protest? Who sets the limits against which our will is tested and proved? No one; Nobody. No test; no commitment; no liberating experience; no freedom. This is a formula for death and despair, not death and rebirth. Yet this is the pattern that so actively grips our unsure, uncommitted adults and our craving youth. Each misguidedly presses the other and then yields; few make the vital commitments that can eventually become liberating.

The loving battle is a useful metaphor to describe the conditions essential to our personal growth. Out of battle between committed opponents can emerge the insights of the liberating experience. This is a battle *in love* and *for love*, not a clawing caring that drowns and encapsulates or an aggressive display that seeks to destroy. The open-window and the laissez faire nobody-ruling authority care little to make those personal declarations and commitments that can result in *any* battles, let alone those carried on in the name of love.

Opponents in loving battle feed each other's growth; without an opponent, we all too readily fold up with despair and self-pity. The window and nonguiding authority motivate our despair more than our freedom. A self-pitying, despairing ego is not ready to meet the transcendent process; the fighting ego, strong and secure in its commitments, is ripe for new growth.

The seeds of the liberating experience lie in security, strength, and commitment. Without strength and security our ego denies itself contact with those very experiences that lie within our experiential stream. Without commitment, there can be neither disillusionment nor action, and thus neither enlightenment nor growth. Actions taken in loving battle and in the name of personal commitments move us ever closer into contact with that ego-alien transcendent perspective. Strong commitments unite our thought with action, much as in their primary form, and thereby break down the separation that our ego's everyday perspective has so carefully maintained.

In the heat of battle and personal commitment, we reveal our inner spirit shorn of its everyday clothing. Out of our intensity of will and commitment we carry our vague projects into action. Having acted spontaneously and with a unity heretofore concealed, our egos now come to reflect upon what has been done. The reflection is enlightening; it reveals the primary unity of our experiential stream; it opens up new vistas and horizons from which our ego can grow. Actions emerging from commitment reveal an inner truth that slices through our ego's web of defending denials and counter-arguments.

We cannot take back what we have done.[9] We can regret it; we can apologize for it; we can pity ourselves for being so foolish. But what is done is done. Even in regret our ego is fascinated. We did it. It was we. Urgently, we may claim that we were following orders, performing our role, acting too hastily. Claim as we may, the nagging recognition remains: it was *our* action.

If in anger I shout that "I hate you," I may come shortly to apologize, to regret having said it, to claim it was the whiskey, the pressures of the day, etc.; but not too far beyond the horizon of my ego's everyday awareness there lurks the nagging suspicion that *I* said that, *I* uttered it aloud. Therefore hate must lie within me; it is part of me.

This first revelation may be too disturbing for the ego to face; thus we deny it as rapidly as possible, seeking to put it out of mind even as it lurks in the background. The more the liberating transition has been accomplished, the more readily our egos can recognize the fact that indeed hate and love exist within, jointly, indivisible, timeless, perfect and whole. Seeing thusly, our ego need not shy away from the realization of its hate, for it also is aware of the totality within itself, and thus of its love.

It is a puzzling thing, this mind of ours; and no more puzzling than in these present instances. Our gain demands that our ego lose itself and merge with our transcendent stream. The gain in this case involves a better ability in our everyday perspective to tolerate, to own up to, and to appreciate the totality of experiences that is *our* fundamental condition and that of all mankind. The ego is liberated when it permits itself to surrender to the unfolding experiential stream and experience as a friend a world that was once its alien partner.

24

Ego at the Threshold

Although the ego has a central position in the world of the everyday natural standpoint, in the transcendent perspective it moves out to the edge; as Sartre[1] has described it, the ego appears not directly but on the horizon of the spontaneity that marks the transcendent process. The ego's presence is noted, if at all, only vaguely, as though it were a passive spectator to the unfolding spontaneous flow.

Repeated encounters between the ego and the transcendent serve as an important source of new material with which to reconstitute the ego's own perspective. The newly liberated ego can become adept at moving itself off to the edge and permitting the experiential stream to flow forth unimpeded, unmonitored, unreflected, unbounded. In this sense the ego may be said to be open, passively receptive, simply letting itself be,[2] going along with the unfolding stream.

We walk a delicate balance between two extremes, both of which represent loss of real liberation-in-the-world. At the one extreme, the ego steadfastly defends itself from intrusions that would cast its stance in doubt, weaken its integrity, or challenge it too much; at the other, the ego's natural perspective, hard won and difficult to maintain even in the everyday world, is lost entirely and forever to the transcendent.

The first extreme overadapts us to the existing structures of reality, creates a rigid, machinelike interpersonal world, and takes away any vestiges of personal freedom; we become reasonably well functioning, reasonably efficient machines, cogs in a social network performing our duties out of habit. The second, the irrevocable submission of the ego to the transcendent stream, places the individual in a state that is entirely and uniquely his own, *never* differentiating between dreams and everyday reality, between history and potentiality, between himself and others. Anyone dwelling in this extreme could never be free. The cooperative ventures necessary for communal survival would be lost. Ours is a social world of obligations and reciprocities; we could never understand it or cope with it if we lived without an ego. The person who sees too deeply and too much can make no contribution to real freedom or spontaneity unless he is able to function effectively within the social context.

Balance is required—the ability to let the ego move downstream, to fade into the distant horizon, to lose its centrality and control, to give in, submit, enjoy and pleasure itself in the floodtide of becoming and then return to its central point enriched by its adventure; strengthened in its weakness, in its recognition of the limitations imposed by living entirely within the world of the natural standpoint. Balance is achieved when the natural standpoint and the transcendent meet in an atmosphere that permits the transcendent to provide more than lip-service guidance to our everyday lives; with such balance we can extend ourselves beyond the everyday and experience a world always available, always there, but rarely counted among our enduring riches. Balance is achieved when the ego moves off to the side, enjoying living life, not merely thinking about it.

If we know ourselves, we are not free; freedom is based on being unpredictable to our ego, surprising even ourselves by our spontaneous actions. While we cannot program ourselves to be spontaneous, courageous, and free, we can admire our courage when we show it; we can take pleasure in engaging in spontaneous activities we could not have predicted for ourselves.

Know thyself, the usual advice given to those who would be free, derives from the belief that without self-knowledge and self-consciousness we could not control the unconscious forces that shape our lives. Yet I have just said that in real freedom our ego is surprised by our actions; real freedom is being unknown even to the self. Self-consciousness interferes with the free, spontaneous flow of living. This does not mean that self-knowledge is not part of the process of liberation; it means that the process must go well beyond self-knowledge before real freedom can occur.

Every therapist and patient is aware of this dilemma. In successful therapy, the patient comes to know himself; that is, he or she comes to understand some of the bases for his neurotic symptoms. Yet *knowing* has not changed behavior; life continues much the same, but now perhaps with a bit more sense of impotence or despair.

Knowing, while the first step beyond ordinary ignorance, is really just that—a first step. The second step involves the integration of that knowledge with our total being; this requires the knowledge to become a part of our intuitive, instinctive repertoire of living: a part of the transcendent stream, flowing out naturally, spontaneously, and without self-consciousness.³

Self-knowledge is but the first step in the process of freeing ourselves from the predictability of our everyday routine. Knowledge is essential to transcending the everyday, but the process is not complete until the ego has removed itself from its central position and the transcendent stream becomes our guide. In that moment we surprise ourselves (i.e., our ego), never really knowing just how our knowledge will appear when it flows forth. In that moment, we are at the same point in our relationship to ourselves as other people are: we and they are witness to the emergence of our own transcendent stream. Its emergence may bring anger or joy; whatever it brings, old patterns will have been broken and disrupted and new patterns will emerge that have a validity, coherence, and unity that can exist only by trusting ourselves to be ourselves.

We can never really know life; we can know about it or we can live it. Knowledge can enrich living but never substitute for it. Those who live life can have more knowledge than those who only read and think about it. We may try to put living experience into words, but words pale before experience itself. This is not an anti-intellectual stance—far from it, especially during these days in which it is so fashionable to reject reason. Living life is not an anti-intellectual, undisciplined activity; it is an activity that takes pleasure in doing and doing well, living freely, not tied to worry or shame or doubt.[4]

It is truth we seek, shorn of all its illusions, its distortions, its apparent glamour. Real truth: pure, beautiful, or ugly, but truth. Driven by our curiosity, our ego's openness, tamed and channeled but never fully destroyed, we may even strike truth one day and back off hurriedly lest we be overwhelmed by our discovery. The mystery carries us along as much as the mastery.

Actually, it is anti-intellectual to deny realities that do not conform readily to one framework for understanding them. The totality of truth will never reveal itself to the person who retires from life to reflect and thereby moves away from living. Nor will it be revealed to the person who never pauses to reflect upon and learn from the spontaneity of living. Only those who live *both* spontaneously and reflectively can discover a real range of truths.

Reflection provides only a partial picture of our total life, since reflection is always limited by the framework within which the ego exists. In everyday affairs, it may be useful to pause for a moment to reflect on what has just happened; such activity may help us gain insights and even extend ourselves beyond the limits by which we typically think out our lives. But the truth that transcends the everyday occurs first and primarily through the loss of that reflective ego, by placing it off to the side, at the threshold where experience flows forth, unabated and unfettered.

The spontaneity of life-as-lived can be captured only by living-becoming; in reflection, however brilliant and insightful, something vital is lost. The moment-just-passed is not the same as the moment-in-creation; this latter moment, so free and unfolding, we can only become aware of by experiencing its occurrence.

Intellectual acts are thus limited in their ability to take us fully into our own lives or those of others. The depths of a living life can never be fully plumbed by a reflective act of the ego.[5] But we cannot fully understand ourselves or others without a reflective act of the ego. Either ego or transcendent perspectives taken alone provide only a partial view of our fundamental nature and lives.

Many social scientists balk at this manner of thinking, for it removes from scientific analysis a vital aspect of each of us. But those who, in the name of existing science, deny a basic quality of humanity, fail in their mission as truth seekers. Denying a vital but difficult aspect of reality in order to explain what is left, albeit a rather large and important remainder, surely is not the way to conduct scientific business.

I have suggested that the liberating experience is indeed just that: an experience. There are preliminary periods during which the movement of our ego away from its central locus and off toward the threshold becomes more than a tentative gesture. The movement into transcendence, coming in a tranquil moment or in a sudden flash, and perhaps disappearing just as suddenly, stands at the end of a phase, the beginnings of which were in evidence before the move itself was made. The doubt cast upon our ego from disconfirming encounters, its open curiosity about the world, and the momentary movements and yieldings to the transcendent flow precede the key moment of liberating insight. What occurs all of a sudden or in a quiet moment has a history and a career.

The insight, having occurred, can motivate still further ventures into this new realm. The vitality and impact of the insight at the moment of liberation may both enlighten and frighten. If it enlightens, it serves to motivate even further movements of our ego to the threshold; if it frightens, it may more severely harden the ego's need to fight for its integrity. The cutting edge is thin; we topple this way and that, over and over, before the insight serves its major function of pushing the transition farther along than before.

Because transcendence is a process, not a state or stage, the transition between the ego's natural perspective and the perspective of transcendence does not happen all at once—it is not as if it were a door that is passed through once and for all into a new room. The notion of an ego that is forever enlightened because it joined with the transcendent flow in a moment of insight is a faulty notion indeed. The process of living is just that: a process, ever moving, ever flowing, ever in transition. Our ego, now enlightened, is ever reaching out toward transcendence while remaining master within its own realm, fending off forces that threaten its centrality and dominance. It is not so much a matter of our ego's passing through a door as it is a matter of our ego's continually coming to the threshold and passing through, going back, coming to the threshold again, and passing through, going back, coming to the threshold and . . .

No state of nirvana or enlightenment will last forever. We live our lives in an everyday world, one that will always require our ego to be carefully attuned to its realities and principles. Our ego's placement within that world is vital. The transition into transcendence is an excursion to a threshold and beyond, into a region and then back again; and so on endlessly through life.

The cost, of course, can be extremely high; each voyage and each return changes our ego in often imperceptible ways in its natural perspective. On its return, it is torn between the pleasures and freedoms uncovered and the demands of everyday reality as socially constituted. It will continually compromise between what is and what might be; its choices and opportunities will have been increased, but compromise it will and compromise it must. Seeing through the maya may help us live more peacefully; it may also frustrate and disturb. Knowing what might be and then having to settle for what will be cannot be all milk and honey.

The process involves a continual movement back and forth, never fully attaining rootedness in either realm, yet never ceasing to take the trip. There is no final breath of joy taken with that shouted "I've made it!" Nothing could be more unrealistic. Life is a process, rooted in two worlds, one created and one in creation.

We must always transcend whatever exists routinely to be transcended; this never ends until our death. The unbroken becoming of the transcendent perspective is always emerging and always becoming; it is always just beyond whatever we happen to be. It is not a place to get to and rest, but a continuously flowing process in which we participate and live.

The pink-pill set finds such a viewpoint annoying; its members want the little pill that will push them beyond into the never-never world of total joy and pleasure, full-scale nirvana, once and forever. To be sure, they do find their little pills, in a variety of forms, that push them through new doors and open new horizons of experience and knowledge. But too often they fail to realize that beyond the door just passed there lies still another door and beyond that still another, and so on infinitely. And these are not doors that lead deeper into layers upon layers of consciousness; these are doors which metaphorically characterize the continuous unfolding quality of transcendence. It is forever out there, beyond; even as we reach it, it is beyond again, and just beyond again. It is the creation of life which is forever unfolding and forever being created. The job is never done, never over; the perspectives are forever expanding, forever opening up, forever creating.

In general, transcendence is described as something to be sought, something that some few persons have achieved and toward which others ought to be striving. This view implies that the world may be divided roughly into two types of persons: the damned and the saved, the enlightened and the mundane, the good and the evil. A second implication is that transcendence is a state of being, a threshold beyond which we step into a new world, a nirvana.

I take exception to both these prevalent notions, which not coincidentally lead to a condition in human affairs that works directly opposite to the apparent desire of all, including those "most transcendent." For if I am saved and you are damned, I must pity you or fight to contain you or convert you; and if you are damned and must confront someone with such moral superiority as myself, then surely for your own sanity and preservation, you must lock me up, or in some other way rid the world of so dangerous a soul as saved, transcendent me.

Many youthful transcendence seekers have no use at all for those who are not precisely the same as they, labeling those who differ from them *blind machines*. But this view overlooks the machine in the existential and the existential in the machine. The labelers, perhaps out for their own gain or cadre of servile followers, fail to appreciate how each and every one of them enacts his everyday life in ways no different from everyman. They fail to see in others the occurrence of what Maslow[6] has termed the peak experience and others the "creative flash"—in other words, the perspective of transcendence. We all are able to transcend the everyday and do, every day in any number of ways.

When as a young man I read about my favorite poets, painters, and musicians, I sought in their lives a sign of madness and insanity, of the sort that would validate an unusual life style. Alas, for every creative madman, I found a creative sane man—one who dwelt more fully in the everyday. Even those most mad, most above and beyond it all, returned to earth again each day with a thud. One's heroes should be more like gods than men; but they are as much men as you and I, rooting their lives in the petty squabbles, jealousies, and routines of everyday life. But they ascend well beyond and touch the heights. It was I, not they, who sought transcendent and heroic purity in their every deed. They seemed satisfied to live their lives in my world as well, while stretching to touch the stars beyond.

25

The Fundamental Duality of the Human Condition

We are dualistic in our fundamental nature, possessing within us two perspectives. We are indeed, as Martin Buber[1] noted, both an *I* and a *Thou*; we are Hesse's[2] man and wolf. We are person and machine, free and prisoner, determined and indeterminate, created and creating, being and becoming. We cannot be otherwise. Though one perspective may dominate, the other is there also, in the shadows. The lucid man has his mad moments; the madman, his lucid ones.

Our ego is a construction, a social product, partly conscious, partly unconscious. Our ego's world encompasses the Freudian trilogy of an impulse-laden id, a conscience-laden superego, and a reality-focused ego.[3] Our transcendent perspective is a becoming, an emergent, not a product; it is neither conscious nor unconscious but rather the soil out of which consciousness and unconsciousness are formed. Our ego is influenced by experiences in the world of everyday living; our transcendent process *is* the unfolding immediate experience of our everyday living. Our ego learns and is shaped by social factors; our transcendent is simply the process of our becoming, neither learning from experience nor being shaped by experience. It is the process of experience flowing forth.

We can grasp our ego's conscious and unconscious aspects; to the extent that we do, prediction and control are possible.

Psychoanalytic therapy, for example, seeks to help the ego attain conscious mastery over its heretofore unconscious life. But we can never grasp the transcendent process; prediction and control are out of the question. Our ego's efforts to monitor, guide, and master this realm are the very conditions that thwart its free emergence. We can only hope to understand the transcendent perspective in reflection *after* the fact of its emergence, never before.

The ego is man's greatest creation, giving him control over himself and others. Our ability to reflect upon our own actions and those of others is an achievement that has made civilization possible. But the ego is also the prison guard, the destroyer. Although rationality is located within the ego, so is irrationality. Transcendence houses neither. This is perhaps the most crucial point.

Normally, we think of ego loss—the process of letting go—as leading to frightful surges of forbidden, disastrous impulses that would more readily destroy than build, and so our ego's romance with the transcendent is usually experienced in terms of fright, loss, and anxiety, as a leap into the darkness of an abyss. But though the abyss is indeed there, it is not the creation of the transcendent process. For it is the ego's world, this masterful social construction, that is the source of what we term good or evil. Our basic human nature will not lead us astray; if we have been led astray, it is because of social learnings that are rooted in our ego's perspective.

Those impulses that civilization seeks to control, the sexual and aggressive surges of which Freud speaks, are not biologically rooted givens basic to all mankind. Popular analyses see man as an animal with aggression and violence inherent in his nature;[4] aggression, however, is a socially learned product of the ego's world, derived from the confrontation between our biology and our sociology.

In a recent comment, a world-renowned brain researcher noted that "man's aggression against man stems not from his primitive irrational instincts, but from that same rationality which has distinguished him in all his enterprises . . . the normal brain is beautiful, there is no demoniacal animal lying within."[5] The ego, responsible for our great rational achievements, is also responsible for our great destructive and seemingly irrational behavior.

The great sociologist Max Weber[6] made much the same point in his analysis of the social processes of *rationalization*. Bureaucracies are human constructions that seek to organize men rationally to achieve valued ends. The processes of rationalization within such organizations require that we relate to each other as impersonal roles functioning by impartial rules rather than by traditional, communal, and personally idiosyncratic methods. This great achievement, however, is a dual-edged sword; at the same time it creates an elegant organizational solution to a problem of human survival, it puts people in an inhumane, depersonalized, mind-rotting context. The rational processes that free also entrap and destroy.

The ego, our civilizer and our destroyer, is a social product, a derivative of the requirements of our living. If there is an evil monster within each of us, it is a beast of our own learning. This does not make it less horrible, but rather places the burden more squarely where it belongs, on our social arrangements, not our fundamental nature. Our fundamental nature interacts with social factors to create the sexual and aggressive id-like being within our ego's unconscious. If there is anything inevitable about the matter, it is that in our growth we will develop an impulse-laden unconscious process within our ego. Things that are inevitable are often erroneously attributed to a biological root rather than to a social one; the latter, in fact, offers us as many inevitabilities as the former.

If the impulse-laden world of our aggression and violence is a fundamental given, never to be changed but only to be carefully guarded and controlled by a watchful ego or a coercive society, then we are stuck, unable to better our lot. If our violent and disruptive qualities are not fundamental to the human species, however, but are part of our social learning histories, we may have hope of transforming those learnings and thereby of creating more altruism and good than aggression, war, and evil.[7]

However, there is an inevitability within the human equation. The confrontation between person and society, between biology and sociology, creates an inevitable array of interpersonal emergents, including the good and the evil with which all civilizations and all social systems must deal. While changed arrangements of social living may diminish the impact of these emergents, they can never be fully eliminated—not because that is the way we are fundamentally, but because that is the way we meet society fundamentally. Out of this meeting our ego is born, soon to contain within it, primarily in its unconscious aspect, the kinds of impulse-laden processes whose release into the light of day we so fear.

To modify the conditions of our social learning in order to reinforce the good rather than the evil outcomes of this meeting between person and society can be helpful, but can never fully eliminate the impulse-laden residues that remain our ego's unconscious heritage. Regardless of whatever else is done, the typical child *will* be toilet trained; this training brings out a conflict between biological and social arrangements. The outcome of this confrontation is the development of an ego that is toilet trained. But the residue left behind, as Freud and others have noted, can involve a sense of aggression, anger, inferiority, loss of autonomy, and so forth. This is inevitable, though clearly something that can be ameliorated by using positive reinforcements rather than punitive ones.

In the view I've taken, our ego, a social product, is the hero *and* the villain; it contains as interpersonal outcomes the processes that have been described as good and evil. From my perspective, all these processes are learned social products that have originated out of interactions between biological pressures and social arrangements. What has emerged is a part of our ego in its natural standpoint. It is this ego, in its conscious and unconscious aspects, that is overlaid on top of the transcendent process, imprisoning us while rewarding us for accepting our prison.

Given this view, our fundamental freedom does not derive from making conscious the unconscious parts of our ego in order to enable the ego to gain mastery. While this is a vital accomplishment, it is nevertheless only a partial freedom. It is true that as long as a major portion of our ego's everyday life is governed by forces of which it is not aware—whether the internally based unconscious factors that psychoanalytic theory concentrates on or the socially based unconscious factors that Marxian theory seeks to illuminate—our freedom is vastly restricted. Thus all approaches that endeavor to bring these unconscious factors under conscious ego control permit our ego to expand its everyday freedom.

But the limits of our freedom are not to be approached until those moments in which our actions are under the guidance of the unfolding spontaneous flow of our transcendent stream. As long as we remain influenced by those parts of us that have been culturally determined, we remain within the natural perspective, known and predictable. It is only when we become fully the author of our destiny by letting be that part of ourselves that simply is always becoming that we reach beyond, transcend the limits of the everyday, and move into the realm of absolute freedom. In those moments and in those domains, we may indeed be said to have a discontinuity in our existence; where the past no longer speaks adequately for the future; where conceptual rules that applied no longer hold; where we emerge and reveal our fundamental humanity.

Most psychology, sociology, and other social scientific disciplines deal with the conscious and unconscious aspects of the constituted ego's experience; they limit themselves, often unwittingly, to the world of everyday reality. Some persons may appear to reach toward the transcendent; what they touch is only the ego's unconscious. Because it is a social product, the ego's unconscious world can never fully open the door to the options and alternatives of the transcendent process. Our horizons may indeed expand, but the horizon still beyond remains beyond; true freedom escapes us just at the moment when its presence has become a more real possibility.

In the sense I've been using it, freedom does not mean consciously seeing alternatives and then choosing among them.

The freedom of transcendence does not derive from facing and choosing among fully conscious choice-options, but rather from choosing through becoming.

As long as freedom entails an ego that faces paths on which to wander, freedom is bounded by already given categories of experience. When, however, our ego lets go, we do not stand back in a linear mode choosing this route rather than that; the routes and the paths we take determine themselves entirely. Freedom in this sense is not the freedom to choose out of knowledge of options. Freedom, here, is not caused by but causes; it is not *determined by*, but *determines*. Choices emerge from our active living; they are not chosen by an ego.

It should now be clear that in my discussion of ego loss I was using the term in a way that differs from its common usage in psychological theory, which describes it as involving unconscious aspects of the ego flooding its conscious aspects, removing the ego from its touch with reality, engulfing it in fears, repressed memories, forbidden wishes, and such. In my usage, the term involves permitting the ego, which is always in charge of its own conscious and unconscious aspects, to lose itself to the emerging stream of experience. A strong ego, one that occupies a central controlling and synthesizing function, is necessary to prevent unconscious rule; it is likewise necessary before the ego can be abandoned to voyage toward the transcendent threshold and beyond. A vital precursor to the transition into the transcendent process is an ego that has adequately dealt with its own unconscious. An ego that has not dealt with its own unconscious life is not likely to yield itself readily or completely to the transcendent process; the weak ego senses the difficulty it would face were it to venture forth and never return. It takes a strong ego (i.e., control over its own house) to have a weak ego (i.e., letting be), which permits a new, emerging, reconstituted ego.

The fear that we and others have of letting go or letting be, of yielding our ego, is a fear rooted in the traditional rather than the revised sense of the concept of ego loss. If letting go means permitting the unconscious, impulse-laden spheres of the ego's world to run about unchecked and unmonitored, it is correct for us and for civilization to fear and distrust such a process. However, if letting go refers to a process in which an ego in disciplined command of its inner world ventures off to the side, there is little to fear and little to distrust. In the wildly faddish moments of contemporary life, when the undisciplined and amateurish play about with losing their egos, there is more to fear than to trust. Few have learned enough about themselves to venture beyond their ego's world with more benefit than harm.

As our ego comes to terms with its own unconscious, in particular with those repressed residues of our personal biography that continue to make claims on our present life, it gains in strength; we become more free in that we become consciously aware of the formerly unconscious factors that *automatically* determined our lives. We can be as imprisoned by unconscious impulses as by socially routinized forces. The person who is driven onward blindly (i.e., unconsciously) out of fear, hate, envy, and such is trapped no less than the person who is consciously fearful or blind to the social routines that govern his daily life. Both require an inner enlightenment before their egos can move toward transcendence. Since our individual biographies are always social biographies as well,[8] both psycho- and socioanalyses are necessary to make these unconscious forces conscious. Freud and Marx are joined in this venture. The outcome of these analyses involves a growth in self-consciousness: an ego better able consciously to deal with unconscious forces.[9]

This is the *first* step; however fundamental and important it may be, it is just a first step, not one to stop with, though indeed few even reach this point of awareness, let alone seek to adventure beyond. An ego that has not yet come to terms with itself is not ready to move toward the threshold of the transcendent process. Chance intrusions of this alien perspective will be experienced, if at all, as too foreign and as too overwhelming for us to wish to move therein again. The temporal and spatial qualities of our ego's unconscious world are sufficiently similar to those of the transcendent experience to permit an ego that has mastered the former to face the latter without shrinking in fear.

The transition toward transcendence demands an ego that has become disciplined, that has mastery over its unconscious aspects. Intrusions of transcendence will of course occur without such discipline and self-consciousness; as we have seen, this transcendent part of ourselves remains forever present and forever available to be yielded to, if even inadvertently. However, the transition in which our ego is significantly reconstituted as a function of its continual and repeated meetings with the transcendent process demands more than these causual intrusions. It requires discipline and control to change our ego's everyday reality, to permit transcendence to become more the norm than the exception.

An ego that is transcendentally reconstituted is one that is qualitatively different in its natural perspective than it was before its movement toward and across the threshold. It is also an ego that is open to continual reconstitution. In this view, our ego is always at the threshold, always moving beyond; attaining, yet never having attained, realizing, yet never having realized, reconstituting, yet never having reconstituted.

The new world in which this reconstituting ego lives is one which is continually opening up, continually expanding; horizons out there are just beyond; places to move toward are just out of reach. It is a world in which our ego's presence is but a whisper, never a shout; a world in which everything is now and forever; all is mystery and unfathomable, but neither frightening nor destructive. Within this world there are no creators and creations, no destroyers and destroyed: creator is creation; destroyer is destroyed.

The world in which the reconstituting ego dwells is a world of unity; there is no ego apart from living; no person separate from world; no me separate from you; no actor separate from action. The distinctions made in our everyday world are not made so readily in this world of the reconstituting ego. This is a world of freedom. It is a world that forever remains beyond the realm of deterministic prediction and control. This world beyond social determinism nevertheless contributes to the constitution of the determined social world.

The ego is a construction of a social world, of the interaction of persons and institutions. If egos stand at the threshold and move across into the world of transcendence, their reconstitution on their return to the everyday world provides new components for the constitution of that everyday social world. This psychological transformation opens the door to a new everyday world. Persons whose reconstituting egos permit them to relate differently to others form a fundamentally new constituent element of the everyday world. Thus, over time, egos that are socialized within this new setting will reflect those very differences that owe their origins to the movements toward transcendence.

A reconstituting ego influences others' constituting egos. We enter each other's worlds as conditions of our mutual growth and development. The presence of persons whose reconstituting egos reveal alternative perspectives therefore produces a new setting within which the everyday world is played out. Yet, we are talking about processes that are always in flux, always emerging; we cannot take the overly simplistic view that this will create a utopian world.

In the first place, the reconstituting process for any one person is a continuing dialectic, never ending until his death. Secondly, the requirements of organized social life always demand the existence of a constructed ego. Even if the components of its construction change over time, as they inevitably do, it is nevertheless a fundamentally socialized ego that sets the limits for its own freedom in its very construction. Utopia is not a place or a form of social organization that is achieved or achievable; rather, it is the name for a continually emerging process, one that began with the presence of man and will continue until he is no longer around. This is true whether we speak about nirvana for a given individual or utopia for a given society.

The point, necessary to repeat, is that the process of transcendence is always moving beyond, reaching ahead of wherever life has been constituted; it is a restless, never settled becoming. Freedom, nirvana, or utopia lie in the process of their becoming, not in their attainment. Attainment spells the cessation of living; there can be no ego reconstituting unless there is forever transcendence. Crossing the threshold is not over once one has crossed. That is only the beginning of a story without ending. Individual biographies end; the process continues.

We each have touched the transcendent yet find few rewards for pursuing the matter further. After all, our everyday lives are busy; we are not rewarded for exploring much beyond the places we now occupy. Conditions of socialization and social organization press us to maintain the integrity of an ego cut off both from itself (i.e., its unconscious life) and from the transcendent realm within. But there are those moments, those exceptional instances, in which we extend ourselves and see what lies just beyond the next turn by taking that turn. The courage to be what we can be, however, is not so readily available nor so readily reinforced; so we sink back into the everyday world and busy ourselves with our maintenance within it. None of this is puzzling; if anything, it is puzzling, but beyond our present scope, to ascertain why some persons push onward anyway, in spite of it all.

Notes

Titles of works by, and publishing information for, the authors cited in these Notes can be found in the References section.

INTRODUCTION

1. Mumford, 1972.
2. Ibid., p. 96.
3. Ibid.

CHAPTER 1. The Nature of Persons: An Image for Man

1. These represent a sampling of classic views of man's fundamental nature, ranging from the writing of Sophocles, Protagoras, and Mohammed to those of Mark Twain.
2. Recent authors have stressed the distinction between the images of man associated with the behaviorist view and the more cognitive, constructivist view: e.g., Hitt, 1969; Lumpkin, 1970. The position I develop argues that these distinctions are only the surface of an otherwise fundamentally similar base.
3. E.g., Hull, 1943; Pavlov, 1960; Skinner, 1948, 1953, 1971; Watson, 1925.
4. Skinner, 1948, 1953, 1971.

5. Watson, 1925.
6. Much this same argument is heard with respect to the use of mind-altering drugs. One side maintains that our minds are our personal possession; if we wish to alter them, that is our business—as long as it does no harm to others. The other side argues that society has a vital interest in the nature of our minds; as such, even as private a thing as "mind" must come under societal scrutiny and perhaps even control.
7. McConnell, 1970.
8. Wooldridge, 1968.
9. See, for example, such constructivist and interactionist perspectives as those of Heider, 1958, 1959; Kelly, 1955, 1963; Lewin, 1935, 1948, 1951; Piaget, 1932, 1952, 1954; Thomas, 1951; Weber, 1930, 1946, 1947; plus the general approach in social science known as cognitive theory: e.g., Scheerer, 1954.
10. E.g., Wheelis, 1969.
11. Jessor (1956) provides a good statement of the detailed theoretical differences and similarities between the S-R behaviorist view and the R-R constructivist view.
12. Skinner, 1971.
13. See Cassirer, 1946, 1957, 1970; Duncan, 1968; Mead, 1934.
14. Cassirer, 1946, 1957, 1970; Church, 1961; Whorf, 1956.
15. Carmichael, Hogan, and Walter, 1932.
16. Brown (1958) and Ervin-Tripp (1969) offer good summaries of the approaches of psycholinguistics and sociolinguistics.
17. Fishman, 1960; Sapir, 1956; Whorf, 1956. Also see Cassirer, 1946, 1957, 1970.
18. Jung, 1939, 1949.
19. See, e.g., Berger and Luckman, 1966, on this point.
20. Ibid.
21. E.g., Becker, 1963; Lemert, 1967; Scheff, 1966; Schur, 1971.
22. Becker, 1963.
23. Szasz, 1960, 1961.
24. E.g., Greenspoon (1955) and Verplanck (1955) provide experimental evidence on this matter of conditioning without awareness.
25. Laing (1967) makes much this same point in arguing that people can be controlled by leading them to experience things in the same way.
26. Carmichael and Hamilton, 1967.
27. See Morris and Jeffries, 1967.

28. See Asch, 1952.
29. This is a fundamental argument of Gestalt psychology. See, e.g., Asch, 1952.

CHAPTER 2. The Person as a Machine

1. See especially Garfinkel, 1967, and Schutz, 1967, 1970, 1971, on this matter of the common-sense world of our everyday life.
2. See Biddle and Thomas, 1966, and Sarbin and Allen, 1968, for an analysis of role theory.
3. Garfinkel, 1967.
4. Schachter, 1951.
5. Sampson and Brandon, 1964.
6. Milgram, 1963.
7. Ibid., p. 377.
8. Berger and Luckman, 1966; Gouldner, 1960; Parsons, 1951; Parsons and Shils, 1951; Parsons, Bales, and Shils, 1953.
9. Bruner, 1961; Freud, 1924–50.
10. Garfinkel, 1967.
11. See Tillich, 1952; also see Laing, 1965, 1967, for a discussion on what we give up in order to maintain order and keep chaos at bay.

CHAPTER 3. Image, Paradigm, and Policy

1. Kuhn, 1962.
2. Eddington, 1928.
3. See especially Argyris, 1969; Kelley, 1971.
4. Rosenthal, 1968; see also Merton's discussion, 1957.
5. The history of industrial social psychology provides insights into two contrasting theories of worker motivation and therefore of proper managerial behavior. The classic, machine view, is to be contrasted with the more modern human relations

perspective. See, for example, Bennis, 1959; McGregor, 1960; and Sampson, 1971, (chap. 19).

6. Berger and Luckman, 1966; Szasz, 1960, 1961.
7. Breer and Locke, 1965.
8. See for example, Memmi (1967) and Sampson (1971, chap. 17) for a discussion and analysis of the master-slave ideology and the reality it conspires to create and maintain.
9. Cassirer, 1970, p. 66. Recently, Carl Rogers (1973) has strongly implored social scientists to accept the challenge of systematically investigating "other realities," in recognition of the possibility, if not the fact, "that there may indeed be a number of 'realities' " (p. 385).
10. Argyris, 1969, and Kelley, 1971, have more to say on this same matter.

CHAPTER 4. The Perspective of the Natural Standpoint of Everyday Life: *An Overview*

1. Eliot, 1930.
2. Auden, 1940.
3. Brecht, 1947.
4. Marquis, 1958.
5. Wilson, 1956.
6. Schutz, 1967, 1970, 1971a, 1971b.
7. Husserl, 1931, 1943, 1964.
8. Schutz, 1971a, p. 229.
9. Garfinkel, 1967.
10. Watts, 1961.
11. Heidegger, 1962.
12. Laing's (1967) analysis of ontological security is based on much this same notion of the illusions of the maya.
13. Berger and Luckman, 1966.
14. Ibid., pp. 101–2.
15. Schachter, 1951.
16. Riesman, 1950. Efforts to understand and further validate Riesman's typology have been conducted by researchers such as Centers, 1962; de Charms and Moeller, 1962; Kassarjian, 1962.
17. Garfinkel, 1967.

18. Argyris, 1969.
19. E.g., Egan, 1970; Perls, Hefferline, and Goodman, 1965; Rogers, 1967, 1969.
20. Sampson, Fisher, Angel, Mulman, and Sullins, 1969.

CHAPTER 5. The Stranger Within: The Interpersonal World of Everyday Life: *Dimension I*

1. Laing, 1965.
2. Saint-Exupéry, 1943.
3. Freud, 1954, especially chap. 7, provides an insightful analysis of the two worlds of our existence: the primary process of our dreams vs. the secondary process of our everyday waking reality.
4. Sampson, Fisher, Angel, Mulman, and Sullins, 1969.
5. The name is fictitious and all quotes are paraphrased from the actual interview data.

CHAPTER 6: On Risk-Taking and Security: *Dimension II*

1. See, e.g., Schutz's notion of the *epoché* of the natural standpoint referred to in Chapter 4 and in note 8 of that chapter.
2. Camus, 1958.
3. Rahe, McKean, and Arthur (1967) provide some valuable data on the illness consequences of life changes. I think it reasonable to conclude that any major life change introduces sufficient insecurity to lead most of us to try to avoid needless change.
4. Berger and Luckman (1966) discuss the potential conflict existing between generations who are just now learning the social constructions of their elders; Sampson (1971, chap. 23) provides further analysis of generational conflict and youth protest. Discussions of "the stranger" by Schutz (1971b) and of the "sojourner" by Brein and David (1971) raise a similar matter in examining this person who stands at the boundary

between the everyday world of one group and his own still-uninitiated perspective.

5. Harvey, Hunt, and Schroder (1961) offer a perspective on rebellion or negativism as being parallel to conformity; Bennis and Shepard's 1956 analysis of dependency and counter-dependency in small-group interaction offers yet another parallel view on rebellion as conformity. Merton (1957) suggests yet another relationship between conformity and rebellion, arguing that resistance in one context usually involves conformity in another context.

6. Numerous analysts writing from different perspectives in different contexts have focused on our human demand for minimal surprise to our everyday living. White (1959) discusses our need to develop competence and mastery in our world. From the perspective of anthropology, Wallace (1961) suggests the importance of our forming complex and orderly cultural "mazeways" to maximize the meaningfulness of our experience; theories of cognitive consistency within social psychology make much this same point: e.g., Festinger, 1957; Heider, 1958; Newcomb, 1953, 1959; and many, many others.

CHAPTER 7. On Secrecy and Vulnerability: *Dimension III*

1. Rubin (1973, especially chap. 8) offers a valuable summary of some of the empirical work done on power and self-disclosure. Jourard's (1964, 1968) work is also important to consider in this context.
2. Bakan, 1965.
3. Simmel, 1950.
4. Bakan, 1965.

CHAPTER 8. Our Other-Directed Character: *Dimension IV*

1. Riesman, 1950.
2. E.g., Festinger, 1954a, 1954b.
3. Sherif (1935) used the autokinetic effect to demonstrate the

convergence of a group toward a common norm or frame of reference for judging ambiguous events.

4. Asch, 1952.

5. This is one of the basic concepts in the several theories of cognitive balance, symmetry, consistency, and consonance: e.g., Festinger, 1957; Heider, 1958; Newcomb, 1953, 1959. See Sampson, 1971, chaps. 7, 8, and 9 for a further discussion and analysis of these theories.

6. See note 5 references, but especially Sampson, 1971, for a summary of some of the validating research.

7. See Laing's (1967) notion of excommunication of the deviant. Also recall from Chapter 4 in this volume Schachter's study in which the deviating group member was cast out as the group redefined its membership boundaries so as to exlude him. And in that same chapter, the Sampson and Brandon study in which the deviating accomplice was actively ignored as though she did not exist.

8. Stouffer (1955) studied issues of civil liberties during the McCarthy era, providing one of many examples of our general intolerance of persons who deviate from community or personal norms.

CHAPTER 9. Other-Directedness: Trust and Intimacy

1. See especially Carl Rogers' notion of positive self-regard (1951), Heidegger's view (1962) of authenticity, and Jung's notion of persona (1939, 1949).

2. Goffman, 1959.

3. Schachter and Singer (1962) present an interesting finding regarding the importance of social comparison in the label we attach to our own emotional experience. Whether we experience joy and anger, for example, is a complex function of both internal physiological arousal and the presence of information from others regarding the likely referent for these stirrings within. Thus an angry person in our midst, given our own arousal, provides cues that lead us to experience that arousal as "I am angry"; on the other hand, a joyful person leads us to conclude that we too must be joyful. It seems then

that even the emotional experience we have is influenced by social-comparative cues.

4. Berger and Luckman, 1966; Laing, 1967.

5. Goffman, 1959.

6. Goffman, 1963, 1972.

7. Lewin, 1948.

8. Perhaps one of the most blatant packaged cures is presented in a recorded program for couples, entitled *Intimacy* and designed to instruct couples to accomplish this highly desired goal within their relationship.

9. May, 1969.

10. Buber, 1958.

11. Bernard, Ottenberg, and Redl, 1968.

12. See Lifton, 1967, on this point in his study of the Hiroshima survivors.

13. Adelson, 1971.

14. Weber (1946, 1947) offers an analysis of impersonality and rationalization as characteristics vital to bureaucratic forms of social organization.

15. The reader will note that in several places throughout this chapter I have made a distinction discussed earlier between a fundamental quality of the human condition of everyday life and a heightened or exaggerated form of this fundamental condition. The point, to repeat, is that while I have been dealing with basic qualities relevant to all persons in their collective everyday lives, specific societal conditions can create a context within which these attributes and their associated outcomes (e.g., trust and intimacy) are more or less manifest. In other words, while all persons everywhere are social-comparative creatures, a particular society, or part of a society, at a particular point in its own developmental history may manifest this quality and its derivatives in an exaggerated form. In turn, the exaggeration of any quality of the natural standpoint makes its uncovering that much easier for the social science investigator. Recall that in examining the natural standpoint, we are examining the fabric of a society that is normally taken for granted; in exaggeration, what is routinely background more readily emerges into foreground awareness. It is normal and even essential for us to have bacteria in our intestinal tracts; in heightened form, under certain conditions, this normal background can become a diseased and destructive foreground.

16. The psychoanalytic literature suggests the fear the child has of giving in to his sexual longings and merging with his mother and thereby of losing himself.

17. Bennis and Shepard (1956) provide an interesting analysis of the overpersonal group member who seems to seek great intimacy but who in fact so fears rejection that he avoids all real intimate contacts with others. Being overpersonal, in this case, is a defense against achieving true intimacy.

18. Applications of the psychoanalytic perspective to the area of small-group dynamics and interpersonal relations, especially the work of Bennis and Shepard (1956), Erikson (1959), Freud (1922), and Schutz (1960), show how issues of authority and personal identity must be resolved before issues of intimacy can possibly be dealt with.

CHAPTER 10. Other-Directedness: Shaming, Teasing, and Social Protest

1. E.g., Benedict, 1946; Whiting, 1959.

2. Freud, 1924–50.

3. See, for example, Lynd's (1969) comments on protest in the United States.

4. Accounts of social control within China suggest how important public-ridicule techniques are in getting people to perform their jobs. Local members of the community repeatedly call upon the lagging member, using nothing more potent than their claim upon his public life, to ridicule and shame him into fulfilling his functions. It would seem that in China, a combination of strong community loyalty and the threat of public ridicule serve as effective managers of individual behavior.

5. Asch, 1952. Also see Chapter 8 of this book for a summary of this study.

CHAPTER 11. On Responsibility and Apathy: *Dimension V*

1. Moreno (1944, 1946, 1959) has been especially noted for introducing psychodramatic and sociodramatic techniques into social psychology.

2. See, e.g., Goffman, 1961; Janis and King, 1965; Lifton, 1961.
3. Bettelheim, 1958.
4. Milgram, 1965.
5. Heider, 1958; Jones, 1964; Jones and Davis, 1965; Kelley, 1967.
6. Peters' (1958) analysis of the concept of motivation in psychological theories reaches a conclusion similar to that which the attribution-theory models (see his note 6) present.
7. Bennis and Shepard (1956) and Argyris (1969) offer a similar perspective on the desirability of being able to own up to one's own feelings and behavior: to take responsibility for one's self.
8. Parsons, Bales, and Shils, 1953; Parsons and Shils, 1951.
9. Kelman (1961) offers a valuable and related analysis of influence processes.
10. Sanford and Comstock, 1970.
11. See Sampson (1971, especially Part 1) for a discussion of the important role of perceptual selectivity for organismic survival and effective daily functioning.

CHAPTER 12. The Developmental Thesis: The Production and Maintenance of the Natural Standpoint: *Argument I*

1. Mead, 1934.
2. Marx, 1956.
3. Cassirer, 1957.
4. Ibid., pp. 89–90.
5. Schachtel, 1959.
6. Sartre, 1954.
7. Cooley, 1902.
8. Flavell, 1963; Piaget, 1952, 1954.

CHAPTER 13. The Functional Thesis: *Argument II*

1. Merton (1957) offers an excellent analysis of functional theory.
2. Hoebel, 1966; Rasmussen, 1927.

3. The theme of mastery plays a major role in many theories including, for example, White's (1959) discussion of competence motivation and Kelley's (1967) view of the attribution process. Sampson (1971, chap. 9, and 1969) provides a discussion and a summary of some of these perspectives on mastery.
4. E.g., Toffler, 1970.
5. Personal communication from R. Buckhout.
6. Marquis, 1958.
7. See Tillich, 1952.
8. The notion of having one's self validated by friends is at the theoretic root of consistency or balance theories: e.g., Newcomb, 1953, 1959; Secord and Backman, 1965.
9. See Fromm, 1941.

CHAPTER 14. The Population-Technology Thesis: *Argument III*

1. Barker, 1960, 1965; Barker and Barker, 1963; Barker and Wright, 1955.
2. Ellul, 1964.
3. Barker and Wright, 1955.
4. Barker and Gump, 1964.
5. Barker, 1960, 1965.
6. Parsons (1951), Parsons, Bales, and Shils (1953), and Parsons and Shils (1951) discuss this distinction between performances and qualities.
7. Fromm (1941) and Parsons (1968) make a similar point.
8. Weber (1930) outlines this Calvinistic view and several of its consequences.
9. Mills, 1959.

CHAPTER 15. The Perspective of Transcendence: *An Overview*

1. E.g., Castaneda (1968, 1971, 1972) offers an excellent view of the mystic's thought. Also see Watts, 1961.

2. E.g., Church, 1961; Flavell, 1963; Freud, 1924–50; Harvey, Hunt, and Schroder, 1961; Piaget, 1952, 1954; Schachtel, 1959.

3. Lee, 1950.

4. See, e.g., Rosner and Abt, 1970.

5. Maslow, 1954, 1955, 1959.

6. E.g., Hampden-Turner, 1970; Sartre, 1957a, and other works; Tillich, 1952; Wheelis, 1969; Wilson, 1956.

7. Maslow, 1954, 1955, 1959.

8. Werner, 1940.

9. Freud, 1954, 1924–50; Piaget, 1952, 1954. Also see Flavell, 1963.

10. Cassirer, 1957, p. 449.

11. Ibid., p. 200.

12. Rosner and Abt (1970) offer numerous illustrations of this point.

13. Erikson, 1969.

14. Deikman, 1963, 1966.

15. One might say that Deikman's instructions to his subjects paralleled Buber's analysis (1958) of man's two attitudes: the analytic "I-it" vs. the nonanalytic, personal, and fused "I-thou."

16. Garfinkel, 1967.

17. Castaneda, 1968, 1971, 1972.

18. See Erikson, 1969.

19. Lee, 1950; Malinowski, 1922.

20. Watts, 1961.

21. E.g., Marcuse, 1966; Marx, 1956.

22. Weber, 1930.

23. From a personal document circulated to explain this academic's personal and political motives.

24. Wilson, 1956.

25. Tillich, 1952.

26. Faith in the sense that Kierkegaard (1941) has developed the concept.

27. See especially Fromm, 1941; Harvey, Hunt and Schroder, 1961; Levy, 1955.

28. Sartre, 1957a.

29. Flavell (1963) offers a good statement of Piaget's position.

30. Husserl, 1931, 1943, 1964. Also see Mann and Kreyche, 1966; Pivcevic, 1970; Schutz, 1967, 1970, 1971a, 1971b; Tymieniecka, 1962.

CHAPTER 16. Into a Different World

1. Maslow, 1955, 1959.
2. See Lewis's (1971) writings on ecstatic religious experiences.
3. There is an especially interesting book by Young (1965) that offers us a view of the adult world from the child's perspective. In a similar manner, Piaget's contributions to developmental theory help us realize that the child is *not* simply a tiny version of the adult but lives in an entirely different cognitive-and-experiential world with a different outlook regarding the nature of social and physical reality.
4. See, e.g., Church, 1961; Wolff, 1967.

CHAPTER 17. The Reconstitution of Experience in the Ego's World

1. Schutz, 1970, 1971a, 1971b.
2. Schutz, 1971a, p. 70.
3. Ibid., p. 71.
4. Mead, 1934.
5. Ibid., p. 243.
6. Ibid., p. 249.
7. Strauss, 1969, p. 31.
8. James, 1890.
9. Parmenides assumed that fundamentally objects were solid and inert, whereas Heraclitus began with the assumption that change rather than stasis was the one inescapable fact of existence.
10. Kummel (1966) makes much this same point.
11. Schutz, 1971a, p. 109.
12. Kummel, 1966, p. 51.
13. Ibid., p. 40.
14. Eliot, 1943, p. 40.
15. Mead, 1934.
16. This is Mead's conception of the thinking process.
17. Cooley, 1902.

18. E.g., Goffman, 1959.
19. Mead, 1934, p. 259.
20. A similar notion of mediation is at the root of the cognitive model (e.g., Heider, 1958; Scheerer, 1954), as is the parallel view that we take our phenomenal world to be directly given and are rarely aware of the mediating processes involved in our perceptual-cognitive activities.
21. This is an important implication of the approach that has been called *self-attribution theory*; e.g., Bem, 1967.
22. See the James-Lange theory of emotions as presented by James (1884) and Lange (1922).
23. E.g., Rogers, 1951.
24. Schutz, 1970, 1971a, 1971b.
25. This is the essence of the Marxist view as well, which sees consciousness as an emergent from persons' relationship to means of production. In other words, their consciousness derives from their experiences in the economic system of a society. Behavior is the independent variable and consciousness, the dependent variable, thus reversing the usual social psychological mode of analysis.
26. Ryle, 1950.
27. Mead (1934) makes this one of the key implications of this distinction between *I* and *me*.

CHAPTER 18. A Step into the Future?

1. See Schutz, 1967, on this point.
2. Watts, 1961.
3. E.g., Fishman, 1960; Sampson, 1971, chap. 2.
4. Ryle, 1950.
5. Maslow, 1955; Rosner and Abt, 1970; Watts, 1961.
6. Rosner and Abt, 1970, pp. 381–82.
7. Garfinkel (1967) provides an interesting perspective on a "documentary analysis" of interaction.
8. E.g., Ekman, 1965; Hall, 1959; also see the 1971 *Nebraska*

Symposium on Motivation for an important series of articles by Ekman, Exline, and Mehrabian.

9. Schutz, 1971a, p. 69.
10. Bergson, 1913, 1923; also Schutz, 1970, 1971a, 1971b.
11. Corliss Lamont (1969) provides a valuable discussion of the free-will position.
12. Erikson, 1959.
13. In Kierkegaard's (1941) sense of the term, faith.
14. The continuity-discontinuity argument is heard especially in analyses of societal futures, with persons such as Drucker (1968) and Theobald (1968) presenting the discontinuity position—i.e., that we cannot predict to the year 2000 from extrapolations of today—and Kahn and Wiener (1967), the continuity position.

CHAPTER 19. The Transcendent Origins: In the Beginning Was Not the Word

1. Schutz, 1971a, p. 112.
2. Ibid.
3. Sartre, 1957b, p. 79.
4. Ibid., p. 96.
5. Cassirer, 1946, 1957, 1970.
6. Flavell, 1963; Freud, 1924–50, 1954, 1961; Piaget, 1932, 1952, 1954. Also see Werner, 1940.
7. This is a major point of the Sapir-Whorf hypothesis of linguistic relativity: e.g., Fishman, 1960; Sapir, 1956; Whorf, 1956.
8. Cassirer (1957, p. 115) uses this example of the Heraclitean view that one cannot step twice into a stream.
9. Cassirer, 1946, p. 38.
10. Ibid., p. 83.
11. Cassirer, 1957, p. 115.
12. Cassirer, 1946, pp. 71, 73, 74.
13. Ibid., p. 76.
14. Sartre, 1957b, pp. 98–99.
15. Ibid., p. 22.

16. Cassirer, 1946, p. 98.
17. Einstein, 1971, 1972.
18. Cassirer, 1946, pp. 91–92.
19. Ibid.
20. Ibid., p. 90.
21. See Lewis (1971) for a description of ecstatic religious experiences that share this same primary mode of experiencing.
22. Lewis (1971) makes this point in his discussion of possession (e.g., p. 57): "This gift of illumination, in return for a surrendering of the self or part of the self . . . a fusing of man and divinity . . . is part of controlled spirit possession everywhere."
23. See note 6.
24. E.g., Church, 1961.
25. Ibid., p. 17.
26. Wolff, 1967, p. 325.
27. Freud, 1954, especially chap. 7.
28. E.g., Hartmann, 1958; Schachtel, 1959.
29. Erikson, 1959.
30. Gill, 1967; Holt, 1967.
31. Holt, 1967.

CHAPTER 20. Interpersonal Themes Within the Transcendent World

1. Buber, 1958.
2. Maslow, 1959.
3. Skinner, 1971.
4. The distinction between *erklären* and *verstehen* was made by Dilthey (see Mann and Kreyche, 1966); it expresses the difference between the laws and approaches appropriate to the physical sciences (i.e., *erklären*) and those suited to the behavioral and cultural sciences (i.e., *verstehen*). The writings of Max Weber and those of Alfred Schutz further outline the appropriateness of the *verstehen* approach in the social sciences.
5. Hitt (1969) makes somewhat this same point in concluding that both the behavioral and the existential paradigms provide an accurate analysis of our lives.

6. See Fromm, 1941.
7. We have already seen reference to this same point by Castaneda and the British radical professor (see Chapter 15).
8. R. D. Laing referred to this kind of dilemma repeatedly in his aptly titled work *Knots*, 1970.
9. Watts, 1961, p. 143.
10. Fromm, 1941.

CHAPTER 21. The Crisis of Liberation

1. Recall that Ryle (1950) uses as an example of the elusiveness of our *I* in the present moment the impossibility of jumping on the shadow of our own head.
2. Maslow, 1955; Watts, 1961.
3. I am referring here to the growing number of "groupy" fads that promise instant cure of our individual and collective ills if we will only invest so much money into this weekend retreat here or that week-long workshop there, all under the able guidance of guru what's-his-name.
4. This is a key argument made by Freud in his analysis of instinct as an inner stimulus from which we cannot escape, as compared with external stimuli from which we can actively remove ourselves.
5. This view should be familiar to those who know the writings of Piaget and those developmental theories that have flowed from his ideas. We have examined it in Chapter 19.
6. The concept of a personal, positive disintegration finds a key place in the interesting little book on this topic by Dabrowski (1964).
7. Sartre, 1959a.
8. The parallel to religious views on death and rebirth which runs throughout this analysis reveals the close relationship between the religious experience and the primitive form of the transcendent process, as noted in Chapter 19. Robert Lifton's work on thought reform (1961) likewise focuses on much this same notion.
9. The idea that our fear of death keeps us from truly living

finds an important place in the writings of Brown (1959) as well as those of Laing (1965, 1967) and Tillich (1952).
10. Selznick, 1948.
11. Regression in the service of the ego has been related to creativity by Kris (1952) and Wild (1965), among others.

CHAPTER 22. Experiences That Disconfirm and Broaden

1. Mannheim, 1936.
2. Berger and Luckman, 1966.
3. Kohlberg, 1969.
4. Mead, 1934.
5. E.g., Sampson, Weiss, Mlodnosky, and Hause, 1972; Weiss, 1971. Lifton (1961) suggests much this same point in his study of thought reform, noting how growth experiences under extreme pressure build upon a groundwork of high ego strength.
6. Weiss, 1952.
7. Noyes, 1972.
8. E.g., Bem, 1967; Festinger, 1957.
9. The issue of personal volition has hounded dissonance theorists. For the most part, they define an action as voluntary, and thus as capable of producing substantial cognitive dissonance, if it has little external as compared with internal cause. Thus, for example, if I tell a lie under high external pressure (e.g., threats of substantial punishment or promises of high reward), I will experience less dissonance than if I tell a lie with minimal pressure (see, for example, Festinger and Carlsmith [1959] and Sampson [1971, pp. 108–14]). In this latter case, I have acted voluntarily and my ego must now cope with this dissonant piece of information about myself. The point that I am making is that actions that occur beyond the range of any apparent ego control are *truly* surprising and thus should evoke the greatest dissonance with which our ego's must later come to deal reflectively. Lifton's (1961) study of thought reform suggested this factor, when substantial milieu control led the

person to act in ways surprising even to himself, providing new material with which he has to deal. These "surprising" actions put our ego in touch with aspects of ourselves, including the transcendent, which under circumstances of ego strength outlined previously can provide substantial enlightenment and personal liberation.

CHAPTER 23. Commitment and the Liberating Experience

1. Sartre, 1959b.
2. Frankl, 1959.
3. Wilson, 1956.
4. Tillich, 1952.
5. In this regard, Lippitt and White's (1958) early experiments on different leadership styles are instructive in showing how the laissez faire style created as much tension, frustration, and disruption as did the more authoritarian style and thereby limited group growth and development.
6. Levi, Stierlin, and Savard, 1972.
7. Erikson, 1969.
8. Arendt, 1969.
9. This is a major thesis of the theory of cognitive dissonance (e.g., Festinger, 1957) that maintains that since we cannot take back what have already done, we change out attitudes to fit our behavior.

CHAPTER 24. Ego at the Threshold

1. Sartre, 1957b.
2. Maslow, 1955, 1959; Watts, 1961.
3. It should be understood from this analysis that we may achieve knowledge and ego mastery in a limited domain within which

we can act as the professional, i.e., spontaneously and without substantial ego intervention or guidance. Furthermore, the fundamental freedom that such spontaneity offers is itself limited by those domains within which our ego has become sufficiently strong and confident to yield its control. The professional dancer, for example, may yield in the dance but in little else; the carpenter may submit in carpentry but in little else. Living *all of life* fully as the professional is an unlikely possibility; yet the sphere of that *some of life* surely can become expanded.

4. Castaneda's analysis of don Juan makes a similar point, in particular emphasizing the importance of living life each day *impeccably*: as a pro.

5. This is similar to the point made by Jaspers (1947, 1948) which emphasized the need to participate with another in order to know him; it is also similar to Buber's view (1958) of the I-Thou relationship.

6. Maslow, 1955, 1959.

CHAPTER 25. The Fundamental Duality of the Human Condition

1. Buber, 1958.
2. Hesse, 1963.
3. Freud, 1924–50, 1954, 1961. Also see Chapter 19 in this volume.
4. E.g., Ardrey 1966, 1967; Morris, 1967.
5. Pribram, 1972.
6. Weber, 1946, 1947.
7. Skinner likewise (1948, 1971) is hopeful that human nature can be changed by changing the condition of social learning.
8. This is the thesis of Marxist theory and of the perspective of the sociology of knowledge as presented by Mannheim, for example.
9. From previous discussions, it should also be apparent that regardless of what domain of human living is involved—e.g., dance or carpentry, writing or athletics—self-conscious ego mastery is the vital first step to acting as a pro. Whatever

endeavor is involved, the professional's ego must be disciplined, open, and aware so that when its guidance is yielded, the freely emerging performance comes forth without doubt or hesitation, but rather intuitively, spontaneously, and uniquely representing a solidly shaped core of skills and knowledges.

References

Adelson, J. "Inventing the Young." *Commentary*, May 1971.

Ardrey, R. *The Territorial Imperative*. New York: Atheneum, 1966.

———. *African Genesis*. New York: Dell, 1967.

Arendt, H. "Reflections on Violence." *The New York Review of Books*, February 27, 1969, 12:19–31.

Argyris, C. "The Incompleteness of Social-psychological Theory." *American Psychologist*, 1969, 24:893–908.

Asch, S. E. *Social Psychology*. Englewood Cliffs, N.J.: Prentice-Hall, 1952.

Auden, W. H. "The Unknown Citizen." In W. H. Auden, *Another Time*. New York: Random House, 1940.

Bakan, D. "The Mystery-Mastery Complex in Contemporary Psychology." *American Psychologist*, 1965, 20:186–101.

Barker, R. G. "Ecology and Motivation." In *Nebraska Symposium on Motivation*, edited by M. R. Jones. Lincoln: University of Nebraska Press, 1960.

———. "Explorations in Ecological Psychology." *American Psychologist*, 1965, 20:1–14.

———, and Barker, L. S. "Social Actions in the Behavior Streams of American and English Children." In *Stream of Behavior: Ex-*

plorations of Its Structure and Content, edited by R. G. Barker. New York: Appleton-Century-Crofts, 1963.

———, and Gump, P. V. *Big School, Small School: High School Size and Student Behavior*. Stanford, Calif.: Stanford University Press, 1964.

———, and Wright, H. F. *Midwest and Its Children: The Psychological Ecology of an American Town*. Evanston, Ill.: Row, Peterson, 1955.

Becker, H. S. *Outsiders*. New York: Free Press, 1963.

Bem, D. J. "Self-perception: An Alternative Interpretation of Cognitive Dissonance Phenomena." *Psychological Review*, 1967, 74:183–200.

Benedict, R. *The Chrysanthemum and the Sword: Patterns of Japanese Culture*. Boston: Houghton Mifflin, 1946.

Bennis, W. G. "Leadership Theory and Administrative Behavior: The Problem of Authority." *Administrative Science Quarterly*, 1959, 4:259–301.

———, and Shepard, H. A. "A Theory of Group Development." *Human Relations*, 1956, 9:415–38.

Berger, P. L., and Luckman, T. *The Social Construction of Reality*. New York: Doubleday, 1966.

Bergson, H. *Time and Free Will*. New York: Macmillan, 1913.

———. *Durée et Simultanéité*. Paris: F. Alcan, 1923.

Bernard, V. W.; Ottenberg, P.; and Redl, F. "Dehumanization: A Composite Psychological Defense in Relation to Modern War." In *The Triple Revolution: Social Problems in Depth*, edited by R. Perrucci and M. Pilisuk. Boston: Little, Brown, 1968.

Bettelheim, B. "Individual and Mass Behavior in Extreme Situations." In *Readings in Social Psychology*. 3d ed. Edited by E. E. Maccoby, T. M. Newcomb, and E. L. Hartley. New York: Holt, Rinehart & Winston, 1958.

Biddle, B. J., and Thomas, E. J. eds. *Role Theory: Concepts and Research*. New York: Wiley, 1966.

Brecht, B. "To Posterity." In *Selected Poems*. New York: Grove Press, 1947.

Breer, P. E., and Locke, E. A. *Task Experiences as a Source of Attitudes*. Homewood, Ill.: Dorsey Press, 1965.

Brein, M., and David, K. H. "Intercultural Communication and the Adjustment of the Sojourner." *Psychological Bulletin*, 1971, 76:215–30.

Brown, N. O. *Life Against Death: The Psychoanalytical Meaning of History*. Middletown, Conn.: Wesleyan University Press, 1959.

Brown, R. W. *Words and Things*. New York: Free Press, 1958.

Bruner, J. S. "The Cognitive Consequences of Early Sensory Deprivation." In *Sensory Deprivation*, edited by P. Solomon, P. E. Kubzansky, et al. Cambridge, Mass.: Harvard University Press, 1961.

Buber, M. *I and Thou*. New York: Scribner's, 1958.

Camus, A. *Caligula*. New York: Vintage, 1958.

Carmichael, L.; Hogan, H. P.; and Walter, A. A. "An Experimental Study of the Effect of Language on the Reproduction of Visually Perceived Form. *Journal of Experimental Psychology*, 1932, 15:73–86.

Carmichael, S., and Hamilton, C. V. *Black Power: The Politics of Liberation in America*. New York: Random House, 1967.

Cassirer, E. *Language and Myth*. New York: Harper, 1946.

———. *The Philosophy of Symbolic Forms*, vol. 3: *The Phenomenology of Knowledge*. New Haven: Yale University Press, 1957.

———. *An Essay on Man*. New York: Bantam, 1970.

Castaneda, C. *The Teachings of Don Juan: A Yaqui Way of Knowledge*. Berkeley: University of California, 1968.

———. *A Separate Reality: Further Conversations with Don Juan*. New York: Simon & Schuster, 1971.

Castaneda, C. *Journey to Ixtlan: The Lessons of Don Juan.* New York: Simon & Schuster, 1972.

Centers, R. "An Examination of the Riesman Social Character Typology: A Metropolitan Survey." *Sociometry*, 1962, 25:232–40.

Church, J. *Language and the Discovery of Reality.* New York: Random House, 1961.

Cooley, C. H. *Human Nature and the Social Order.* New York: Scribner's, 1902.

Dabrowski, K. *Positive Disintegration.* Boston: Little, Brown, 1964.

de Charms, R., and Moeller, G. H. "Values Expressed in American Children's Readers: 1800–1950." *Journal of Abnormal and Social Psychology*, 1962, 64:136–42.

Deikman, A. J. "Experimental Meditation." *Journal of Nervous and Mental Disorders*, 1963, 136:329–73.

———. "Deautomization and the Mystic Experience." *Psychiatry*, 1966, 29:329–43.

Drucker, P. F. *The Age of Discontinuity.* New York: Harper & Row, 1968.

Duncan, H. D. *Symbols in Society.* New York: Oxford University Press, 1968.

Eddington, A. S. *The Nature of the Physical World.* New York: Wiley, 1928.

Egan, G. *Encounter: Group Processes for Interpersonal Growth.* Belmont, Calif.: Brooks/Cole, 1970.

"Einstein Papers: A Three-Part Series by W. Sullivan." *The New York Times*, March 27, 28, 29, 1972. Also, *The Born-Einstein Letters.* New York: Walker & Company, 1971.

Ekman, P. "Communication Through Nonverbal Behavior: A Source of Information about Interpersonal Relations." In *Affect, Cognition, and Personality: Empirical Studies*, edited by S. S. Tomkins and C. E. Izard. New York: Springer, 1965.

Eliot, T. S. *The Complete Poems and Plays.* New York: Harcourt, Brace & World, 1930.

————. *Four Quartets.* New York: Harcourt, Brace & World, 1943.

Ellul, J. *The Technological Society.* New York: Knopf, 1964.

Erikson, E. "Identity and the Life Cycle." In *Psychological Issues.* New York: International Universities Press, 1959.

————. *Gandhi's Truth.* New York: Norton, 1969.

Ervin-Tripp, S. "Sociolinguistics." In *Advances in Experimental Social Psychology,* vol. 4, edited by L. Berkowitz. New York: Academic Press, 1969.

Festinger, L. "A Theory of Social Comparison Processes." *Human Relations,* 1954a, 7:117–40.

————. "Motivations Leading to Social Behavior." In *Nebraska Symposium on Motivation,* edited by M. R. Jones. Lincoln: University of Nebraska Press, 1954b.

————. *A Theory of Cognitive Dissonance.* Evanston, Ill.: Row, Peterson, 1957.

————, and Carlsmith, J. M. "Cognitive Consequences of Forced Compliance." *Journal of Abnormal and Social Psychology,* 1959, 58:203–10.

Fishman, J. A. "A Systematization of the Whorfian Hypothesis." *Behavioral Science,* 1960, 5:323–39.

Flavell, J. H. *The Developmental Psychology of Jean Piaget.* Princeton, N.J.: Van Nostrand, 1963.

Frankl, V. E. *Man's Search for Meaning.* Boston: Beacon Press, 1959.

Freud, S. *Group Psychology and the Analysis of the Ego.* New York: Boni & Liveright, 1922.

————. *Collected Papers.* 5 vols. London: Hogarth Press and the Institute of Psychoanalysis, 1924–50.

————. *Interpretation of Dreams.* London: Allen & Unwin, 1954.

————. *The Ego and the Id.* London: Hogarth Press, 1961.

Fromm, E. *Escape from Freedom*. New York: Holt, Rinehart & Winston, 1941.

Garfinkel, H. *Studies in Ethnomethodology*. Englewood Cliffs, N.J.: Prentice-Hall, 1967.

Gill, M. M. "The Primary Process." In *Motives and Thought*, edited by R. R. Holt. New York: International Universities Press, 1967.

Goffman, E. *The Presentation of Self in Everyday Life*. Garden City, N.Y.: Doubleday, 1959.

———. *Asylums*. Chicago: Aldine, 1961.

———. *Behavior in Public Places*. New York: Free Press, 1963.

———. *Relations in Public*. New York: Harper & Row, 1972.

Gouldner, A. W. "The Norm of Reciprocity: A Preliminary Statement." *American Sociological Review*, 1960, 25:161–78.

Greenspoon, J. "The Reinforcing Effect of Two Spoken Sounds on the Frequencies of Two Responses." *American Journal of Psychology*, 1955, 68:409–16.

Hall, E. T. *The Silent Language*. Garden City, N.Y.: Doubleday, 1959.

Hampden-Turner, C. *Radical Man*. Cambridge, Mass.: Schenkman, 1970.

Hartmann, H. *Ego Psychology and the Problem of Adaptation*. New York: International Universities Press, 1958.

Harvey, O. J.; Hunt, D. E.; and Schroder, H. M. *Conceptual Systems and Personality Organization*. New York: Wiley, 1961.

Heidegger, M. *Being and Time*. London: SCM Press, 1962.

Heider, F. *The Psychology of Interpersonal Relations*. New York: Wiley, 1958.

———. "On Perception, Event Structure and the Psychological Environment." *Psychological Issues*, 1959, 1.

Hesse, H. *Steppenwolf*. New York: Holt, Rinehart & Winston, 1963.

Hitt, W. D. "Two Models of Man." *American Psychologist*, 1969, 24:651–58.

Hoebel, E. A. *Anthropology*. New York: McGraw-Hill, 1966.

Holt, R. R. "The Development of the Primary Process: A Structural View." In *Motives and Thought*, edited by R. R. Holt. New York: International Universities Press, 1967.

Hull, C. L. *Principles of Behavior: An Introduction to Behavior Theory*. New York: Appleton-Century, 1943.

Husserl, E. *Ideas*. New York: Macmillian, 1931.

———. See M. Farber. *The Foundations of Phenomenology*. Cambridge, Mass.: Harvard University Press, 1943.

———. *The Phenomenology of Internal Time Consciousness*. Bloomington: Indiana University Press, 1964.

Intimacy: An Encounter Program for Couples. Human Development Institute, Atlanta, Georgia.

James, W. "What Is an Emotion?" *Mind*, 1884, 9:188–205.

———. *Principles of Psychology*. 2 vols. New York: Holt, 1890.

Janis, I. L., and King, B. T. "The Influence of Role-Playing on Opinion Change." *Journal of Abnormal and Social Psychology*, 1965, 1:17–27.

Jaspers, K. *Von der Wahrheit*. Berlin: Springer, 1947.

———. *Philosophie*. 2d. ed. Berlin: Springer, 1948.

Jessor, R. "Phenomenological Personality Theories and the Data Language of Psychology." *Psychological Review*, 1956, 63:173–80.

Jones, E. E. *Ingratiation: A Social Psychological Analysis*. New York: Appleton-Century-Crofts, 1964.

———, and Davis, K. E. "From Acts to Dispositions: The Attribution Process in Person Perception." In *Advances in Experimental Social Psychology*, vol 2, edited by L. Berkowitz. New York: Academic Press, 1965.

Jourard, S. M. *The Transparent Self*. Princeton, N.J.: Van Nostrand, 1964.

———. *Disclosing Man to Himself*. Princeton, N.J.: Van Nostrand, 1968.

Jung, C. G. *The Integration of the Personality*. New York: Farrar & Rinehart, 1939.

———. *Psychology of the Unconscious*. New York: Dodd, Mead, 1949.

Kahn, H., and Wiener, A. J. *The Year 2000*. New York: Macmillan, 1967.

Kassarjian, W. M. "A Study of Riesman's Theory of Social Character." *Sociometry*, 1962, 25:213–30.

Kelley, H. H. "Attribution Theory in Social Psychology." *Nebraska Symposium on Motivation*, 1967, 15:192–240.

———. "Moral Evaluation." *American Psychologist*, 1971, 26:293–300.

Kelly, G. A. *The Psychology of Personal Constructs*. New York: Norton, 1955.

———. *A Theory of Personality: The Psychology of Personal Constructs*. New York: Norton, 1963.

Kelman, H. C. "Processes of Opinion Change." *Public Opinion Quarterly*, 1961, 25:57–78.

Kierkegaard, S. *Fear and Trembling and The Sickness unto Death*. Princeton, N.J.: Princeton University Press, 1941.

Kohlberg, L. "Stage and Sequence: The Cognitive-developmental Approach to Socialization." In *Handbook of Socialization Theory and Research*, edited by D. A. Goslin. Chicago: Rand McNally, 1969.

Kris, E. *Psychoanalytic Explorations in Art*. New York: International Universities Press, 1952.

Kuhn, T. S. *The Structure of Scientific Revolutions*. Chicago: University of Chicago Press, 1962.

Kummel, F. "Time As Succession and the Problem of Duration." In *The Voices of Time*, edited by J. T. Fraser. New York: Braziller, 1966.

Laing, R. D. *The Divided Self*. Baltimore, Md.: Penguin, 1965.

————. *The Politics of Experience*. Baltimore, Md.: Penguin, 1967.

————. *Knots*. New York: Pantheon, 1970.

Lamont, C. *Freedom of Choice Affirmed*. Boston: Beacon Press, 1969.

Lange, C. G. *The Emotions*. Baltimore, Md.: Williams & Wilkins, 1922.

Lee, D. "Codifications of Reality: Lineal and Nonlineal." *Psychosomatic Medicine*, 1950, 12:89–97.

Lemert, E. *Human Deviance, Social Problems, and Social Control*. Englewood Cliffs, N.J.: Prentice-Hall, 1967.

Levi, L. D.; Stierlin, H.; and Savard, R. "Fathers and Sons: The Interlocking Crises of Integrity and Identity." *Psychiatry*, 1972, 35:48–56.

Levy, D. M. "Oppositional Syndromes and Oppositional Behavior." In *Psychopathology of Childhood*, edited by P. H. Hock and J. Zubin. New York: Grune & Stratton, 1955.

Lewin, K. *Dynamic Theory of Personality*. New York: McGraw-Hill, 1935.

————. *Resolving Social Conflicts*. New York: Harper & Row, 1948.

————. *Field Theory in Social Science: Selected Theoretical Papers*, edited by D. Cartwright. New York: Harper & Row, 1951.

Lewis, I. M. *Ecstatic Religion*. Baltimore, Md.: Penguin, 1971.

Lifton, R. J. *Thought Reform and the Psychology of Totalism: A Study of "Brainwashing" in China*. New York: Norton, 1961.

Lifton, R. J. *Death in Life*, New York: Random House, 1967.

Lippitt, R., and White, R. K. "An Experimental Study of Leadership and Group Life." In *Readings in Social Psychology*. 3d. ed. Edited by E. E. Maccoby, T. M. Newcomb, and E. L. Hartley. New York: Holt, Rinehart & Winston, 1958.

Lumpkin, M. "Walden I and II: A Plea for Renewed Balance in the Psychological Pursuit of Science." *American Psychologist*, 1970, 25:1087–90.

Lynd, S. "The New Left." *Annals of the American Academy of Political and Social Science*, 1969, 382:64–72.

Malinowski, B. *Argonauts of the Western Pacific*. London: 1922.

———. *Crime and Custom in Savage Society*. London: Paul, Trench, Trubner, 1932.

Mann, J. A., and Kreyche, G. F., eds. *Reflections on Man: Readings in Philosophical Psychology From Classical Philosophy to Existentialism*. New York: Harcourt, Brace, 1966.

Mannheim, K. *Ideology and Utopia*. New York: Harcourt, Brace, 1936.

Marcuse, H. *One-Dimensional Man: Studies in the Ideology of Advanced Industrial Society*. Boston: Beacon Press, 1966.

Marquis, D. "The Lesson of the Moth." In Marquis, *Archy and Mehitabel*. London: Faber & Faber, 1958.

Marx, K. *Selected Writings in Sociology and Social Philosophy*, edited by T. B. Bottomore and M. Rubel. London: Watts, 1956.

Maslow, A. H. *Motivation and Personality*. New York: Harper & Row, 1954.

———. "Deficiency Motivation and Growth Motivation." In *Nebraska Symposium on Motivation, 1955*, edited by R. M. Jones. Lincoln: University of Nebraska Press, 1955.

———. "Cognition of Being in the Peak Experiences." *Journal of Genetic Psychology*, 1959, 43–66.

May, R. *Love and Will*. New York: Norton, 1969.

McConnell, J. V. "Criminals Can Be Brainwashed Now." *Psychology Today*, 1970, 3:14–18, 74.

McGregor, D. *The Human Side of Enterprise*. New York: McGraw-Hill, 1960.

Mead, G. H. *The Social Psychology of George Herbert Mead*, edited by A. Strauss. Chicago: University of Chicago Press, 1934.

Memmi, A. *The Colonizer and the Colonized*. Boston: Beacon Press, 1967.

Merton, R. S. *Social Theory and Social Structure*. Glencoe, Ill.: Free Press, 1957.

Milgram, S. "Behavioral Study of Obedience." *Journal of Abnormal and Social Psychology*, 1963, 67:371–78.

———. "Liberating Effects of Group Pressure." *Journal of Personality and Social Psychology*, 1965, 1:127–34.

Mills, C. W. *The Sociological Imagination*. New York: Oxford University Press, 1959.

Moreno, J. L. *Sociodrama: A Method for the Analysis of Social Conflicts*. Beacon, N.Y.: Beacon House, 1944.

———. *Psychodrama*, vol. 1. Beacon, N.Y.: Beacon House, 1946.

———. *Psychodrama*, vol. 2. *Foundations of Psychotherapy*. Beacon, N.Y.: Beacon House, 1959.

Morris, D. *The Naked Ape*. New York: McGraw-Hill, 1967.

Morris, R. T., and Jeffries, V. *The White Reaction Study*. Los Angeles: Institute of Government and Public Affairs, University of California, 1967.

Mumford, Lewis. *The Transformations of Man*. New York: Harper Torchbooks, 1972.

Nebraska Symposium on Motivation. Lincoln, Nebraska: University of Nebraska Press, 1971. A. Mehrabian, "Nonverbal Communication"; R. Exline, "Visual Interaction: The Glances of Power and Preference"; P. Ekman, "Universals and Cultural Differences in Facial Expressions of Emotion."

Newcomb, T. M. "An Approach to the Study of Communicative Acts." *Psychological Review*, 1953, 60:393–404.

———. "Individual Systems of Orientation." In *Psychology: A Study of a Science*, vol. 3. Edited by S. Koch. New York: McGraw-Hill, 1959.

Noyes, R. Jr. "The Experience of Dying." *Psychiatry*, 1972, 35:174–84.

Parsons, T. *The Social System*. Glencoe, Ill.: Free Press, 1951.

———. "The Position of Identity in the General Theory of Action." In *The Self in Social Interaction*, edited by C. Gordon and K. J. Gergen. New York: Wiley, 1968.

———; Bales, R. F.; and Shils, E. A. *Working Papers in the Theory of Action*. Glencoe, Ill.: Free Press, 1953.

———, and Shils, E. A., eds. *Toward a General Theory of Action*. Cambridge, Mass.: Harvard University Press, 1951.

Pavlov, I. P. *Conditioned Reflexes*. New York: Dover, 1960.

Perls, F.; Hefferline, R. F.; and Goodman, P. *Gestalt Therapy*. New York: Delta, 1965.

Peters, R. S. *The Concept of Motivation*. New York: Humanities Press, 1958.

Piaget, J. *The Moral Judgment of the Child*. New York: Harcourt, Brace, 1932.

———. *The Origins of Intelligence in Children*. New York: International Universities Press, 1952.

———. *The Construction of Reality in the Child*. New York: Basic Books, 1954.

Pivcevic, E. *Husserl and Phenomenology*. London: Hutchinson University Library, 1970.

Pribram, K. As reported in *APA Monitor*, 1972, No. 4, 3:3.

Rahe, R. H.; McKean, J. D.; and Arthur, R. J. "A Longitudinal Study of Life-change and Illness Patterns." *Journal of Psychosomatic Research*, 1967, 10:355–66.

Rasmussen, K. *Across Arctic America*. New York & London: Putnam's, 1927.

Riesman, D. *The Lonely Crowd: A Study of the Changing American Character*. New Haven: Yale University Press, 1950.

Rogers, C. R. *Client-Centered Therapy*. Boston: Houghton Mifflin, 1951.

———. "The Process of the Basic Encounter Group." In *Challenges of Humanistic Psychology*, edited by J. F. T. Bugental. New York: McGraw-Hill, 1967.

———. "The Group Comes of Age." *Psychology Today*, 1969, 3:27–31, 58–61.

———. "Some New Challenges." *American Psychologist*, 1973, 28:379–87.

Rosenthal, R. *Pygmalion in the Classroom*. New York: Holt, Rinehart, & Winston, 1968.

Rosner, S., and Abt, L. E. *The Creative Experience*. New York: Dell, 1970.

Rubin, Z. *Liking and Loving*. New York: Holt, Rinehart & Winston, 1973.

Ryle, G. *The Concept of Mind*. New York: Barnes & Noble, 1950.

Saint-Exupéry, A. de. *The Little Prince*. New York: Harcourt, Brace & World, 1943.

Sampson, E. E. *Social Psychology and Contemporary Society*. New York: Wiley, 1971.

———, and Brandon, A. C. "The Effects of Role and Opinion Deviation in Small Group Behavior." *Sociometry*, 1964, 27:261–81.

———; Fisher, L.; Angel, A.; Mulman, A.; and Sullins, C. "Two Profiles: The Draft Resister and the ROTC Cadet." Unpublished report, University of California, 1969.

Sampson, H.; Weiss, J.; Mlodnosky, L.; and Hause, E. "Defense Analysis and the Emergence of Warded Off Mental Contents: An Empirical Study." *Archives of General Psychiatry*, 1972.

Sanford, N., and Comstock, C., eds. *Sanctions for Evil*. San Francisco: Jossey-Bass, 1970.

Sapir, E. *Culture, Language and Personality*, edited by D. G. Mandelbaum. Berkeley: University of California Press, 1956.

Sarbin, T. R., and Allen, V. L. "Role Theory." In *Handbook of Social Psychology*, vol. 1. Edited by G. Lindzey and E. Aronson. Reading, Mass.: Addison-Wesley, 1968.

Sartre, J. P. *No Exit*. New York: Knopf, 1954.

———. *Being and Nothingness*. London: Methuen, 1957a.

———. *The Transcendence of the Ego*. New York: Noonday, 1957b.

———. *Nausea*. Norfolk, Conn.: New Directions, 1959a.

———. "La République du Silence." In *The Alienation of Modern Man*, edited by F. Pappenheim. New York: Modern Reader Paperbacks, 1959b.

Schachtel, E. G. *Metamorphosis*. New York: Basic Books, 1959.

Schachter, S. "Deviation, Rejection and Communication." *Journal of Abnormal and Social Psychology*, 1951, 46:190–207.

———, and Singer, J. S. "Cognitive, Social and Physiological Determinants of Emotional State." *Psychological Review*, 1962, 69:379–99.

Scheerer, M. "Cognitive Theory." In *Handbook of Social Psychology*, vol. 1. Edited by G. Lindzey. Cambridge, Mass.: Addison-Wesley, 1954.

Scheff, T. J. *Being Mentally Ill*. Chicago: Aldine, 1966.

Schur, E. M. *Labeling Deviant Behavior*. New York: Harper & Row, 1971.

Schutz, A. *The Phenomenology of the Social World*. Evanston, Ill.: Northwestern University Press, 1967.

———. *Collected Papers*, vol. 3: *Studies in Phenomenological Philosophy*. The Hague: Martinus Nijhoff, 1970.

———. *Collected Papers*, vol. 1: *The Problem of Social Reality*. The Hague: Martinus Nijhoff, 1971a.

————. *Collected Papers*, vol. 2: *Studies in Social Theory*. The Hague: Martinus Nijhoff, 1971b.

Schutz, W. C. *FIRO: A Three-dimensional Theory of Interpersonal Behavior*. New York: Holt, Rinehart, & Winston, 1960.

Secord, P. F., and Backman, C. W. "An Interpersonal Approach to Personality." In *Progress in Experimental Personality Research*, vol. 2. Edited by B. A. Maher. New York: Academic Press, 1965.

Selznick, P. "Foundations of the Theory of Organization." *American Sociological Review*, 1948, 13:25–35.

Simmel, G. *The Sociology of Georg Simmel*, translated and edited by K. H. Wolff. Glencoe, Ill.: Free Press, 1950.

Sherif, M. A. "A Study of Some Social Factors in Perception." *Archives of Psychology*, 1935, vol. 27, no. 187.

Skinner, B. F. *Walden Two*. New York: Macmillian, 1948.

————. *Science and Human Behavior*. New York: Macmillian, 1953.

————. *Beyond Freedom and Dignity*. New York: Knopf, 1971.

Stouffer, S. A. *Communism, Conformity, and Civil Liberties*. Garden City, N.Y.: Doubleday, 1955.

Strauss, A. L. *Mirrors and Masks*. San Francisco: Sociology Press, 1969.

Szasz, T. S. "The Myth of Mental Illness." *American Psychologist*, 1960, 15:113–18.

————. "The Uses of Naming and the Origin of the Myth of Mental Illness." *American Psychologist*, 1961, 16:59–65.

Tedeschi, J. T.; Schlenker, B. R.; and Bonoma, T. V. "Cognitive Dissonance: Private Ratiocination or Public Spectacle?" *American Psychologist*, 1971, 26:685–95.

Theobald, R. "The Implications of American Physical Abundance." *Annals of the American Academy of Political and Social Science*, 1968, 378:11–21.

Thomas, W. I. In *Social Behavior and Personality: Contributions of W. I. Thomas to Theory and Social Research*, edited by E. H. Volkart. New York: Social Science Research Council, 1951.

Tillich, P. *The Courage to Be*. New Haven: Yale University Press, 1952.

Toffler, A. *Future Shock*. New York: Random House, 1970.

Tymieniecka, A. *Phenomenology and Science in Contemporary European Thought*. New York: Noonday, 1962.

Verplanck. W. S. "The Control of the Content of Conversation: Reinforcement of Statements of Opinion." *Journal of Abnormal and Social Psychology*, 1955, 51:668–76.

Wallace, A. F. C. "The Psychic Unity of Human Groups." In *Studying Personality Cross-culturally*, edited by B. Kaplan. Evanston, Ill.: Row, Peterson, 1961.

Watson, J. B. *Behaviorism*. New York: Norton, 1925.

Watts, A. W. *Psychotherapy East and West*. New York: Ballantine, 1961.

Weber, M. *The Protestant Ethic and the Spirit of Capitalism*. New York: Scribner's, 1930.

———. *From Max Weber: Essays in Sociology*, edited by H. H. Gerth and C. W. Mills. New York: Oxford University Press, 1946.

———. *The Theory of Social and Economic Organization*, translated by T. Parsons and A. M. Henderson. New York: Oxford University Press, 1947.

Weiss, J. "Crying at the Happy Ending." *Psychoanalytic Review*, 1952, 39:388.

———. "The Emergence of New Themes: A Contribution to the Psychoanalytic Theory of Therapy." *International Journal of Psychoanalysis*, 1971, 52:459–67.

Werner, H. *Comparative Psychology of Mental Development*. New York: Harper, 1940.

Wheelis, A. "How People Change." *Commentary*, May 1969.

White, R. W. "Motivation Reconsidered: The Concept of Competence." *Psychological Review*, 1959, 66:297–333.

Whiting, J. W. M. "Sorcery, Sin and the Superego." In *Nebraska Symposium on Motivation*, edited by M. R. Jones. Lincoln: University of Nebraska Press, 1959.

Whorf, B. L. *Language, Thought and Reality*, edited by J. B. Carroll. Cambridge, Mass.: Technology Press of MIT, 1956.

Wild, C. "Creativity and Adaptive Regression." *Journal of Personality and Social Psychology*, 1965, 2:161–69.

Wilson, C. *The Outsider*. New York: Dell, 1956.

Wolff, P. H. "Cognitive Considerations for a Psychoanalytic Theory of Language Acquisition." In *Motives and Thought*, edited by R. R. Holt. New York: International Universities Press, 1967.

Wooldridge, D. E. *Mechanical Man*. New York: McGraw-Hill, 1968.

Young, L. *Life Among the Giants*. New York: McGraw-Hill, 1965.

Index